Rick Steves'
SNAPSHOT

Munich, Bavaria & Salzburg

CONTENTS

INTRODUCTION

This Snapshot guide, excerpted from my guidebook *Rick Steves' Germany*, introduces you to Germany's cutest corner, Bavaria, and its showpiece city, Munich. Salzburg, just across the border in Austria, adds sparkle.

Munich—a thriving and livable city—entertains visitors with rollicking beer halls, excellent museums, an inviting traffic-free core filled with grand facades, and a relaxing park that tempts visitors to become temporary *Münchners*. Bavaria is home to Europe's most famous castles—"Mad" King Ludwig's Neuschwanstein and its cousins—and idyllic alpine scenery. Scream down a mountain slope on a luge, ogle the ornate Rococo curlicues of the Wieskirche, glide up a lift to a summit viewpoint, and explore medieval castle ruins on a desolate hilltop. Then dive into the lively, strollable, music-crazy city of Salzburg—home to Mozart and *The Sound of Music*. Just thinking about the attractions in this book makes me want to yodel.

To help you have the best trip possible, I've included the following topics in this book:

• **Planning Your Time,** with advice on how to make the most of your limited time

• **Orientation,** including tourist information (abbreviated as TI), tips on public transportation, local tour options, and helpful hints

• **Sights** with ratings:

▲▲▲—Don't miss

▲▲—Try hard to see

▲—Worthwhile if you can make it

No rating—Worth knowing about

• **Sleeping** and **Eating,** with good-value recommendations in every price range

• **Connections,** with tips on trains, buses, and driving
• **Practicalities,** near the end of this book, has information on money, phoning, hotel reservations, transportation, and more, plus German survival phrases.

To travel smartly, read this little book in its entirety before you go. It's my hope that this guide will make your trip more meaning-ful and rewarding. Traveling like a temporary local, you'll get the absolute most out of every mile, minute, and dollar.

Gute Reise!

Rick Steves

MUNICH

München

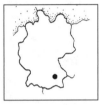

Munich, often called Germany's most livable city, is also one of its most historic, artistic, and entertaining. It's big and growing, with a population of 1.5 million. Until 1871, it was the capital of an independent Bavaria. Its imperial palaces, jewels, and grand boulevards constantly remind visitors that Munich has long been a political and cultural powerhouse. Meanwhile, the concentration camp in nearby Dachau reminds us that 80 years ago, it provided a springboard for Nazism.

Orient yourself in Munich's old center, with its colorful pedestrian zones. Immerse yourself in the city's art and history—crown jewels, Baroque theater, Wittelsbach palaces, great paintings, and beautiful parks. Spend your Munich evenings in a frothy beer hall or outdoor *Biergarten,* prying big pretzels from buxom, no-nonsense beer maids amidst an oompah, bunny-hopping, and belching Bavarian atmosphere.

Planning Your Time

Munich is worth two days, including a half-day side-trip to Dachau. But if all you have for Munich is one day, follow the self-guided walk laid out in this chapter (visiting museums along the way), tour the Residenz museum and treasury, and drink in the beer-hall culture for your evening's entertainment. With a second day, choose from the following: Tour the Dachau Concentration Camp Memorial, rent a bike to enjoy the English Garden, head out to the BMW-Welt and Museum, exhaust yourself at the Deutsches Museum, or—if you're into art—tour your choice of the city's many fine art galleries (especially the Alte Pinakothek). With all these blockbuster sights and activities, the city could

MUNICH

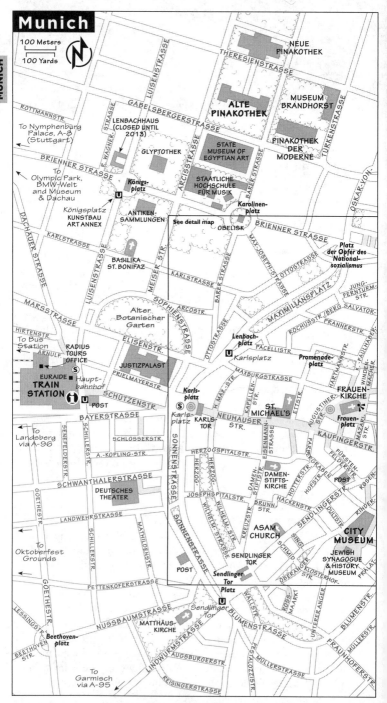

Munich

100 Meters
100 Yards

N

KOTTMANNSTR

To Nymphenburg
Palace, A-8
(Stuttgart)

BRIENNER STRASSE

To
Olympic Park,
BMW-Welt
and Museum
& Dachau

DACHAUER STRASSE

GABELSBERGERSTRASSE

LUISENSTRASSE

R. WAGNER

LENBACHHAUS
(CLOSED UNTIL
2013)

GLYPTOTHEK

Königsplatz

U

Königsplatz
KUNSTBAU
ART ANNEX

ANTIKEN-
SAMMLUNGEN

THERESIENSTRASSE

ARCISSTRASSE

BAKER STRASSE

NEUE
PINAKOTHEK

ALTE
PINAKOTHEK

STATE
MUSEUM OF
EGYPTIAN ART

STAATLICHE
HOCHSCHULE
FÜR MUSIK

Karolinen-
platz

See detail map   OBELISK

MUSEUM
BRANDHORST

PINAKOTHEK
DER
MODERNE

TÜRKENSTRASSE

OSKAR-VON-

BRIENNER STRASSE

Platz
der Opfer des
National-
sozialismus

KARLSTRASSE

BASILIKA
ST. BONIFAZ

MARSSTRASSE

HIRTENSTR
To Bus
Station

EURAIDE
TRAIN
STATION

RADIUS
TOURS
OFFICE
ARNULF

LUISENSTRASSE

MEISER STR.

SOPHIENSTRASSE

Alter
Botanischer
Garten

ELISENSTR.

JUSTIZPALAST

Hauptbahnhof

PRIELMAYERSTR.

ARCOSTR

KARLSTRASSE

BAKER STRASSE

MAX-JOSEPH-STRASSE

OTTOSTRASSE

Lenbach-
platz

U

Karlsplatz

Karls-
platz

S

Karls-
platz

KARLS-
TOR

MAXIMILIANSPLATZ

JUNG-
FERNTURM-
STR.

ROCHUSSTR / BERG SALVATOR

PRANNERSTR.

PACELLISTR

H.-MAX-STR.

MAXBURGSTRASSE

NEUHAUSER

KAPELLEN-STR.

Promenade-
platz

FRAUEN-
KIRCHE

AUGUSTINER-STR.

Frauen-
platz

WINDEN-FAULHABER-

MAZAR

POST

BAYERSTRASSE

SCHÜTZENSTR.

U

POST

SENEFELDERSTR.

To
Landsberg
via A-96

SCHILLERSTR.

GOETHESTR.

To
Oktoberfest
Grounds

SCHLOSSERSTR.

A.-KOPLING-STR.

SCHWANTHALERSTRASSE

LANDWEHRSTRASSE

MATHILDENSTR.

DEUTSCHES
THEATER

SONNENSTRASSE

ST
MICHAEL'S

STR.

EISENMANN-STRASSE

HERZOGSPITALSTR.

HERZOG

DAMEN-STIFTS

JOSEPHSPITALSTR.

WILHELM-STR.

BRUNN-STR.

KREUZSTR.

HACKENSTR.

ASAM
CHURCH

SENDLINGER
TOR

POST

KAUFINGERSTR.

FÜRSTEN-
FELDERSTR.

HOFSTR.

SENDLINGERSTR

SENDLINGER

SCHMID

SING-

OBERANGER

KLOSTERHOF.

ROSEN-

KINDER-

DULTST.

CITY
MUSEUM

JEWISH
SYNAGOGUE
& HISTORY
MUSEUM

PRÄLAT-

PETTENKOFERSTRASSE

Sendlinger
Tor
Platz

Sendlinger
Tor

U

BLUMENSTRASSE

KOB-
MAART-

UNTERERANGER-

BLUMENSTR.

FRAUNHOFERSTR.

LESSINGSTR.

BEETHOVEN-STR.

Beethoven-
platz

NUSSBAUMSTRASSE

MATTHÄUS-
KIRCHE

LINDWURMSTRASSE

GOETHESTR.

To
Garmisch
via A-95

AUGSBURGERSTR.

MÜLLERSTR.

HOLZ-

FESTAVOZISTR.

REISINGERSTRASSE

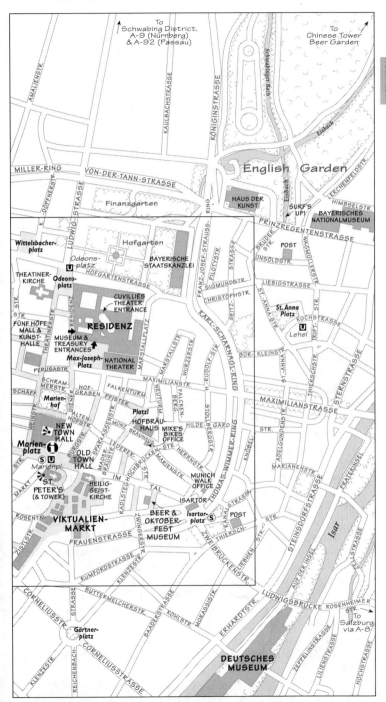

easily fill three days. And remember, many visitors spend an entire day side-tripping south to "Mad" King Ludwig's Castles. Austria's Salzburg (1.5-2 hours one-way by train) is also within day-tripping distance.

Orientation to Munich

(area code: 089)

The tourist's Munich is circled by a ring road (site of the old town wall) marked by four old gates: Karlstor (near the main train station—the Hauptbahnhof), Sendlinger Tor, Isartor (near the river), and Odeonsplatz (no surviving gate, near the palace). Marienplatz marks the city's center. A great pedestrian-only zone (Kaufingerstrasse and Neuhauser Strasse) cuts this circle in half, running neatly from the Karlstor and the train station through Marienplatz to the Isartor. Orient yourself along this east-west axis. Ninety percent of the sights and hotels I recommend are within a 20-minute walk of Marienplatz and each other.

Despite its large population, Munich feels small. This big-city elegance is possible because of its determination to be pedestrian- and bike-friendly, and because of a law that no building can be taller than the church spires. Despite ongoing debate about changing this policy, there are still no skyscrapers in downtown Munich.

Tourist Information

Munich has two helpful city-run TIs (www.muenchen.de). One is in front of the **main train station** (with your back to the tracks, walk through the central hall, step outside, and turn right; Mon-Sat 9:00-20:00, Sun 10:00-18:00, hotel reservations tel. 089/2339-6500—no info at this number). The other TI is on Munich's main square, **Marienplatz,** below the glockenspiel (Mon-Fri 10:00-19:00, Sat 10:00-17:00, Sun 10:00-14:00).

At either TI, pick up brochures and a city map (€0.40, better than the free map in hotel lobbies—especially for anyone using public transit), and confirm your sightseeing plans. Consider the *Monatsprogramm* (€2, German-language list of sights and events calendar) and the free, twice-monthly magazine *In München* (in German, lists all movies and entertainment in town). The TI can book you a room (you'll pay about 10 percent here, then pay the rest at the hotel), but you'll get a better value by contacting my recommended hotels directly. If you're interested in a Gray Line tour of the city or to nearby castles, don't buy your ticket at the TI; instead, you can get discounted tickets for these same tours at EurAide.

The **City Tour Card,** which covers public transportation and gives stingy discounts at minor sights, is a bad deal (€10/1 day, €19/3 days, sold at TIs). Two or more people traveling on a Munich "partner" all-day transit pass blow this deal out of the water (for details, see "Getting Around Munich," later).

The 14-day **Bavarian Castles Pass** covers admission to Munich's Residenz and Nymphenburg Palace Complex, as well as other castles and palaces in Bavaria (€24, €40 family/partner pass, annual pass also available, not sold at TI—purchase at participating sights, www.schloesser.bayern.de). For avid castle-goers, this is a deal: Two people will save €5 with a family/partner pass even if only visiting the two Munich sights.

EurAide

At counter #1 in the train station's main *Reisezentrum* (travel center), the hardworking, eager-to-help EurAide desk is a godsend

for Eurailers and budget travelers. Alan Wissenberg and his EurAide staff can answer your train-travel and accommodations questions in clear American English. Paid by the German rail company to help you design your train travels, EurAide makes reservations and sells tickets, *couchettes*, and sleepers for the train at the same price you'd pay at the other counters (open April-Oct Mon-Fri 10:00-19:00, closed Sat-Sun and Nov-March). EurAide sells a €0.50 city map and offers a free, information-packed newsletter, *The Inside Track* (always available in a rack at their door; also see www.euraide.com). As EurAide helps about 500 visitors per day in the summer, a line can build up; do your homework and have a list of questions ready. Chances are that your questions are already answered in *The Inside Track* newsletter—grab it and scan it first.

EurAide also sells tickets for Munich Walk city walking tours and Gray Line city bus tours, as well as for Gray Line tours to Neuschwanstein and Linderhof castles (all described later, under "Tours in Munich"). They offer a discount on these tickets to travelers with this book.

Arrival in Munich

By Train: Munich's main train station (München Hauptbahnhof) is a sight in itself—one of those places that can turn a homebody into a fancy-free vagabond.

Clean, high-tech **public toilets** are downstairs near track 26

(€1, showers-€7). For a quick rest stop, Burger King's toilets (upstairs) are as pleasant and accessible as its hamburgers.

Check out the bright and modern **food court** opposite track 14. For sandwiches and prepared meals to bring on board, I shop at **Yorma's** (two branches: one by track 26, another outside the station, next to the TI).

You'll find a city-run **TI** (out front of station and to the right) and **lockers** (€3-5, opposite track 26). **Car-rental agencies** are up the steps opposite track 21. A quiet, non-smoking **waiting room** *(Warteraum)* is open to anybody (across from track 23 and up the escalator), but the nearby, plush **DB Lounge** is only for those with a first-class ticket issued by DeutscheBahn (railpasses don't get you in). The **k presse + buch** shop (across from track 23) is great for English-language books, newspapers, and magazines. **Radius Tours** (at track 32) rents bikes and organizes tours.

Subway lines, trams, and buses connect the station to the rest of the city (though many of my recommended hotels are within walking distance of the station). If you get lost in the underground maze of subway corridors while you're simply trying to get to the train station, follow the signs for *DB* (DeutscheBahn) to surface successfully. Watch out for the hallways with blue ticket-stamping machines in the middle—these lead to the subway, where you could be fined if nabbed without a validated ticket.

By Bus: Munich's central bus station, called the **ZOB,** is by the Hackerbrücke S-Bahn station (from the train station, it's one S-Bahn stop, two stops on the #16/#17 tram, or a 10-15 minute walk; www.muenchen-zob.de). The Romantic Road bus leaves from here, as do many buses to Eastern Europe and the Balkans.

By Plane: For airport information, see "Munich Connections" at the end of this chapter.

Helpful Hints

Museum Hours: Sights closed on Monday include the Alte Pinakothek, Munich City Museum, Jewish Museum, Pinakothek der Moderne, Museum Brandhorst, Glyptothek, Bavarian National Museum, Beer and Oktoberfest Museum, Dachau Concentration Camp, and BMW-Welt and Museum. The Neue Pinakothek closes Tuesday. The art galleries are generally open late one night a week. On Sunday, the Pinakotheks, Glyptothek, Museum Brandhorst, and Bavarian National Museum cost just €1 apiece, but you'll pay extra for the usually free audioguides.

Internet Access: Hole-in-the-wall call centers near the train station and all over town have Internet terminals. **Internet Cafe München,** underneath the train station, feels wholesome and has long hours and low prices (€2.40/hour; go down stairs by track 26, then pass the WC and go left after the Rischart bakery, or find Arnulfsstrasse 10 and go down the stairway with the S-Bahn sign between #10 and #12; Mon-Fri 8:00-23:00, Sat-Sun 12:00-23:00, tel. 089/5161-7995).

Bookstore: The German bookstore chain **Hugendubel** runs a good English-language store at Salvatorplatz 2, between Marienplatz and Odeonsplatz (Mon-Sat 10:00-19:00, closed Sun, tel. 01801/484-484).

Need a Toilet? Munich had outdoor urinals until the 1972 Olympics and then decided to beautify the city by doing away with them. What about the people's needs? By law, any place serving beer must admit the public (whether or not they're customers) to use the toilets.

Pharmacy: Go out the front door of the train station, turn left, and walk a block to the corner of Elisenstrasse and Luisenstrasse (Mon-Fri 8:00-19:00, Sat 9:00-14:00, closed Sun, Elisenstrasse 5, tel. 089/595-444); another one is just below Marienplatz at Im Tal 13 (Mon-Fri 8:30-19:30, Sat 8:30-18:00, closed Sun, tel. 089/292-760).

Laundry: A handy self-service **Waschcenter** is a 10-minute walk from the train station (€7/load, €12 for larger machines, drop-off service €12/load, daily 7:00-23:00, English instructions, Paul-Heyse-Strasse 21, near intersection with Landwehrstrasse). Taking the U-4 or U-5 to Theresienwiese actually brings you a little closer to the laundry than getting off at the train station.

Bikes and Pedestrians: Signs painted on the sidewalk or blue-and-white street signs show which part of the sidewalk is designated for pedestrians and which is for cyclists. The strip of pathway closest to the street is usually reserved for bikes. Pedestrians wandering into the bike path may hear the cheery ding-ding of a cyclist's bell just before being knocked unconscious.

Taxi: Call 089/21610 for a taxi.

Private Driver: Johann Fayoumi is reliable and speaks English (€60/hour, mobile 0174-183-8473, www.firstclasslimousines .de, johannfayoumi@gmail.com).

Car Rental: Several car-rental agencies are located upstairs at the train station, opposite track 21 (open daily, hours vary).

***The Inside Track* Train Travelers' Newsletter:** Anyone traveling by train should pick up this wonk-ish yet brilliant quarterly newsletter published by Alan Wissenberg at EurAide (free, always available at the EurAide counter in the train station—described earlier, under "Tourist Information"). You'll find all the tedious but important details on getting to Neuschwanstein, Dachau, Nymphenburg, and Prague; the ins and outs of supplements and reservations necessary for railpass-holders; a daily schedule of various tours in Munich; and (of course) plenty of tips on how to take advantage of EurAide's services.

Great City Views: Downtown Munich's three best city viewpoints (all described in this chapter) are from the towers of St. Peter's Church (stairs only), Frauenkirche (stairs plus elevator), and New Town Hall (elevator).

What's with Monaco? People walking around with guidebooks to Monaco aren't lost. "Monaco di Baviera" means "Munich" in *Italiano*.

Getting Around Munich

Much of Munich is walkable. To reach sights away from the city center, use the efficient tram, bus, and subway systems. Taxis are honest and professional, but expensive and generally unnecessary.

By Public Transit

Subways are called U-Bahns and S-Bahns (S-Bahns are actually commuter railways that run underground through the city). The U-Bahn lines mainly run north-south, while the S-Bahn lines are generally east-west. All S-Bahn lines converge on the central axis running from the Hauptbahnhof to Marienplatz. Subway lines are numbered (for example, S-3 or U-5). Eurailpasses are good on the S-Bahn (but not the U-Bahn), but if you use a flexipass, it activates the use of a travel day. Trams are more convenient than subways for some destinations (such as Nymphenburg Palace); one bus (#100) is useful for getting to the Alte Pinakothek and other major museums.

The entire transit system (subway/bus/tram) works on the same tickets, sold at TIs, at booths in the subway, and at easy-to-use ticket machines marked *MVV* (which take coins and €5 and €10 bills). There are four concentric zones—white, green, yellow, and orange. Almost everything described in this chapter is within the white/inner zone, except for Dachau (green zone) and the airport (orange zone).

A one-zone **regular ticket** *(Einzelfahrkarte)* costs €2.50 and is good for three hours in one direction, including changes and stops. For short rides (four stops max, only two of which can be on the subway lines), buy the €1.20 *Kurzstrecke* ("short stretch") ticket. The €5.40 **all-day pass** *(Single-Tageskarte)* for the white/inner zone

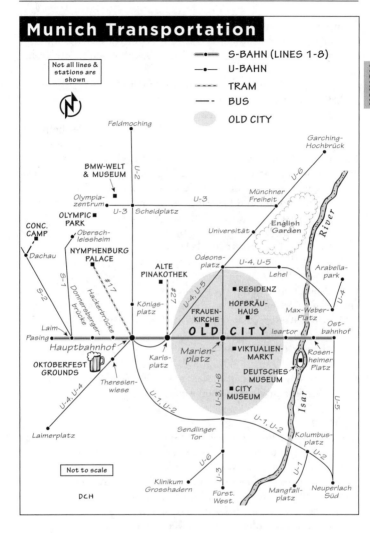

Munich Transportation

Not all lines & stations are shown

- ●━━ S-BAHN (LINES 1-8)
- ━●━ U-BAHN
- ⋯⋯ TRAM
- ━ ─ BUS
- ⬭ OLD CITY

Feldmoching

Garching-Hochbrück

BMW-WELT & MUSEUM

Olympia-zentrum

OLYMPIC PARK

Oberschleissheim

CONC. CAMP

Dachau

NYMPHENBURG PALACE

Münchner Freiheit

Scheidplatz

U-2

U-3

Universität

English Garden

River

ALTE PINAKOTHEK

Odeons-platz

U-4, U-5

Lehel

Arabella-park

RESIDENZ

HOFBRÄU-HAUS

Königs-platz

FRAUEN-KIRCHE

Max-Weber-Platz

Laim

Pasing

Hauptbahnhof

Marien-platz

OLD CITY

Isartor

Ost-bahnhof

Hackerbrücke

Donnersberger-brücke

Karls-platz

VIKTUALIEN-MARKT

Rosen-heimer Platz

OKTOBERFEST GROUNDS

Theresien-wiese

DEUTSCHES MUSEUM

CITY MUSEUM

Isar

Laimerplatz

Sendlinger Tor

Kolumbus-platz

Klinikum Grosshadern

Fürst. West.

Mangfall-platz

Neuperlach Süd

Not to scale

DCH

---

is a great deal for a single traveler. If you're going to Dachau, buy the *XXL* version of the *Single-Tageskarte,* which also includes the green zone (€7.30); the *Gesamtnetz* version of the pass covers all four zones and gets you to the airport (€10.80).

All-day small-group passes *(Partner-Tageskarte)* are an even better deal—they cover all public transportation for up to five adults and a dog (two kids count as one adult, so two adults, six kids, and a dog can travel with this ticket). A *Partner-Tageskarte* for the white/inner zone costs €9.40. The *XXL* version, which includes Dachau, costs €12.30; and the *Gesamtnetz* version, including the airport, costs €19.60. These partner tickets—while seemingly impossibly cheap—are for real. Read it again and do the arithmetic. Even two people traveling together save money, and for groups, it's a real steal. The only catch is that you've got to stay together.

For longer stays, consider a **three-day ticket** (€13.30/person, €22.80/partner ticket for the gang, white/inner zone only, does not include transportation to Dachau).

Maps of the transit system, available everywhere, help you navigate. To find the right platform, look for the name of the last station in the direction you want to travel. The name of this end-station is posted on trains and signs using the word *Richtung* ("direction"). Know where you're going relative to Marienplatz, the Hauptbahnhof, and Ostbahnhof, as these are so important to navigation that they are often referred to as end points.

In Munich, you must stamp all tickets with the date and time prior to using them (for an all-day or multi-day pass, you only have to stamp it the first time you use it). For the subway, punch your ticket in the blue machine *before* going down to the platform. For buses and trams, stamp your ticket once on board. Plainclothes ticket-checkers enforce this honor system, rewarding freeloaders with stiff €40 fines. All-day and multi-day passes are valid until 6:00 the following morning.

There's a transit customer-service center underground at Marienplatz (Mon-Fri 9:00-20:00, Sat 9:00-16:00, closed Sun, go down stairs by Beck's department store). For more transit info, call 01803/442-266 or visit www.mvv-muenchen.de.

By Bike

Level, compact, and with plenty of bike paths, Munich feels made for those on two wheels. When biking in Munich, follow these simple rules: You must walk your bike through pedestrian zones; you can take your bike on the subway, but not during rush hour and only if you have an extra ticket; and cyclists are expected to follow the rules of the road, just like drivers.

You can **rent bikes** quickly and easily from three great places: Radius Tours (in the train station), Mike's Bikes (near Marienplatz), and Munich Walk (at the Isartor). All have an extensive selection of bikes; provide helmets, maps, and route advice; and offer bike tours. Radius and Munich Walk give a 10 percent discount with this book in 2012.

Radius Tours (*Rad* means "bike" in German) is in the train station in front of track 32 (3- to 7-speed city bikes-€3/hour, €14.50/day, €17/24 hours, €25/48 hours, fancier bikes cost more, €50 cash or credit-card deposit, April-Oct Mon-Fri 9:00-18:00, Sat-Sun 9:00-20:00, closed Nov-March, tel. 089/543-487-7730, www.radiustours.com).

Mike's Bikes is between Marienplatz and the Hofbräuhaus (€9/3 hours, €15/24 hours, daily mid-April-early Oct 10:00-20:00, March-mid-April and early Oct-mid-Nov 10:30-13:00 & 16:30-17:30, closed mid-Nov-Feb, Bräuhausstrasse 10—enter around corner on Hochbrückenstrasse, tel. 089/2554-3987, www.mikes biketours.com).

Munich Walk is at the other end of the tourist zone from the train station, right by the Isartor (€4/hour, €18/24 hours, €12 from 14:30 until the next morning, 2-hour minimum, open daily 10:00-23:00, Thomas-Wimmer-Ring 1, storefront says *Tourist info*, tel. 089/2423-1767, www.munichwalktours.de).

For a great city ride, consider this day on a bike: From the station (where you rent your bike), take the bike path on Arnulfstrasse, pedaling along the canal out to Nymphenburg Palace. Ride around the palace grounds, then head to Olympic Park and BMW-Welt, and finish at the English Garden (for the late-afternoon or early-evening scene) before returning to the center. Or go for the Isar River bike ride.

Tours in Munich

Munich's two largest conventional tour companies, Radius Tours and Munich Walk, both run bike tours (described earlier), walking tours, and day trips to Dachau Concentration Camp Memorial, Neuschwanstein Castle, and other places. Radius and Munich Walk compete directly with each other, and in my experience, they're comparable. **Radius Tours** has a convenient office and meeting point in the main train station, in front of track 32 (tel. 089/543-487-7720, www.radiustours .com, run by Gabi Holder). **Munich Walk** has their office near the Isartor at Thomas-Wimmer-Ring 1, and uses Marienplatz as their meeting point (tel. 089/2423-1767, www.munichwalk tours.de, tours@munichwalktours.de, Ralph Lünstroth). Both companies offer €2 off their walking tours with this book—don't forget to show this book and request your discount. There's also **Gray Line,** which runs sightseeing buses around town and on day trips (tel. 089/5490-7560, sightseeing-munich.com), and a couple of bike tour companies: Mike's Bikes and Lenny's (see later). You can buy discounted tickets for Gray Line and Munich Walk tours at EurAide.

"Free" Tours: You'll encounter brochures advertising "free" walking and biking tours. These tours aren't really free—tipping is expected, and the guides actually have to pay the company a cut for each person who takes the tour—so unless you tip at least a few euros per person, they don't make a penny. The tours tend to be light on history, and the guides work hard to promote their company's other tours (which are not free). Unless you're a poor backpacker, my advice is to favor the more established companies' tours, where you pay for a hardworking guide who can make the city's history come alive—and who is paid by the tour company.

Within Munich

Walking Tours—**Munich Walk** offers two daytime tours (€2 Rick Steves discount on each tour): a "City Walk" (€12, daily year-round at 10:45, May-mid-Oct also daily at 14:45, 2.25 hours) and "Hitler's Munich" (€12, daily at 10:15, 2.5 hours, extended €22 five-hour version Mon and Sat only). Their "Beer and Brewery" tour is more mature than your typical hard-partying pub crawl. You visit Paulaner, Munich's oldest brewery, to learn, eat, and drink in the city that made beer famous. The price includes three different beers in the brewery; afterward, the tour ends at the Hofbräuhaus (€20, May-mid-Sept daily at 18:15, fewer tours off-season, 3.5 hours). They also offer a Bavarian food-tasting tour, where you visit the Viktualienmarkt for lunch (€22 includes food), and a €14 Haunted Munich evening tour (check their website for schedules). All Munich Walk tours depart from under the glockenspiel on Marienplatz. You don't need to reserve—just show up.

Radius Tours runs two city walking tours, both with reliably good guides: "Priceless Munich" (no up-front charge but tip for guide requested, daily at 10:10, 2 hours) and "Birthplace of the Third Reich" (€12, €2 Rick Steves discount, April-mid-Oct daily at 15:00; mid-Oct-March Mon, Tue, Fri, and Sun at 11:30; 2.5 hours). They also offer an educational "Bavarian Beer and Food" tour that includes a visit to the Beer and Oktoberfest Museum, samples of four varieties of beer, and regional food (€27, €2 Rick Steves discount; Tue, Thu, and Sat at 18:00; also Wed and Fri at 18:00 April-mid-Oct; no tours during Oktoberfest; 3 hours). All tours depart from the Radius office (in front of track 32 at the train station). No need to reserve—just show up.

Local Guides—A guide can be a great value—especially if you assemble a small group. Six people splitting the cost can make the luxury of a private guide affordable. I've had great days with two good guides, each charging the same price (€130/3 hours): **Georg Reichlmayr** (tel. 08131/86800, mobile 0170-341-6384, program explained on his website, www.muenchen-stadtfuehrung .de, info@muenchen-stadtfuehrung.de) and **Monika Hank** (tel. 089/311-4819, mobile 0175-923-2339, monika.hank@web.de). They've helped me with much of the historical information in this chapter.

Bike Tours—Munich lends itself to bike touring, and four outfits fit the bill. You don't need to reserve for any of these—just show up—but do confirm times in advance online or by phone.

Munich Walk offers 3.5-hour bike tours around Munich (€20, €2 Rick Steves discount, April-Oct only, daily at 10:45, depart from under the glockenspiel on Marienplatz). They also have a four-hour mountain bike tour out into the countryside along the Isar River, including a lunch stop at a beer garden (€29, €2 Rick Steves discount, Sat at 10:00, May-Oct only; departing from their Isartor office). Confirm times at www.munichwalktours.de.

Radius Tours has similar 3.5-hour bike tours on Tuesdays, Thursdays, and Sundays (€19.50, €1.50 Rick Steves discount, May-mid-Oct only at 10:30). Tours leave from the Radius office at track 32 in the train station (confirm times at www.radiustours.com).

Mike's Bike Tours, popular with the college crowd, are four hours of entertainment on wheels. The tours are high-energy, if a bit clunky with pacing, and the guides are better comedians than historians. Still, you get a great ride through the English Garden (€29, 1-hour break in Chinese Tower beer garden, daily mid-April-Aug at 11:30 and 16:00, March-mid-April and Sept-mid-Nov at 12:30, meet under tower of Old Town Hall on Marienplatz; tel. 089/2554-3987, mobile 0172-852-0660, www.mikesbiketours .com).

Lenny's Bike Tours has a €10 tour (with a request for tips at the end) that is generally led by young Brits (3.5 hours with an hour at the Chinese Tower beer garden, in English only, starts at the fish fountain in Marienplatz, daily mid-April-Aug at 11:30 and 16:00, March-mid-April and Sept-mid-Nov at 12:30, tel. 089/4202-4505, mobile 0176-8114-3062, www.discovermunichnow.com).

Quickie Orientation City Bus Tour—Gray Line Tours has hop-on, hop-off bus tours that leave from in front of the Karstadt department store at Bahnhofplatz, directly across from the train station. Choose from a basic, one-hour "Express Circle" that heads past the Pinakotheks, Marienplatz, and Karlsplatz (3/hour, 9:00-17:30); or the more extensive "Grand Circle" that lasts 2.5 hours and also includes the Nymphenburg Palace and BMW-Welt/Museum (1/hour, 9:00-16:00). If you plan on visiting Nymphenburg and the BMW center, this is a very efficient way to see both—just plan your visits to these sights around the tour schedule (bus generally leaves from Nymphenburg at :30 past the hour, and from BMW at :55 past). This tour is actually well worthwhile—sitting upstairs on the topless double-decker bus, you'll see lots of things missed by the typical visitor wandering around the center. It comple-ments the information in this book, though the live narration (in German and English) is delivered as stiffly as a tape recording. Just show up and pay the driver (cash only), or get a €1-2 discount by buying your ticket in advance at EurAide (€13 Express tour, €19 Grand tour, daily in season, tel. 089/5490-7560, www.sightseeing -munich.com).

MUNICH

Beyond Munich

While you can do all these day trips from Munich on your own by train, going as part of an organized group can be convenient—especially to Neuschwanstein.

"Mad" King Ludwig's Castle at Neuschwanstein—Choose between an escorted tour to Neuschwanstein by train and local bus, or guided private bus tours that include extras such as Linderhof Castle. Though they're a little more expensive, I prefer the bus tours—you're guaranteed a seat (public transport to Neuschwanstein is routinely standing-room only in summer), and you get to see more. All these tours can sell out, especially in summer, so it's wise to buy your ticket a day ahead (for information on visiting the castle on your own, see the next chapter).

Gray Line Tours offers rushed all-day bus tours of Neuschwanstein that also include Ludwig's Linderhof Castle and 30 minutes in Oberammergau (€49, €7 Rick Steves discount if you buy your ticket at EurAide—cash only, two castle admissions-€17 extra, daily April-Oct, no tours Mon Nov-March, www.sight seeing-munich.com). Tours meet at 8:10 and depart at 8:30 from the Karstadt department store (across from the station). While tours are designed to be in both English and German, if groups are large they may split them up and you'll get only English. **Munich Walk** advertises a tour that sounds similar—because they're simply selling tickets for this Gray Line trip.

Mike's Bike Tours runs a similar private bus tour with an outdoor theme—a bike ride and short hike near Neuschwanstein are included (€49, or €39 without bike ride; Neuschwanstein admission-€9 extra; June-mid-Sept at least Mon, Thu, and Sat at 8:35, during Oktoberfest at 9:35 but without bike ride, meet at Mike's Bike office, Bräuhausstrasse 10—enter around corner on Hochbrückenstrasse, tel. 089/2554-3987, mobile 0172-852-0660, www.mikesbiketours.com).

Radius Tours runs all-day tours to Neuschwanstein Castle using public transportation. Your guide will escort you onto the train to Füssen and then the bus from there to the castle, give you some general information, and help you into the castle for the standard tour that's included with any admission ticket (€32 with this book, €25 with railpass, castle admission-€9 extra; daily mid-April-Sept at 9:30, back by 19:00; Oct-mid-April tours run Mon, Wed, Fri, Sat, and Sun at 9:30; smart to reconfirm times, departs from the Radius office near track 32 in the train station, www .radiustours.com).

Dachau Concentration Camp—While several companies do Dachau tours, only Radius Tours and Munich Walk are allowed to actually guide inside the camp. The camp is easy to see on your own. But if you'd prefer a guided visit, these tours are a great value, considering how good and passionate their guides are—and that you're only paying about €10 for the guiding, once you factor in transportation costs. Allow about five hours total, and keep in mind that Dachau is closed on Mondays. Both companies charge the same price (€21, includes the €7 cost of public transportation, €3 Rick Steves discount). It's smart to reserve the day before, especially for the morning tours. Choose between **Radius** (April–mid-Oct Tue-Sun at 9:15 and 12:30; mid-Oct–March Tue-Sun at 10:00) and **Munich Walk** (April-Oct Tue-Sun at 10:15 and 13:15; Nov-March Tue-Sun at 10:15).

Nürnberg—Just an hour away by fast train, this makes a great day trip from Munich. Do it on your own using this book, or take the **Radius Tours** all-day excursion (see their website for details—www.radiustours.com).

Other Day Tours—Radius Tours also offers all-day trips to Salzburg, Augsburg, and the castles at Herrenchiemsee (details at radiustours.com). Munich Walk does Salzburg tours (www.munichwalktours.com). These trips cost around €35-40 and include public transport there and back.

Self-Guided Walk

Munich City Walk

I've laced the top sights in the old town center into a ▲▲▲ walk, starting at Marienplatz and ending at the Hofgarten. You can do these sights in any order and take a break from the walk to tour the museums (details about visiting sights are included later, under "Sights in Munich"), but if you want to cover the center in a logical way, this is a great template. I've included basic walking directions linking the sights.

• *Begin your walk at the heart of the old city, with a stroll through...*

▲▲Marienplatz

Riding the escalator out of the subway into sunlit Marienplatz ("Mary's Square") gives you a fine first look at the glory of Munich: great buildings bombed flat and rebuilt, outdoor cafés, and people bustling and lingering like the birds and breeze with which they share this square. Take in the ornate facades of the gray, pointy Old Town Hall and the Neo-Gothic New Town Hall, with its beloved glockenspiel.

MUNICH

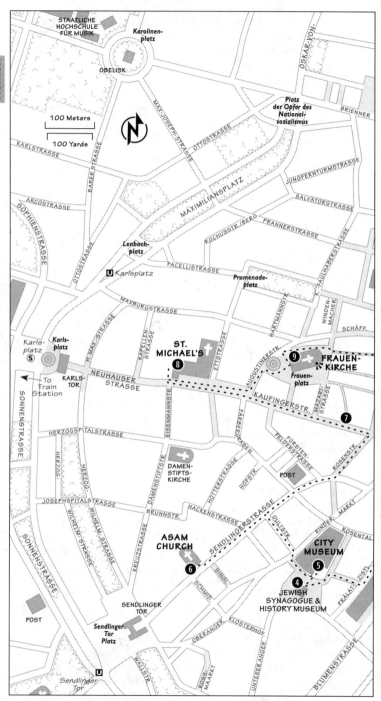

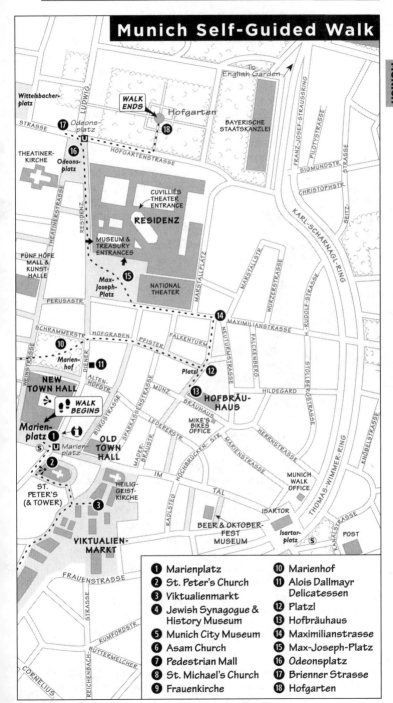

Munich Self-Guided Walk

WALK ENDS

Hofgarten

1 Marienplatz
2 St. Peter's Church
3 Viktualienmarkt
4 Jewish Synagogue & History Museum
5 Munich City Museum
6 Asam Church
7 Pedestrian Mall
8 St. Michael's Church
9 Frauenkirche
10 Marienhof
11 Alois Dallmayr Delicatessen
12 Platzl
13 Hofbräuhaus
14 Maximilianstrasse
15 Max-Joseph-Platz
16 Odeonsplatz
17 Brienner Strasse
18 Hofgarten

The **New Town Hall** (Neues Rathaus), built from 1867 until 1908, dominates Marienplatz. This very Neo-Gothic structure is a fine example of the same Historicism (mixing-and-matching of historical styles) that you see in nearby Neuschwanstein, London's Houses of Parliament, Budapest's Parliament, and other buildings of that era. Notice the politics of the statuary: The 40 statues—though sculpted only in 1900—decorate the New Town Hall not with civic leaders, but with royals and blue-blooded nobility. Because this building survived the bombs and had a central location, it served as the US military headquarters in 1945.

The New Town Hall is famous for its **glockenspiel**—dating from 1908—which "jousts" daily at 11:00 and 12:00 all year (also at 17:00 May-Oct). The *Spiel* re-creates a royal wedding from the 16th century: The duke and his bride watch the action as the groom's Bavarian family (in Bavarian white and blue) joyfully jousts with the bride's French family (in red and white). Below, the barrel-makers—famous for being the first to dance in the streets after a deadly plague lifted—do their popular jig.

At the very top of the New Town Hall is a statue of a child with outstretched arms, dressed in monk's garb and holding a book in its left hand. This is the **Münchner Kindl,** the symbol of Munich (the city's name comes from *Kloster von Mönchen*—"cloister of monks"). You'll spot this mini-monk all over town, on everything from posters to tram cars (often holding other objects, like a bundle of radishes or a giant beer). Over the centuries, the monk has gone through several transformations. He started as a grown man, wearing a gold-lined black cloak and red shoes. Artists later represented him as a young boy, then a gender-neutral child, and, more recently, a young girl. Every year, a young woman dressed as the *Kindl* kicks off Oktoberfest by leading the opening parade on horseback, and then serves as the mascot throughout the festivities.

The New Town Hall tower offers **views** of the city (€2.50, elevator from under glockenspiel; May-Oct daily 10:00-19:00; Nov-April Mon-Fri 10:00-17:00, closed Sat-Sun).

Marienplatz is marked by a statue of the square's namesake, the **Virgin Mary,** moved here in 1638 from its original location in the Frauenkirche in thanks that the Swedes didn't sack the town during their occupation. It was also a rallying point for the struggle against the Protestants. The cherubs are fighting the four great biblical enemies of civilization: the dragon of war, the lion of hunger, the rooster-headed monster of plague and disease, and the serpent of heresy (Protestantism). The serpent that's being stepped upon represents the "wrong faith," a.k.a. Martin Luther.

The **Old Town Hall** (Altes Rathaus; at the right side of the square as you face New Town Hall) was completely destroyed by WWII bombs and later rebuilt. Ludwig IV, an early Wittelsbach who was Holy Roman Emperor back in the 14th century, stands in the center of the facade. He donated this great square to the people. On the bell tower, find the city seal with its monk/*Kindl* and towers. Munich flourished because, in its early days, all salt trade had to stop here on Marienplatz.

• *Just beyond the southeast corner of Marienplatz, with its steeple poking up above a row of buildings, is...*

St. Peter's Church

The oldest church in town, St. Peter's overlooks Marienplatz from its perch near the Viktualienmarkt. It's built on the hill where

Munich's original monastic inhabitants probably settled. (Founded in 1158, the city celebrated its 850th birthday in 2008.) Outside, notice the old tombstones plastered onto the wall—a reminder that in the Napoleonic age, the cemeteries surrounding most city churches were (for hygienic and practical space reasons) dug up and moved.

St. Peter's was badly damaged in World War II. Inside, photos show the bomb damage (near the entrance). As part of the soul of the city (according to a popular song, "Munich is not Munich without St. Peter's"), the church was lovingly rebuilt—half with Augustiner beer money, the rest with private donations—and the altar and ceiling frescoes were marvelously restored (possible with the help of Nazi catalog photos).

Apostles line the nave, leading up to St. Peter above the altar. On the ceiling, you'll see Peter crucified upside-down. The finely crafted gray iron chapel fences were donated after World War II by the local blacksmiths of the national railway. The precious and fragile sandstone Gothic chapel altar (front left) survived the war

The History of Munich: Part 1
Monastic Beginnings to the Age of Kings

Born from Salt (1100-1500)

Munich began in the 12th century, when Henry the Lion (Heinrich der Löwe) muscled in on the lucrative salt trade, burning a rival's bridge over the Isar River and building his own near a monastery of "monks"—München. (The town's coat of arms features the Münchner Kindl, a child in monk's robes, see page 18.) Henry built walls and towers and opened a market, and peasants flocked in from the countryside. Marienplatz was the center of town and the crossroads of the Salzstrasse (Salt Road) from Salzburg to Augsburg. After Henry's death, the town was taken over by an ambitious merchant family, the Wittelsbachs (1240), and became the capital of the region (1255). Munich-born Louis IV (1282-1347) was elected king of Germany and Holy Roman Emperor, temporarily making Munich a major European capital.

By the 1400s, Munich's maypole-studded market bustled with trade. Besides salt, Munich gained a reputation for beer. More than 30 breweries pumped out the golden liquid that lubricated both trade and traders. The Bavarian Beer Purity Law assured quality control. Wealthy townspeople erected the twin-domed Frauenkirche and the Altes Rathaus on Marienplatz, and the Wittelsbachs built a stout castle that would eventually become the cushy Residenz. When the various regions of Bavaria united in 1506, Munich (pop. 14,000) was the natural capital.

Religious Wars, Plagues, Decline (1500-1800)

While Martin Luther and the Protestant Reformation raged in northern Germany, Munich became the ultra-Catholic heart of the Counter-Reformation. The devout citizens poured enormous funds into building the massive St. Michael's Church (1583) as a home for the Jesuits, and into the Residenz (early 1600s) as home of the Wittelsbachs. Both were showpieces of conservative power and the Baroque and Rococo styles.

During the Thirty Years' War, the Catholic city was surrounded by Protestants (1632). The Wittelsbachs surrendered quickly and paid a ransom, sparing the city from pillage, but it was soon hit by the bubonic plague. After that passed, the leaders erected the Virgin's column on Marienplatz to thank God for killing only 7,000 citizens. (Munich's many plagues are also remembered today when the glockenspiel's barrel-makers do their daily dance to ward off the plague.)

The double whammy of invasion and disease left Munich bankrupt and powerless, overshadowed by the more powerful Habsburgs of Austria. The Wittelsbachs took their cultural cues from France (Nymphenburg Palace is a mini-Versailles), England (the English Garden), and Italy (the Pitti Palace-inspired Residenz). While the rest of Europe modernized and headed toward democracy, Munich remained conservative and backward.

The Kings (1806-1918): Max I, Ludwig I, Max II, Ludwig II, Ludwig III

When Napoleon's army surrounded the city (1800), the Wittelsbachs again surrendered hospitably. Napoleon rewarded the Wittelsbach "duke" with more territory and a royal title: "king." Maximilian I (r. 1806-1825), a.k.a. Max Joseph, now ruled the Kingdom of Bavaria, a nation bigger than Switzerland, with a constitution and parliament. When Max's popular son Ludwig married (Sept 1810), it touched off a two-week celebration that became an annual event: Oktoberfest.

As king, Ludwig I (r. 1825-1848) set about rebuilding the capital in the Neoclassical style we see today. Medieval walls and ramshackle houses were replaced with grand buildings of columns and arches (including the Residenz and Alte Pinakothek). Connecting these were broad boulevards and plazas for horse carriages and promenading citizens (Ludwigstrasse and Königsplatz). Ludwig established the university and built the first railway line, turning Munich (pop. 90,000) into a major transportation hub, budding industrial city, and fitting capital.

In 1846, the skirt-chasing King Ludwig (see Nymphenburg's Gallery of Beauties, page 55) was beguiled by a notorious Irish dancer named Lola Montez. She became his mistress, and he fawned over her in public, scandalizing Munich. The Münchners resented her spending their tax money and dominating their king (supposedly inspiring the phrase "Whatever Lola wants, Lola gets"). In 1848, as Europe was swept by a tide of revolution, the citizens rose up and forced Ludwig to abdicate. His son Maximilian II (r. 1848-1864) continued Ludwig's enlightened program of modernizing, while studiously avoiding dancers from Ireland.

In 1864, 18-year-old Ludwig II (r. 1864-1886) became king. He invited the composer Richard Wagner to Munich, planning a lavish new opera house to stage Wagner's operas. Munich didn't like the idea, and Ludwig didn't like Munich. For most of his reign, Ludwig avoided the Residenz and Nymphenburg, instead building castles in the Bavarian countryside at the expense of Munich taxpayers. (For more on the king, see page 105.)

In 1871, Bavaria became part of the newly united Germany, and overnight, Berlin overtook Munich as Germany's power center. But turn-of-the-century Munich was culturally rich, giving birth to the abstract art of Wassily Kandinsky, Paul Klee, and the Blue Rider group. But this artistic flourishing didn't last long. World War I devastated Munich. Poor, hungry, disillusioned, unemployed Münchners roamed the streets. Extremists from the left and right battled for power. In 1918, a huge mob marched to the gates of the Residenz and drove the forgettable King Ludwig III (r. 1913-1918)—the last Bavarian king—out of the city, ending nearly 700 years of continuous Wittelsbach rule.

For "The History of Munich: Part 2," see page 26.

only because it was buried in sandbags.

Munich has more relics than any city outside of Rome. For more than a hundred years, it was the pope's bastion against the rising tide of Protestantism in northern Europe during the Reformation. Favors done in the defense of Catholicism earned the Wittelsbachs neat relic treats. For instance, check out the tomb of Munditia (second side chapel on left as you enter). She's a third-century martyr (note the ancient Roman tombstone with red lettering), whose remains were given to Munich by Rome in thanks and as a vivid reminder that those who die for the cause of the Roman Church go directly to heaven without waiting for Judgment Day.

It's a long climb to the top of the **spire** (306 steps, no elevator)—much of it with two-way traffic on a one-lane staircase—but the view is dynamite (€1.50, Mon-Fri 9:00-18:30, Sat-Sun 10:00-18:30, off-season until 17:30, last exit 30 minutes after closing). Try to be two flights from the top when the bells ring at the top of the hour. Then, when your friends back home ask you about your trip, you'll say, "What?"

• *Just behind and beyond (downhill from) St. Peter's, join the busy commotion of the...*

▲▲Viktualienmarkt

Early in the morning, you can still feel small-town Munich here, long a favorite with locals for fresh produce and good service (open Mon-Sat, food stalls open late, closed Sun).

The most expensive real estate in town could never really support such a market, but Munich charges only a percentage of the gross income, enabling these old-time shops to carry on (and keeping out fast-food chains).

The huge **maypole** is a tradition. Fifteenth-century town market squares posted a maypole as a practical information post—decorated with various symbols to explain which crafts and merchants were doing business in the market. Munich's maypole shows the city's six great brews, and the crafts and festivities associated with brewing. (You can't have a kegger without coopers—find the merry barrel-makers.)

Notice the **beer counter.** Munich's breweries take turns here. Changing every day or two, a sign *(Heute im Ausschank)* announces which of the six brews is being served today. Here, under the standard beer-garden chestnut trees, you can order just half a liter—unlike at other *Biergarten*s (handy for shoppers who want to have

a quick sip and then keep on going). The Viktualienmarkt is ideal for a light meal.
• *Leave the Viktualienmarkt from the far side, then walk two blocks (ask anyone: "Synagogue?") to find the...*

Jewish Synagogue and History Museum (Jüdisches Museum München)

Thanks to Germany's acceptance of religious refugees from former Soviet states, Munich's Jewish population has now reached its pre-Nazi size—10,000 people. The city's new synagogue and Jewish

History Museum anchor a revitalized Jewish quarter, which includes a kindergarten and day school, children's playground, fine kosher restaurant (at #18), and bookstore.

While the **synagogue** is shut tight to non-worshippers, its architecture is striking from the outside. Lower stones of travertine evoke the Wailing Wall in Jerusalem, while an upper section represents the tent that held important religious wares during the 40 years of wandering through the desert until the Temple of Solomon was built, ending the Exodus. The synagogue's door features the first 10 letters of the Hebrew alphabet, symbolizing the Ten Commandments.

The cube-shaped **museum** (behind the cube-shaped synagogue) is stark, windowless, and as inviting as a bomb shelter. Its small permanent exhibit in the basement is disappointing. The two floors of temporary exhibits might justify the entry fee.

Cost and Hours: Museum-€6, discount with Munich City Museum, Tue-Sun 10:00-18:00, closed Mon, St.-Jakobs-Platz 16, tel. 089/2339-6096, www.juedisches-museum-muenchen.de.
• *Facing the synagogue, on the same square, is the...*

▲▲Munich City Museum (Münchner Stadtmuseum)

Five floors of exhibits in this recently renovated museum tell the story of life in Munich through the centuries, including the history of "monk culture," the development of National Socialism (i.e., Nazism), and World War II—illustrated with paintings, photos, and models. Their good permanent exhibit, called "Typically Munich!", examines the various stereotypes—both positive and negative—that people around the world associate with this city.

Cost and Hours: €4, discount with Jewish History Museum, open Tue-Sun 10:00-18:00, closed Mon, English descriptions in loaner booklets, €3 audioguide, no crowds, bored and playful guards, St.-Jakobs-Platz 1, tel. 089/2332-2370, www.stadtmuseum -online.de.

Eating: The museum's Stadt Café is handy for a good meal (listed under "Eating in Munich," later).

• *Continue another three blocks away from the market—one block to Sendlinger Strasse, then two blocks south (left)—where you'll encounter the...*

Asam Church (Asamkirche)

The private church of the Asam brothers is a gooey, drippy Baroque-concentrate masterpiece by Bavaria's top two Rococonuts. Just 30

feet wide, it was built in 1740 to fit within this row of homes. While it was built as a private initiative by these two brother-architects to show off their work (on their own land, next to their home and business headquarters—to the left), it's also recognized by the Church as a legitimate place of worship.

The church served as a promotional brochure to woo clients, packed with every architectural trick in the books. Imagine approaching the church not as a worshipper, but as a shopper representing your church's building committee. First stand outside: Hmmm, the look of those foundation stones really packs a punch. And the legs hanging over the portico...nice effect. Those star-bursts on the door would be a hit back home, too.

Then step inside: I'll take a set of those over-the-top golden capitals, please. We'd also like to order the gilded garlands draping the church in jubilation, and the twin cupids capping the confessional. Check out the illusion of a dome on the flat ceiling—that'll save us lots of money. The yellow glass above the altar has the effect of the thin-sliced alabaster at St. Peter's in Rome, but it's within our budget! And, tapping the "marble" pilasters to determine that they are just painted fakes, we decide to take that, too... Visiting the Asam Church, you can see why the Asam brothers were so prolific and successful.

Cost and Hours: Free, Sat-Thu 9:15-18:00, closed Fri.

• *Leaving the church, turn left and walk straight up Sendlinger Strasse, and then Rosenstrasse, until you hit Marienplatz and the big, busy...*

Pedestrian Mall

This car-free area (on Kaufingerstrasse and Neuhauser Strasse) leads you through a great shopping district, past carnivals of street entertainers and good old-fashioned slicers and dicers. As one of Europe's first pedestrian zones, the mall enraged shop-keepers when it was built in 1972 for the Olympics. Today, it is Munich's living room. Nearly 9,000 shoppers pass through it each hour. The shopkeepers are happy...and merchants nearby are begging for their streets to become traffic-free. Imagine this street in Hometown, USA.

• *Stroll a few blocks away from Marienplatz toward the Karlstor, until you arrive at the big church on the right.*

St. Michael's Church

While one of the first great Renaissance buildings north of the Alps, this church has a brilliantly Baroque interior. Inspired by the Gesù (the Jesuits' main church in Rome), it was built in the late 1500s as a home to Bavaria's Jesuits (and rebuilt after WWII bombing—see photos in the back). The statue of Michael fighting a Protestant demon (on the front facade) is a reminder that this leader of heaven's army invited the Jesuits to literally counter the Reformation from here. The interior is striking for its barrel vault, the largest of its day. The crypt contains 40 stark royal tombs, including the resting place of King Ludwig II. Judging by all the flowers, romantics are still mad about their "mad" king.

Cost and Hours: Church entry free, daily 9:00-19:00, Thu until 20:45, Sun until 22:00; crypt-€2, Mon-Fri 9:30-16:30, Sat 9:30-14:30, closed Sun, less off-season; frequent concerts—check the schedule outside; www.st-michael-muenchen.de.

• *Backtrack a couple blocks on the pedestrian mall, then turn left at Augustinerstrasse to find Munich's towering, twin-domed cathedral.*

Frauenkirche

These twin onion domes are the symbol of the city. Some say Crusaders, inspired by the Dome of the Rock in Jerusalem, brought home the idea. Others say these domes are the inspiration for the characteristic domed church spires marking villages throughout Bavaria.

Cost and Hours: Free, Sat-Wed 7:00-19:00, Thu 7:00-20:30, Fri 7:00-18:00, www.muenchner-dom.de.

Touring the Church: Go inside. While much of the church was destroyed during World War II (see photos just inside the entrance, on the right), the towers survived, and the rest has been gloriously restored.

Built in Gothic style in the late 1400s, the Frauenkirche

The History of Munich: Part 2
Troubled 20th Century
and Today's Revitalization

This picks up where "Part 1" leaves off (see page 20).

Nazis, World War II, and Munich Bombed (1918-1945)

Germany after World War I was in chaos. In quick succession, the prime minister was gunned down, Communists took power, and the army restored the old government. In the hubbub, one fringe group emerged—the Nazi party, headed by the charismatic war veteran Adolf Hitler.

Hitler—an Austrian who'd settled in Munich—made stirring speeches in Munich's beer halls (including the Hofbräuhaus) and galvanized the city's disaffected. On November 8-9, 1923, the Nazis launched a coup d'état known as the Beer Hall Putsch. They kidnapped the mayor, and Hitler led a mob to overthrow the German government in Berlin. The march got as far as Odeonsplatz before Hitler was arrested and sent to prison in nearby Landsberg. Though the Nazis eventually gained power in Berlin, they remembered their roots, dubbing Munich "Capital of the Movement." The Nazi headquarters stood near today's obelisk on Brienner Strasse, Dachau was chosen as the regime's first concentration camp, and Odeonsplatz was designated as a place where all who passed by were required to perform the Nazi salute.

As World War II drew to a close, it was clear that Munich would be destroyed. Hitler did not allow the evacuation of much of the town's portable art treasures and heritage—a mass emptying of churches and civil buildings would have caused hysteria and been a statement of no confidence in his leadership. While museums were closed (and could be systematically emptied over the war years), public buildings were not. Rather than save the treasures, the Nazis photographed everything.

Munich was indeed pummeled mercilessly by air raids, leveling nearly half the city. What the bombs didn't get was destroyed by 10 years of rain and freezing winters.

(Church of Our Lady) has been the city's cathedral since 1821. Construction was funded with the sale of indulgences, but money problems meant the domes weren't added until Renaissance times. Late-Gothic buildings in Munich were generally built of brick—easy to make locally and cheaper and faster to build than stone. This church was constructed in a remarkable 20 years. It's located on the grave of Ludwig IV (who died in 1347). His big, black, ornate, tomb-like monument (now in the back) was originally in front at the high altar. Standing in the back of the nave, notice

MUNICH

Munich Rebuilds (1945-Present)

After the war, with generous American aid, Münchners set to reconstructing their city. During this time, many German cities established commissions to debate their rebuilding strategy: They could restore the old towns, or bulldoze and go modern. While Frankfurt decided to start from scratch (hence its Manhattan-like feel today), Munich voted—by a close margin—to rebuild its old town.

Münchners took care to preserve the original street plan and re-create the medieval steeples, Neo-Gothic facades, and Neoclassical buildings. They blocked off the city center to cars, built the people-friendly U-Bahn system, and opened up Europe's first pedestrian-only zone (Kaufingerstrasse and Neuhauser Strasse). Only now, nearly 65 years after the last bombs fell, are the restorations—based on those Nazi photographs—finally being wrapped up. And those postwar decisions still shape the city: Buildings cannot exceed the height of the church spires.

The 1972 Olympic Games, featuring a futuristic stadium and a squeaky-clean city, were to be Munich's postwar statement that it had arrived. However, the Games turned tragic when a Palestinian terrorist group stormed a dormitory and kidnapped (and eventually killed) 11 Israeli athletes. In 1989, when Germany reunited, Berlin once again became the focal point of the country, relegating Munich to the role of sleepy Second City.

These days, Munich seems to be comfortable just being itself rather than trying to keep up with Berlin. In fact, the city seems to be on a natural high, especially since the ascension of Joseph Ratzinger (the local archbishop) to the papacy in 2005, his wildly successful homecoming visit in 2006, and Munich hosting the World Cup soccer tournament that same year.

Today's Munich is rich—home to BMW and Siemens, and a producer of software, books, movies, and the latest fashions. It's consistently voted one of Germany's most livable cities—safe, clean, cultured, a university town, built on a people scale, and close to the beauties of nature. Though it's the capital of Bavaria and a major metropolis, Munich's low-key atmosphere has led Germans to dub it *Millionendorf*—the "village of a million people."

how your eyes go right to the altar...Christ...and (until recently) Ludwig. Those Wittelsbachs—always trying to be associated with God. In fact, this alliance was instilled in people through the prayers they were forced to recite: "Virgin Mary, mother of our duke, please protect us." A plaque over the last pew on the left recalls the life story of Joseph Ratzinger, who occupied the archbishop's seat in this very church from 1977 until 1982, when he moved into Pope John Paul II's inner circle in the Vatican, and ultimately became Pope Benedict XVI in 2005.

Other Church Sights: You can ascend the **tower** for the city's highest public viewpoint, at 280 feet (€3, 86 steps to elevator, April-Oct Mon-Sat 10:00-17:00, closed Sun and Nov-March). On many Wednesday evenings in summer, you can catch an **organ concert** here (€10, 19:00, tickets available at München Ticket office inside Marienplatz TI).

• *From here, we'll walk along back streets and squares, eventually ending up at the Hofgarten, the royal gardens. First walk two blocks directly behind the Frauenkirche to find the big, grassy square called...*

Marienhof

This square, tucked behind the New Town Hall, was left as a green island after the 1945 bombings. The square will be dug up for years while Munich builds a new subway tunnel here. With virtually the entire underground system converging on nearby Marienplatz, this new tunnel will provide a huge relief to the city's congested subterranean infrastructure.

• *On the far side of Marienhof is the most aristocratic grocery store in all of Germany...*

Alois Dallmayr Delicatessen

When the king called out for dinner, he called Alois Dallmayr. This place became famous for its exotic and luxurious food items: tropical fruits, seafood, chocolates, fine wines, and coffee (there are meat and cheese counters, too). As you enter, read the black plaque with the royal seal by the door: *Königlich Bayerischer Hof-Lieferant* ("Deliverer for the King of Bavaria and his Court"). Catering to royal and aristocratic tastes (and budgets), it's still the choice of Munich's old rich. Today, it's most famous for its sweets, chocolates, and coffee—dispensed from fine hand-painted Nymphenburg porcelain jugs.

Hours: Mon-Sat 9:30-19:00, closed Sun; two cafés inside—described later, under "Eating in Munich"; Dienerstrasse 13-15, down the street to the right of New Town Hall, www.dallmayr.de.

• *From Marienhof, Hofgraben (which becomes Pfisterstrasse) leads three blocks east, directly to Platzl—"small square." (If you get turned around, just ask any local to point you toward the Hofbräuhaus.)*

Platzl

As you stand here, recall that everything around you was flattened in 1945, and appreciate the facades. Imagine the work that

Oktoberfest

The 1810 marriage reception of King Ludwig I was such a success that it turned into an annual bash. These days, the

Oktoberfest lasts just over two weeks (Sept 22-Oct 7 in 2012), starting on the third Saturday in September and usually ending on the first Sunday in October (but never before Oct 3—the day Germany celebrates its recent reunification).

Oktoberfest kicks things off with an opening parade of more than 6,000 participants. Every night, it fills eight huge beer tents with about 6,000 people each. A million gallons of beer later, they roast the last ox.

It's best to reserve a room early, but if you arrive in the morning (except Fri or Sat) and haven't called ahead, the TI can usually help. The Theresienwiese fairground (south of the main train station), known as the "Wies'n" (VEE-zehn), erupts in a frenzy of rides, dancing, and strangers strolling arm-in-arm down rows of picnic tables while the beer god stirs tons of brew, pretzels, and wurst in a bubbling cauldron of fun. The triple-loop roller coaster must be the wildest on earth (best before the beer-drinking). During the fair, the city functions even better than normal. It's a good time to sightsee, even if beer-hall rowdiness isn't your cup of tea. For details, see www.oktoberfest.de.

If you're not visiting while the party's on, don't worry: You can still dance to oompah bands, munch huge pretzels, and show off your stein-hoisting skills any time of year at Munich's classic beer halls, including the venerable Hofbräuhaus (for descriptions of my favorite beer halls, see page 74).

Also in the city center, check out the humble **Beer and Oktoberfest Museum** (Bier- und Oktoberfestmuseum), which offers a low-tech and underwhelming take on history. Exhibits and artifacts outline the centuries-old quest for the perfect beer (apparently achieved in Munich) and the origins of the city's Oktoberfest celebration. The oldest house in the city center, the museum's home is noteworthy in itself (€4, Tue-Sat 13:00-17:00, closed Sun-Mon, between the Isartor and Viktualienmarkt at Sterneckerstrasse 2, tel. 089/2423-1607, www.bier-und-oktoberfestmuseum.de).

MUNICH

went into rebuilding Munich after World War II. The recon-struction happened in stages: From 1945 to 1950, they removed 12 million tons of bricks and replaced roofs to make buildings weather tight. From 1950 to 1972, they redid the exteriors. From 1972 to 2000, they refurbished the interiors. Today, Platzl hosts a lively mix of places to eat and drink—pop-culture chains like Starbucks and Hard Rock Café alongside top-end restaurants like Schuhbecks.

• *A the bottom of the square (#6), you can experience the venerable...*

▲▲Hofbräuhaus

Whether or not you slide your lederhosen on its polished benches, it's a great experience just to walk through the world's most famous beer hall in all its rowdy glory.

Cost and Hours: Free to enter, daily 9:00-23:30, live oompah music during lunch and dinner; a five-minute walk northeast of Marienplatz at Platzl 6, www.hofbraeuhaus.de.

Touring the Hofbräuhaus: As you wander the Hofbräuhaus (HOAF-broy-howze), look for the various *Stammtisch* signs (meaning "reserved" for regulars), hanging above tables where different clubs meet regularly; don't sit here unless you're specifically invited. Racks of locked steins, made of pottery and metal, are for regulars. You'll see locals stuffed into lederhosen and dirndls; giant ginger-bread cookies that sport romantic messages; and postcards of the German (and apparently beer-drinking) pope.

After being bombed in World War II, this palace of beer was quickly rebuilt (reflecting the durability of traditional German priorities) and back in business within a few years. Notice the quirky 1950s-style painted ceiling, with Bavarian colors, grapes, chestnuts, and fun "eat, drink, and be merry" themes. A slogan on the ceiling above the band reads, *Durst ist schlimmer als Heimweh* ("Thirst is worse than homesickness").

A bouncer at the door once told me he nabs 20-50 people (mostly Italians, he says) each day trying to steal mugs as souve-nirs. The staircase to the left of the entrance displays historic old Hofbräuhaus photos and prints; there's a more extensive historical display on the second floor (daily 9:00-17:00).

• *Leaving the Hofbräuhaus, turn right and walk two blocks up to the street called...*

Maximilianstrasse

This boulevard is known as the home of Munich's most exclusive shops. Ludwig I made the grand but very impersonal Ludwigstrasse. In the 1850s, as a reaction to the unpopularity of that street and its namesake king, his son Maximilian II (father of "Mad" King Ludwig) built a street designed for the people and for shopping. It leads from the National Theater, over the Isar River, to the Bavarian parliament (which you can see from the theater end).

• *Walk left on Maximilianstrasse to the big square facing both the Residenz and the National Theater.*

Max-Joseph-Platz

The giant building wrapping around the square is the **Residenz,** the palace of the Wittelsbach royal family. Munich's best palace interior to tour, it features a museum (including some of the complex's most sumptuous staterooms), an impressive treasury, and the fine Cuvilliés Theater.

The centerpiece of the square is a grand statue of King Maximilian I, a.k.a. **Max Joseph,** who was installed as Bavaria's king in 1806 by Napoleon. Because Napoleon was desperate to establish his family as royal, Max Joseph was crowned on one condition: that his daughter marry Napoleon's stepson.

Later, with the Holy Roman Empire gone and Napoleon history, modern 19th-century kings had little choice but to embrace constitutions that limited their power. (Remember that the country of Germany was only created in 1871. Until then, Bavaria was an independent and middle-sized power.) Max Joseph liberalized his realm with a constitution, emancipated Protestants and Jews, and established the Viktualienmarkt. He was a particularly popular king, and both his reign and his son's reign were full of grand

building projects designed to show that Bavaria was an enlightened state, Munich was a worthy capital, and the king was an equal with Europe's other royalty. The **National Theater** (fronting this square), which opened in 1818, celebrated Bavaria's strong culture, roots, and legitimacy. The Roman numerals MCMLXIII (1963) mark the year the theater reopened after WWII bombing restoration.

• *Leave Max-Joseph-Platz at the top corner, walking alongside the Residenz on Residenzstrasse to the next grand square.*

MUNICH

Munich at a Glance

In the Center

▲▲Marienplatz Munich's main square, at the heart of a lively pedestrian zone, watched over by New Town Hall (and its glockenspiel show). **Hours:** Always open; glockenspiel jousts daily at 11:00 and 12:00, plus 17:00 May-Oct; New Town Hall tower elevator runs May-Oct daily 10:00-19:00; Nov-April Mon-Fri 10:00-17:00, closed Sat-Sun. See page 15.

▲▲Viktualienmarkt Munich's "small-town" open-air market, perfect for a quick snack or meal. **Hours:** Mon-Sat, *Biergarten* open until late, closed Sun. See page 22.

▲▲Munich City Museum The city's history in five floors. **Hours:** Tue-Sun 10:00-18:00, closed Mon. See page 23.

▲▲Hofbräuhaus World-famous beer hall, worth a visit even if you're not chugging. **Hours:** Daily 9:00-23:30. See page 30.

▲▲The Residenz The elegant family palace of the Wittelsbachs, awash with Bavarian opulence. Complex includes the Residenz Museum (private apartments), Residenz Treasury (housing Wittelsbach family crowns and royal knickknacks), and the impressive, just-restored Cuvilliés Theater. **Hours:** Museum and treasury—daily April-mid-Oct 9:00-18:00, mid-Oct-March 10:00-17:00; theater—April-mid-Sept daily 9:00-18:00; mid-Sept-March Mon-Sat 14:00-17:00, Sun 10:00-17:00. See page 35.

▲▲Alte Pinakothek Bavaria's best painting gallery, with a wonderful collection of European masters from the 14th through the 19th centuries. **Hours:** Wed-Sun 10:00-18:00, Tue 10:00-20:00, closed Mon. See page 42.

▲▲Deutsches Museum Germany's version of our Smithsonian Institution, with 10 miles of science and technology exhibits. **Hours:** Daily 9:00-17:00. See page 50.

▲Neue Pinakothek The Alte's twin sister, with paintings from 1800 to 1920. **Hours:** Thu-Mon 10:00-18:00, Wed 10:00-20:00, closed Tue. See page 46.

▲Pinakothek der Moderne Hip contemporary-art museum near the Alte and Neue Pinakotheks—housed in a building that's as interesting as the art. **Hours:** Tue-Sun 10:00-18:00, Thu until 20:00, closed Mon. See page 46.

▲Museum Brandhorst Munich's newest art museum, with collections from the turn of the 21st century. **Hours:** Tue-Sun 10:00-

18:00, Thu until 20:00, closed Mon. See page 47.

▲**English Garden** The largest city park on the Continent, packed with locals, tourists, surfers, and nude sunbathers. (On a bike, I'd rate this ▲▲.) **Hours:** Always open. See page 48.

St. Peter's Church Munich's oldest church, packed with relics. **Hours:** Church—long hours daily; spire climb—Mon-Fri 9:00-18:30, Sat-Sun 10:00-18:30, off-season until 17:30. See page 19.

St. Michael's Church Renaissance church housing Baroque decor and a crypt of 40 Wittelsbachs. **Hours:** Church—daily 9:00-19:00, Thu until 20:45, Sun until 22:00; crypt—Mon-Fri 9:30-16:30, Sat 9:30-14:30, closed Sun, less off-season. See page 25.

Frauenkirche Huge, distinctive twin-domed church looming over the city center. **Hours:** Church—Sat-Wed 7:00-19:00, Thu 7:00-20:30, Fri 7:00-18:00; tower climb—April-Oct Mon-Sat 10:00-17:00, closed Sun and Nov-March. See page 25.

Away from the Center
▲▲**Nymphenburg Palace** The Wittelsbachs' impressive summer palace, featuring a hunting lodge, coach museum, fine royal porcelain collection, and vast park. **Hours:** Daily April-mid-Oct 9:00-18:00, mid-Oct-March 10:00-16:00. See page 53.

▲▲**BMW-Welt and Museum** The carmaker's futuristic museum and floating-cloud showroom shows you BMW past, present, and future in some unforgettable architecture. **Hours:** BMW-Welt—building open 9:00-24:00, exhibits open 9:00-18:00; museum—Tue-Sun 10:00-18:00, closed Mon. See page 57.

▲▲**Dachau Concentration Camp** Notorious Nazi camp on the outskirts of Munich, now a powerful museum and memorial. **Hours:** Tue-Sun 9:00-17:00, closed Mon. See page 59.

▲**Museum of Transportation** Deutsches Museum's cross-town annex devoted to travel. **Hours:** Daily 9:00-17:00. See page 51.

▲**Andechs Monastery** Baroque church, hearty food, and Bavaria's best brew, in the nearby countryside. **Hours:** *Biergarten* daily 10:00-20:00, church open until 18:00. See page 65.

Olympic Park Munich's 1972 Olympic stadium, now a lush park with a view tower and pool. **Hours:** Grounds always open; tower daily 9:00-24:00, pool daily 7:00-23:00. See page 58.

MUNICH

Odeonsplatz

This square is a part of the royal family's grand imperial Munich vision. The church on Odeonsplatz (Theatinerkirche) contains about half of the Wittelsbach tombs. The loggia on Odeonsplatz (honoring Bavarian generals) is modeled after the famous Renaissance-style loggia in Florence. And two grand boulevards, Ludwigstrasse and Brienner Strasse, lead away from there.

Ludwigstrasse leads to a Roman-type triumphal arch that hovers in the distance. Though Max Joseph was himself a busy and visionary leader, it was his son and successor, the builder-king Ludwig I, who made Munich into a grand capital. His street, Ludwigstrasse, remains an impressive boulevard, with 60-foot-tall buildings stretching a mile from Odeonsplatz to the Arch of Victory, capped with a figure of Bavaria riding a lion-drawn chariot. (And it was this Ludwig's wedding festival in 1810 that became an annual bash, giving Munich perhaps its greatest claim to fame: Oktoberfest.)

• *From Odeonsplatz, face west, and look (or wander) down the grand...*

Brienner Strasse

This street gives you a taste of the Wittelsbachs' ambitious city planning. In the distance, on Karolinenplatz, the black obelisk commemorates the 30,000 Bavarians who marched with Napoleon to Moscow and never returned. Beyond that is the grand Königsplatz, or "King's Square," with its stern Neoclassicism, evocative of ancient Greece (and home to Munich's cluster of art museums).

Between here and the obelisk, Brienner Strasse goes through a square called **Platz der Opfer des Nationalsozialismus** ("Square of the Victims of Nazism"). It's the site of Himmler's Gestapo headquarters for the entire Third Reich, now entirely gone. If you went farther along, past the obelisk toward Konigsplatz, you'd find two former Nazi administration buildings; one, with recognizably fascist architecture, was Hitler's main residence while in Munich (it's now the music academy; a plaque in the street explains the buildings' history).

• *Backtrack to Odeonsplatz, then finish your walk just beyond Ludwigstrasse in the royal gardens or the genteel café at the...*

Hofgarten

The elegant court garden *(Hofgarten)* is a delight on a sunny afternoon. The "Renaissance" temple centerpiece has great acoustics (and usually a musician performing for tips from listeners). The lane leads to a building that houses the government of Bavaria and the Bavarian war memorial, which honors the fallen *heroes* of World War I, but only the *fallen* of World War II. The venerable old **Café Tambosi,** with an Italian-influenced menu, Viennese elegance inside, and a relaxing garden setting outside, is a good antidote to all the beer halls (daily 8:00-24:00, €10 lunch specials, Odeonsplatz 18, tel. 089/298-322). Just beyond is a lazy gravel *boules* court.

• *With this city walk completed, you've seen the essential Munich. From here, you can walk a couple of blocks to the museum quarter (up Brienner Strasse); head through the Hofgarten to the vast English Garden (best on a bike); backtrack a block to tour the museum and treasury at the Residenz (facing Max-Joseph-Platz); or descend into the U-Bahn from the Odeonsplatz stop for points elsewhere. These—and many other— sights are described in the next section.*

If you're ready to eat, you have several choices. Café Tambosi and the elegant Spatenhaus are nearby, and there are more options if you backtrack toward Marienplatz (see "Eating in Munich," later).

Sights in Munich

Most of the top sights in the city center are covered on the self-guided walk, above. But there's much more to see in this city.

The Residenz

For a long hike through corridors of gilded imperial Bavarian grandeur, tour the Wittelsbachs' family palace. The sprawling Residenz, with a facade modeled after the Medici's Pitti Palace in Florence, evolved from the 14th through the 19th centuries—as you'll see on the charts near the entrance—and was largely rebuilt after World War II.

If you're torn between visiting Munich's top two palaces, I'd say the Residenz interior is best, while Nymphenburg has the finest garden.

Orientation: Within the Residenz complex are four sights: the 90-room Residenz Museum, the eight-room Treasury, the Halls of the Nibelungen (currently closed for renovation), and the Cuvilliés Theater. To reach the first three, enter the complex from the main entrance on Max-Joseph-Platz (at the corner of the palace nearest Marienplatz); there's also a side entrance on Residenzstrasse. Inside the main entrance, past the Halls of the Nibelungen, you'll find the ticket office and the entrances to the Museum and Treasury. The separate entrance to the Cuvilliés Theater is a little ways up Residenzstrasse—ask staff to help if you can't find it.

Cost and Hours: €7 each to visit the Residenz Museum

(palace apartments) and the Treasury, including audioguides; €11 combo-ticket covers both; €13 version also covers Cuvilliés Theater; covered by Bavarian Castles Pass. The Halls of the Nibelungen are closed for renovation until at least 2013. All parts of the palace are open daily April-mid-Oct 9:00-18:00, mid-Oct-March 10:00-17:00, last entry one hour before closing. The complex is located three blocks north of Marienplatz. Tel. 089/290-671, www .residenz-muenchen.de.

Halls of the Nibelungen (Nibelungensäle)

The mythological scenes in these halls—currently closed for renovation—were the basis of Wagner's *Der Ring des Nibelungen*. Wagner and "Mad" King Ludwig were friends and spent time hanging out here (c. 1864). The images in this hall could well have inspired Wagner to write his *Ring* and Ludwig to build his "fairy-tale castle," Neuschwanstein.

▲▲Residenz Museum (Residenzmuzeum)

Though called a "museum," what's really on display here are the best parts of the Residenz itself: the palace's spectacular banquet and reception halls, and the Wittelsbachs' lavish private apartments. It's the best place to get a glimpse of the opulent lifestyle of Bavaria's late, great royal family. (Whatever happened to the Wittelsbachs, the longest continuously ruling family in European history? They're still around, but they're no longer royalty, so most of them have real jobs now—you may well have just passed one on the street.)

   ➊ **Self-Guided Tour:** Leave the ticket office and pick up the free audioguide; later, if you visit the Treasury, you'll need to stop by the desk again to have the guide switched over. Ask for a map of the museum (in English, often stacked up in the museum's first room or two).

   You're about to walk through a 90-room residence, including three private chapels and several still-in-use banquet halls. Follow the red arrows along a one-way route made meaningful by the fine—if ponderous—audioguide and the English descriptions in each room. The rooms are numbered (in black on the bilingual information boards; these numbers are on the map too), and you'll also see red signs with numbers that you can punch into the audioguide. This tour just covers the highlights of the route, in the order you'll see them—use the audioguide to learn more about the rooms you find most compelling. Mercifully, you'll find chairs and benches in many rooms, as well as two WCs along the way.
• *One of the first rooms you'll come to is the...*
   Shell Grotto (Room 6, actually outside, facing a courtyard, ground floor): The whole wall in front of you is made from Bavarian

freshwater shells. This artificial grotto was an exercise in man controlling nature—a celebration of humanism. Renaissance humanism was a big deal when this was built in the 1550s. Imagine the ambience here during that time, with Mercury—the pre-Christian god of trade and business—overseeing the action, and red wine spurting from the mermaid's breasts and dripping from Medusa's head in the courtyard. Like the rest of the palace, the grotto was destroyed by Allied bombs. After World War II, Germans had no money to contribute to the reconstruction—but they could gather shells. All the shells you see here were donated by small-town Bavarians, as the grotto was rebuilt according to Nazi photos (see "The History of Munich: Part 2" sidebar). To the right of the shells, the door marked *OO* leads to handy WCs.

• *The next room is the...*

Antiquarium (Room 7, ground floor): In the mid-16th century, Europe's royal families (such as the Wittelsbachs) collected and displayed busts of emperors—implying a connection between

themselves and the ancient Roman rulers. Given the huge demand for these Classical statues in the courts of Europe, many of the "ancient busts" are fakes cranked out by crooked Romans. Still, a third of the statuary you see here is original. This was, and still is, a festival banquet hall. Two hundred dignitaries can dine here, surrounded by allegories of the goodness of just rule on the ceiling. Check out the small paintings around the room—these survived the bombs because they were painted in arches. Of great historic interest, these paintings show 120 Bavarian villages as they looked in 1550. Even today, when a Bavarian historian wants a record of how his village once looked, he comes here. Notice the town of Dachau in 1550 (above the door on the left as you enter).

• *Keep going through a few more rooms, then up a stairway to the upper floor. Now the tour winds through a couple dozen small rooms on either side of a large courtyard—many of them the private apartments of the prince and his consort. In Room 32, detour to the right to see the...*

All Saints' Chapel (Room 32, upper floor): This early-19th-century chapel, commissioned by King Ludwig I, was severely damaged in World War II—and didn't reopen until 2003. It still hasn't been fully decorated and outfitted; photos by the entrance show how it used to look.

• *Keep going along the other side of the courtyard until you come to Room 45, where you'll have a choice between "short" and "long" routes. Unless you're in a real hurry and want to skip some of the best parts of the palace, choose the long route and turn right. You'll wind around through the large Imperial Hall (Room 111) and then through several small rooms, where the centerpiece painting on the ceiling is just blank black, as no copy of the original survived World War II. A little farther on, peek into the...*

Reliquary Room (Room 95, upper floor): This room harbors a collection of gruesome Christian relics (bones, skulls, and even several mummified hands) in ornate golden cases.

• *A few more steps brings you to the balcony of the...*

Chapel (Hofkapelle; the balcony is Room 96, and the chapel itself is Room 89): Dedicated to Mary, this late-Renaissance/early-

Baroque gem was the site of "Mad" King Ludwig's funeral after his mysterious murder—or suicide—in 1886. (He's buried in St. Michael's Church.) Though Ludwig II was not popular in political circles, he was beloved by his people, and his funeral drew huge crowds. About 75 years earlier, his grandfather and namesake (Ludwig I) was married here, in 1810. After the wedding ceremony, carriages rolled his guests to a rollicking reception, which turned out to be such a hit that it became an annual tradition—Oktoberfest.

• *A couple rooms ahead is the...*

Private Chapel of Maximilian I (Room 98, upper floor): Duke Maximilian I, the dominant Bavarian figure in the Thirty Years' War, built one of the most precious rooms in the palace. The miniature pipe organ (from about 1600) still works. The room is sumptuous, from the gold leaf and the fancy hinges to the miniature dome and the walls made of stucco marble. (Stucco marble is fake marble—a special mix of stucco, applied and polished. Designers liked it because it was less expensive than real marble and the color could be controlled.) Note the post-Renaissance perspective tricks decorating the walls; they were popular in the 17th century. The case (on the right wall as you enter) supposedly contains skeletons of three babies from the Massacre of the Innocents in Bethlehem (where Herod, in an attempt to murder the baby

Jesus, ordered all sons of a certain age killed).

• *Now you'll enter a set of rooms (#55–62) known as the Ornate Rooms (Reiche Zimmer), which were used for official business. The Wittelsbachs were always trying to keep up with the Habsburgs, and this long string of ceremonial rooms was all for show. The decor and furniture are Rococo—over-the-top Baroque. The family art collection, now in the Alte Pinakothek, once decorated these walls. The most lavish of these rooms is the...*

Red Room (Room 62, upper floor): The ultimate room is at the end of the corridor—the coral red room from 1740. (Coral red

was *the* most royal of colors in Germany.) Imagine visiting the duke and having him take you here to ogle miniature copies of the most famous paintings of the day, composed with one-haired brushes. Notice the fun effect of the mirrors around you—the corner mirrors make things go forever and ever.

• *From the Red Room, you'll circle around to a stairway that brings you back down to the ground floor, where you'll soon reach the long Ancestral Gallery (Room #4). Before walking down it, detour to the right, into the...*

Porcelain Cabinet (Room 5, ground floor): In the 18th century, the royal family bolstered their status with an in-house porcelain works (just like the one the Wettins, the ruling family of Saxony, had at Meissen, near Dresden). The Wittelsbach family had their own Nymphenburg porcelain made for the palace. See how the mirrors and porcelain vases give the effect of infinite pedestals. If this inspires you to own some pieces of your own, head to the Nymphenburg Porcelain Store at Odeonsplatz (see "Shopping in Munich," later).

• *Now go back into the...*

Ancestral Gallery of the Wittelsbach Family (Room 4, ground floor): This room is from the 1740s (about 200 years younger than the Antiquarium). All official guests had to pass through here to meet the duke (and his 100 Wittelsbach relatives). The family tree in the center is labeled "genealogy of an imperial family." Notice how the tree is shown being actually planted by Hercules, to boost their royal street cred. The big Wittelsbach/Habsburg rivalry was worked out through 500 years of marriages and battles—when they failed to sort out a problem through strategic weddings, they had a war. Opposite the tree are portraits of Charlemagne and Ludwig IV, each a Holy Roman Emperor and each wearing the same crown (now in Vienna). Ludwig IV was the first Wittelsbach HRE—an honor used for hundreds of years to substantiate the family's claim to power. You are surrounded by a scrapbook covering centuries of Wittelsbach family history.

Allied bombs took their toll on this hall. Above, the central ceiling painting has been restored, but since there were no photos of the other two ceiling paintings, those spots remain empty. Looking at the walls, you can see how each painting was hastily cut out of its frame. Museums were closed in 1939, then gradually evacuated in anticipation of bombings. But public buildings like this palace, which remained open to instill confidence in local people, could not prepare for the worst. It wasn't until 1944, when bombs were imminent, that the last-minute order was given to slice all portraits out of their frames and hide them away.

• *The doorway at the end of the hall deposits you back at the museum entrance. If you're also visiting the Treasury, go to the audioguide desk to have them reset your guide.*

▲▲Residenz Treasury (Schatzkammer)

The Treasury, next door to the Residenz Museum, shows off a thousand years of Wittelsbach crowns and knickknacks. Vienna's jewels are better, but this is the best treasury in Bavaria, with fine 13th- and 14th-century crowns and delicately carved ivory and glass.

◉ Self-Guided Tour: A clockwise circle through the eight rooms takes you chronologically through a thousand years of royal treasure. (You can't get lost, as there aren't any side rooms.) You'll see little signs with a headphone icon and black-and-white numbers—punch these into your audioguide for full explanations.

The oldest jewels in the first room are 200 years older than Munich itself. Many of these came from various prince-bishop collections when they were secularized (and their realms came under the rule of the Bavarian king from Munich) in the Napoleonic Era (c. 1800). The tiny mobile altar allowed a Carolingian king (from Charlemagne's family of kings) to pack light in 890—and still have a little Mass while on the road.

In Room 3, study the reliquary with St. George killing the dragon—sparkling with more than 2,000 precious stones. Get up close (it's OK to walk around the rope posts)...you can almost hear the dragon hissing. It was made to contain the relics of St. George, who never existed (Pope John Paul II declared him nothing more than a legend). If you could lift the miniscule visor, you'd see that the carved ivory face of St. George is actually the Wittelsbach duke (the dragon represents the "evil" forces of Protestantism).

In the next room (#4), notice the vividly carved ivory crucifixes from 1630 (#157 and #158, on the right). These incredibly realistic sculptures were done by local artist Georg Petel, a friend of Peter Paul Rubens (whose painting of Christ on the cross—which you'll see across town in the Alte Pinakothek—is Petel's obvious inspiration). Look at the flesh of Jesus' wrist pulling around the nails.

Continue into Room 5. The freestanding glass case (#245)

holds the never-used royal crowns of Bavaria. Napoleon ended the Holy Roman Empire and let the Wittelsbach family rule as kings of Bavaria. As a sign of friendship, this royal coronation gear was made in Paris by the same shop that crafted Napoleon's crown. But before the actual coronation, Bavaria joined in an all-Europe anti-Napoleon alliance, and suddenly these were too French to be used.

Cuvilliés Theater

The exquisite Cuvilliés Theater is in a northern wing of the Residenz complex, best entered from Residenzstrasse. Your visit

consists of just one small but plush theater hall. It's so heavily restored, you can almost smell the paint. In 1751, this was Germany's ultimate Rococo theater. Mozart conducted here several times. Designed by the same brilliant dwarf architect who did the Amalienburg Palace, this theater is dazzling enough to send you back to the days of divine monarchs.

Cost and Hours: €3.50, €11 combo-ticket with Museum and Treasury, covered by Bavarian Castles Pass; April-mid-Sept daily 9:00-18:00; mid-Sept-March Mon-Sat 14:00-17:00, Sun 10:00-17:00; last entry one hour before closing, no English information provided.

Munich's Cluster of Art Museums

This cluster of blockbuster museums (the Alte, Neue, and Moderne Pinakotheks, the Museum Brandhorst, the currently closed Lenbachhaus, and the Glyptothek) displays art spanning from the 14th century to the 21st. The Glyptothek and Lenbachhaus are right by the Königsplatz stop on the U-2 subway line. The three

Pinakothek museums and the Brandhorst are just to the northeast. Handy tram #27 whisks you right to the Pinakothek stop from Karlsplatz (between the train station and Marienplatz). You can also take bus #100 from the train station, or walk 10 minutes from the Theresienstrasse or Königsplatz stops on the U-2 line.

A €12 combo-ticket covers the three Pinakotheks and the Brandhorst, and pays for itself if you visit two museums. On Sundays, these museums and the Glyptothek let you in for just a token €1, but charge for the useful audioguides (normally included).

▲▲Alte Pinakothek

Bavaria's best painting gallery (the "Old Art Gallery," pronounced ALL-tuh pee-nah-koh-TAYK) shows off a world-class collec-

tion of European master-pieces from the 14th to 19th centuries, starring the two tumultuous centuries (1450-1650) when Europe went from medieval to modern. See paintings from the Italian Renaissance (Raphael, Leonardo, Botti-celli, Titian) and the German Renaissance it inspired (Albrecht Dürer). The Reformation of Martin Luther eventually split Europe into two subcultures—Protestants and Catholics—with their two distinct art styles (exemplified by Rembrandt and Rubens, respectively).

Cost and Hours: €7, €1 on Sun, covered by €12 combo-ticket, open Wed-Sun 10:00-18:00, Tue 10:00-20:00, closed Mon, last entry 30 minutes before closing, free and excellent audioguide (€4.50 on Sun), obligatory lockers with refundable €2 deposit, no flash photos; U-2: Theresienstrasse, tram #27, or bus #100; Barer Strasse 27, tel. 089/2380-5216, www.pinakothek.de/alte -pinakothek.

❍ Self-Guided Tour: From the ticket counter, head toward the back wall and walk up the stairway to the left. All the paintings we'll see are on the upper floor, which is laid out like a barbell. Start at one fat end and work your way through the "handle" to the other end. Along the way you'll find the following paintings, roughly in this order.

German Renaissance—Room II: Albrecht Altdorfer's *The Battle of Issus (Schlacht bei Issus)* shows a world at war. Masses of soldiers are swept along in the currents and tides of a battle completely beyond their control, their confused motion reflected in

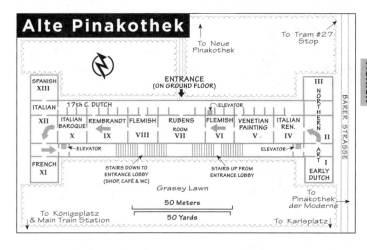

Alte Pinakothek

To Neue Pinakothek

To Tram #27 Stop

SPANISH XIII

ITALIAN XII

17th C. DUTCH

ITALIAN BAROQUE X

REMBRANDT IX

FLEMISH VIII

RUBENS ROOM VII

FLEMISH VI

VENETIAN PAINTING V

ITALIAN REN. IV

ENTRANCE (ON GROUND FLOOR)

ELEVATOR

ELEVATOR

ELEVATOR

FRENCH XI

STAIRS DOWN TO ENTRANCE LOBBY (SHOP, CAFÉ & WC)

STAIRS UP FROM ENTRANCE LOBBY

NORTHERN ART

III

II

I

EARLY DUTCH

BARER STRASSE

MUNICH

Grassy Lawn

50 Meters

50 Yards

To Königsplatz & Main Train Station

To Pinakothek der Moderne

To Karlsplatz

the swirling sky. We see the battle from a great height, giving us a godlike perspective. Though the painting depicts Alexander the Great's victory over the Persians (find the Persian king Darius turning and fleeing), it could as easily have been Germany in the 1520s. Christians were fighting Muslims, peasants battled masters, and Catholics and Protestants were squaring off for a century of conflict. The armies melt into a huge landscape, leaving the impression that the battle goes on forever.

Albrecht Dürer's larger-than-life *Four Apostles* (*Johannes und Petrus* and *Paulus und Marcus*) are saints of a radical new religion:

Martin Luther's Protestantism. Just as Luther challenged Church authority, Dürer—a friend of Luther's—strips these saints of any rich clothes, halos, or trappings of power and gives them down-to-earth human features: receding hairlines, wrinkles, and suspicious eyes. The inscription warns German rulers to follow the Bible rather than Catholic Church leaders. The figure of Mark—a Bible in one hand and a sword in the other—is a fitting symbol of the dangerous times.

Dürer's *Self-Portrait in Fur Coat (Selbstbildnis im Pelzrock)*

looks like Jesus Christ but is actually 28-year-old Dürer himself, gazing out, with his right hand solemnly giving a blessing. This is the ultimate image of humanism: the artist as an instrument of God's continued creation. Get close and enjoy the intricately braided hair, the skin texture, and the fur collar. To the left of the head is Dürer's famous monogram—"A.D." in the form of a pyramid.

Italian Renaissance—Room IV: With the Italian Renaissance—the "rebirth" of interest in the art and learning of ancient Greece and Rome—artists captured the realism, three-dimensionality, and symmetry found in classical statues. Leonardo da Vinci's *Virgin and Child (Maria mit dem Kind)* need no halos—they radiate purity. Mary is a solid pyramid of maternal love, flanked by Renaissance-arch windows that look out on the hazy distance. Baby Jesus reaches out to play innocently with a carnation, the blood-colored symbol of his eventual death.

Raphael's *Holy Family at the Canigiani House (Die hl. Familie aus dem Hause Canigiani)* takes Leonardo's pyramid form and runs with it. Father Joseph forms the peak, with his staff as the strong central axis. Mary and Jesus (on the right) form a pyramid-within-the-pyramid, as do Elizabeth and baby John the Baptist on the left. They all exchange meaningful contact, safe within the bounds of the stable family structure.

In Botticelli's *Lamentation over Christ (Die Beweinung Christi)*, the Renaissance "pyramid" implodes, as the weight of the dead Christ drags everyone down, and the tomb grins darkly behind them.

Venetian Painting—Room V: In Titian's *Christ Crowned with Thorns (Die Dornenkronung)*, a powerfully built Christ sits silently enduring torture by prison guards. The painting is by Venice's greatest Renaissance painter, but there's no symmetry, no pyramid form, and the brushwork is intentionally messy and Impressionistic. By the way, this is the first painting we've seen done on canvas rather than wood, as artists experimented with vegetable oil-based paints.

Rubens and Baroque—Room VII: Europe's religious wars split the Continent in two—Protestants in the northern countries, Catholics in the south. (Germany itself was divided, with Bavaria remaining Catholic.) The Baroque style, popular in Catholic countries, featured large canvases, bright colors, lots of flesh, rippling motion, wild emotions, grand themes...and pudgy winged babies, the sure sign of Baroque. This room holds several canvases by the great Flemish painter Peter Paul Rubens.

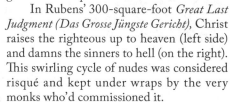

In Rubens' 300-square-foot *Great Last Judgment (Das Grosse Jüngste Gericht)*, Christ raises the righteous up to heaven (left side) and damns the sinners to hell (on the right). This swirling cycle of nudes was considered risqué and kept under wraps by the very monks who'd commissioned it.

Rubens and Isabella Brant shows the artist with his first wife, both of them the very picture of health, wealth, and success. They lean together unconsciously, as people in love will do, with their hands clasped in mutual affection. When his first wife died, 53-year-old Rubens found a replacement—16-year-old Hélène Fourment, shown in an adjacent painting (just to the left) in her wedding dress. You may recognize Hélène's face in other Rubens paintings.

The Rape of the Daughters of Leucippus (Der Raub der Tochter des Leukippos) has many of Rubens' most typical elements—fleshy, emotional, rippling motion; bright colors; and a classical subject. The legendary twins Castor and Pollux crash a wedding and steal the brides as their own. The chaos of flailing limbs and rearing horses is all held together in a subtle X-shaped composition. Like the weaving counterpoint in a Baroque fugue, Rubens

balances opposites.

Notice that Rubens' canvases were—to a great extent—cranked out by his students and assistants from small "cartoons" the master himself made (displayed in the next room).

Rembrandt and Dutch—Room IX: From Holland, Rembrandt van Rijn's *Six Paintings from the Life of Christ* are a down-to-earth look at supernatural events. The *Adoration (Die Anbetung der Hirten)* of Baby Jesus takes place in a 17th-century

Dutch barn with ordinary folk as models. The canvases are dark brown, lit by strong light. The *Adoration*'s light source is the Baby Jesus himself—literally the "light of the world." In the *Deposition (Kreuzabnahme)*, the light bounces off Christ's pale body onto his mother Mary, showing how his death also hurts her. The drama is underplayed, with subdued emotions. Looking on is a man dressed in blue—a self-portrait of Rembrandt.

▲Neue Pinakothek

The Alte Pinakothek's sister is a twin building across the street, showing off paintings from 1800 to 1920: Romanticism, Realism, Impressionism, *Jugendstil*, Claude Monet, Pierre-Auguste Renoir, Vincent van Gogh, Francisco Goya, and Franz von Stuck—Munich's answer to Gustav Klimt.

Cost and Hours: €7, €1 on Sun, covered by €12 combo-ticket, open Thu-Mon 10:00-18:00, Wed 10:00-20:00, closed Tue, well-done audioguide is usually free but €4.50 on Sun, classy Café Hunsinger in basement spills into park; U-2: Theresienstrasse, tram #27, or bus #100; Barer Strasse 29 but enter on Theresienstrasse, tel. 089/2380-5195, www.pinakothek.de/neue-pinakothek.

▲Pinakothek der Moderne

This museum picks up where the other two leave off, covering

the 20th century. Four permanent displays (graphics, design, architecture, and paintings) are layered within the striking minimalist architecture. You'll find works by Pablo Picasso, Salvador Dalí, Joan Miró, René Magritte, Max Beckmann, Max Ernst, and abstract artists. The big, white, high-ceilinged build-

ing itself is worth a look. Even if you don't pay to visit the exhibits, step into the free entrance hall to see the sky-high atrium and the colorful blob-column descending the staircase.

Cost and Hours: €10, €1 on Sun, covered by €12 combo-ticket, open Tue-Sun 10:00-18:00, Thu until 20:00, closed Mon; U-2: Theresienstrasse, tram #27, or bus #100; Barer Strasse 40, tel. 089/2380-5360, www.pinakothek.de/pinakothek-der-moderne. This far-out collection offers little information in English—and there's no English audioguide.

▲Museum Brandhorst

Museum Brandhorst covers the end of the 20th century and the beginning of the 21st, with full English captions. You can't miss  the building—thousands of colored cylinders line the outside. The top floor (of three) is devoted to American artist Cy Twombly. A highlight is an ensemble of 12 Twombly paintings called *Lepanto*, after a 1571 battle in which Venice defeated the Ottoman fleet; six huge canvases of roses fill another room. On the lower floor, I liked the giant medicine cabinet full of multicolored pills by Damien Hirst, and the sizable Andy Warhol collection.

Cost and Hours: €7, €1 on Sun, covered by €12 combo-ticket, audioguide usually free but €4.50 on Sun, open Tue-Sun 10:00-18:00, Thu until 20:00, closed Mon, small café; U-2: Theresienstrasse, tram #27, or bus #100; Theresienstrasse 35a, tel. 089/2380-52286, www.museum-brandhorst.de.

▲Lenbachhaus

Closed for renovation until sometime in 2013, this museum is housed in a beautiful late 19th-century Tuscan-style villa (once owned by painter Franz von Lenbach). It features the most complete collection of the early Modernist movement known as Blaue Reiter (Blue Rider), a branch of Expressionism that flourished from 1911 to 1914. When Wassily Kandinsky, Paul Klee, Franz Marc, Gabriele Münter, and some of their art-school cronies got fed up with being told how and what to paint, they formed the Blaue Reiter around a common ideology: to strive for new forms that expressed spiritual truth. Already controversial in their own day, their work was later targeted by the Nazis as *entartete Kunst* ("degenerate art"). The collection allows visitors to trace Kandinsky's progression from his earlier, more realistic works to the complete abstraction he's best known for. Münter, Kandinsky's lover and a great painter in her own right, donated her entire private collection (90 paintings and 330 other works) to Lenbachhaus in 1957, putting this little museum on the world art map.

Cost and Hours: Closed for renovation; when it reopens: likely €5-10 depending on exhibits, Tue-Sun 10:00-18:00, closed Mon, worthwhile €3 audioguide, €8 guidebook is a nice souvenir but otherwise unnecessary, small café, U-2: Königsplatz, Luisenstrasse 33, tel. 089/2333-2000, www.lenbachhaus.de.

Glyptothek

A collection of Greek and Roman sculpture started by King Ludwig I, the Glyptothek includes the famous *Barberini Faun,*

statues from the Greek Classical period, funerary monuments of wealthy Athenian families, and pediments of the Temple of Aegina. For a Who's Who of ancient celebrities, visit the Room of Ancient Portraits, where you'll come face-to-face with Alexander the Great and other luminaries from ancient political and philosophical spheres.

Cost and Hours: €3.50, €1 on Sun, not much in English so invest in the worthwhile €1 guidebook, Tue-Sun 10:00-17:00, Thu until 20:00, closed Mon, U-2: Königsplatz, on Königsplatz, tel. 089/286-100, www.antike-am-koenigsplatz.mwn.de/glyptothek.

The English Garden and Nearby

▲**English Garden (Englischer Garten)**—Munich's "Central Park," the largest one on the Continent, was laid out in 1789 by

an American. More than 100,000 locals commune with nature here on sunny summer days. The park stretches three miles from the center, past the university to the trendy and bohemian Schwabing quarter. For the best quick visit, follow the river from the surfers (under the bridge just past Haus der Kunst) downstream into the garden. Just beyond the hilltop temple (walk up for a postcard view of the city), you'll find the big Chinese Tower beer garden and other places to enjoy a drink or a meal (described later, under "Eating in Munich"). A rewarding respite from the city, the park is especially fun—and worth ▲▲—on a bike under the summer

Green Munich

Although the capital of a very conservative part of Germany, Munich has long been a liberal stronghold. For nearly two decades, the city council has been controlled by a Social Democrat/Green Party coalition. The city policies are pedestrian-friendly—you'll find much of the town center closed to normal traffic, with plenty of bike lanes and green spaces. As you talk softly and hear birds rather than motors, it's easy to forget you're in the center of a big city. On summer Mondays, the peace and quiet make way for "blade Monday"—when streets in the center are closed to cars and as many as 30,000 inline skaters swarm around town in a giant rolling party.

sun and on warm evenings (unfortunately, there are no bike-rental agencies in or near the park). Caution: While local law requires sun-worshippers to wear clothes on the tram, the park is sprinkled with buck-naked sunbathers—quite a shock to prudish Americans (they're the ones riding their bikes into the river and trees).

Haus der Kunst—Built by Hitler as a temple of Nazi art, this bold and fascist building—a rare surviving example of a purpose-built Nazi structure—is now an impressive shell for various temporary art exhibits. Ironically, the art now displayed in Hitler's "house of art" is the kind that annoyed the Führer most—modern. Its cellar, which served as a nightclub for GIs in 1945, is now the P-1 nightclub.

Cost and Hours: €5-10 per exhibit, combo-tickets save money if seeing at least two exhibits, daily 10:00-20:00, Thu until 22:00, little information in English but some exhibits may have English handouts, at south end of English Garden, tram #17 or bus #100 from station to Nationalmuseum/Haus der Kunst, Prinzregentenstrasse 1, tel. 089/211-270, www.hausderkunst.de.

Nearby: Just beyond the Haus der Kunst, where Prinzregentenstrasse crosses the Eisbach canal, you can watch adventure-seekers surfing in the rapids created as the small river tumbles underground.

Bavarian National Museum (Bayerisches National-museum)—This tired but interesting collection features Tilman Riemenschneider woodcarvings, manger scenes, traditional living rooms, and old Bavarian houses.

Cost and Hours: €5, €1 on Sun, open Tue-Sun 10:00-17:00, Thu until 20:00, closed Mon, tram #17 or bus #100 from station to Nationalmuseum/Haus der Kunst, Prinzregentenstrasse 3, tel. 089/211-2401, www.bayerisches-nationalmuseum.de.

MUNICH

Deutsches Museum

Germany's answer to our Smithsonian National Air and Space Museum, the Deutsches Museum traces the evolution of science and technology. The main branch of the Deutsches Museum is centrally located. The two other branches—the Museum of Transportation and the Flight Museum—are situated outside the city center, but are worth the effort for enthusiasts. You can pay separately for each museum, or buy one €15 combo-ticket, which covers all three. Since this ticket has no time limit, you can spread out your visits to the various branches over your entire stay.

▲▲Deutsches Museum (Main Branch)

Enjoy wandering through well-described rooms of historic airplanes, spaceships, mining, the harnessing of wind and water power, hydraulics, musical instruments, printing, chemistry, computers, astronomy, and nanotechnology...it's the Louvre of technical know-how. The museum is designed to be hands-on; if you see a button, push it. But with 11 acres of floor space and 10 miles of exhibits, from astronomy to zymurgy, even those on roller skates will need to be selective. While the museum was a big deal a generation ago, today it feels to many a bit dated, dusty, and overrated. It's far too vast and varied to cover completely. The key is to study the floor plan that shows all the departments and simply visit the ones that interest you. Many sections of the museum are well-described in English. The much-vaunted high-voltage demonstrations (3/day, 15 minutes, all in German) show the noisy creation of a five-foot bolt of lightning.

Cost and Hours: €8.50, €15 combo-ticket includes Museum of Transportation and Flight Museum, daily 9:00-17:00, worthwhile €4 English guidebook, self-service cafeteria, tel. 089/21791, www.deutsches-museum.de.

Getting There: Take the S-Bahn to Isartor, then walk 300 yards over the river, following signs.

➌ Self-Guided Tour: If you don't mind a very long, winding, one-way route that feels like a subterranean hike, start off in the **mines** (mines closed during daily German-language tours at 9:45 and 13:45). This exhibit traces the history of mining since prehistoric times. Enter just past the coat-check desk (just keep on going—there's only one way) through a vacant mine shaft with lots of old mining gear. While descriptions are only in German, the reconstructions of coal, potash, and salt mines are still impressive. When you emerge from the mines, skip the mineral oil and natural gas section *(Erdöl und Erdgas)* and follow the signs for *Ausgang* (exit).

The fascinating, compact exhibit on **marine navigation** (on the ground floor) has models of sail, steam, and diesel vessels, from early canoes to grand sailing ships. Take the staircase down into the galley, below the main floor, to check out how life on passenger ships has changed—and don't miss the bisected U1 submarine. This first German submarine, dating from 1906, has been in the museum since 1921.

Flying high above the masts of the marine navigation exhibit is the section on **aeronautics** (first floor). Displays cover the most basic airborne flights (flying insects and seed pods), Otto Lilienthal's successful efforts in 1891 to imitate bird flight, and the development of hot-air balloons and gas-powered zeppelins. Many of the planes here are original, including the Wright brothers' Type A (1909), fighters and cargo ships from the two World Wars, and the first functioning helicopter, made in 1936. Climb into the planes whenever permitted, and try out the flight simulator.

The **astronautics** exhibit is located on the second floor. Back in the 1920s, Germany was working on rocket-propelled cars and sleds. Germany's research provided the US and Soviet space teams with much of their technical know-how. Here, you can peer at models of the V-2 (one of the first remote-controlled rockets/ weapons, from World War II), motors from the American Saturn rockets, and various space capsules, including Spacelab. The main focus is the walk on the moon, the Apollo missions, and the dogs-in-space program (monkeys, too)...but if you've ever been curious about how space underwear works, you'll find your answer here.

The third floor traces the **history of measurement,** including time (from a 16th-century sundial and an 18th-century clock to a scary Black Forest wall clock complete with grim reaper), weights, geodesy (surveying and mapping), and computing (from 18th-century calculators to antiquated computers from the 1940s and 1950s).

On your way to the state-of-the-art **planetarium** (worth a visit if open, requires €2 extra ticket, lecture in German), poke your head out into the **sundial garden** located above the third floor. Even if you're not interested in sundials, this is a great place for a view of the surrounding landscape. On a clear day, you can see the Alps.

▲Museum of Transportation (Verkehrszentrum)

You don't need to be an engineer or race-car driver to get a kick out of this fun museum. In 2003, the Deutsches Museum celebrated its centennial by opening this annex across town that shows off all aspects of transport, from old big-wheeled bikes to Benz's first car (a three-wheeler from the 1880s) to sleek ICE super-trains. It's housed in three giant hangar-like exhibition halls near the Oktoberfest grounds, a.k.a. Theresienwiese. All the exhibits are in both English and German.

Cost and Hours: €6, €15 combo-ticket includes Deutsches Museum and Flight Museum, daily 9:00-17:00, Theresienhöhe 14a, tel. 089/5008-06762, www.deutsches-museum.de.

Getting There: Take the U-4 or U-5 to Schwanthalerhöhe and follow signs for *Deutsches Museum* from the platform. The museum is just a few steps from the station exit.

Tours: The free tours daily at 13:30, 14:00, and 14:30 (each focusing on one of the museum's three halls) are primarily in German, but worth tagging along on for a chance to climb into the old carriage in Hall 2 (only allowed as part of the tour). The metal track simulates what it would have felt like to travel in the 18th century over different terrain (grass and cobblestones—pretty uncomfortable).

◒ Self-Guided Tour: True to the Deutsches Museum's interactive spirit, the Museum of Transportation is totally hands-on, and comes with plentiful English explanations. The museum asks what our lives would be like without transportation, and the exhibits show how modes of transportation developed from Neolithic "bone" skates (predecessors to today's inline skates) to 19th-century Lapland skis, to today's snowboards and fast cars.

Hall 1 focuses on urban transport, with special attention to Munich. Climb into the original 1967 U-Bahn car, marvel at a cross-section of the intricate and multi-layered subway system, learn about the history of the bicycle, and admire the vintage cars arrayed into mock traffic jams. Once a day (usually at 11:30; confirm times to be sure) they fire up an S-Bahn simulator and let visitors pretend to drive the train.

Hall 2 gives you a look at the development of long-distance overland travel. The focus here is on trains and coach travel (serious train buffs, however, will be more excited by the Deutsche Bahn Museum in Nürnberg). Don't miss the Maffei S3/6, a.k.a. "The Pride of Bavaria" (in its heyday the fastest steam engine, at nearly 80 miles per hour); climb aboard the clever old postal train car (complete with a mail slot on the side); and check out the 1950s panorama bus that shuttled eager tourists to fashionable destinations such as Italy.

Hall 3 is all about fun: motorcycles, bicycles, skis, and race cars. Famous prewar models include the deluxe Mercedes-Benz 370 (1930s) and the Auto Union Type C "Grand Prix" race car. Other tiny racers—which resemble metal pickles to the uninitiated—include the 1950s Mercedes-Benz 300 SLR and the famous Messerschmitt 200. You'll also find early 18th-century bicycles based on Leonardo da Vinci's drawings. Before the invention of the pedal crank, bikes were just silly-looking scooters for adults.

Flight Museum (Flugwerft Schleissheim)

Fans of all things winged will enjoy the Deutsches Museum's Flight Museum, with more than 50 planes, helicopters, gliders, and an original Europa rocket housed in a historical aerodrome on a former military airfield. Inside the museum is the glass-walled workshop, where visitors can watch as antique planes are restored.

Cost and Hours: €6, €15 combo-ticket includes Deutsches Museum and Museum of Transportation, daily 9:00-17:00; 20-minute S-Bahn trip from Marienplatz, take S-1 direction: Freising Flughafen and get off at Oberschleissheim, trip covered by Munich XXL day pass, Effnerstrasse 18, tel. 089/315-7140, www.deutsches-museum.de.

Sights Outside the City Center

Greater Munich

The following destinations are in Munich, but on the outskirts of town.

Nymphenburg Palace Complex

Nymphenburg Palace and the surrounding one-square-mile park are good for a royal stroll or bike ride. Here you'll find a pair of palaces, the Royal Stables Museum, and playful extras such as a bathhouse, pagoda, and artificial ruins.

Cost and Hours: €6 for just the palace, €11.50 for the palace plus outlying sights, covered by Bavarian Castles Pass. All sights are open daily April-mid-Oct 9:00-18:00, mid-Oct-March 10:00-16:00, except for Amalienburg Palace, which is closed in the winter. The park is open daily 6:30-dusk. Tel. 089/179-080, www.schloss-nymphenburg.de.

Getting There: The palace is three miles northwest of central Munich. From the center, take tram #17 from the Karlstor or the train station (15 minutes to palace), getting off at the Schloss Nymphenburg stop. From the bridge by the tram stop, you'll see the palace—a 10-minute walk away. A pleasant bike path follows Arnulfstrasse from the train station all the way to Nymphenburg (a 30-minute pedal).

▲▲**Nymphenburg Palace**—In 1662, after 10 years of trying, the Bavarian ruler Ferdinand Maria and his wife, Henriette Adelaide of Savoy, finally had a son, Max Emanuel. In gratitude for a male heir, Ferdinand gave this land to his Italian wife, who proceeded to build an Italian-style Baroque palace. Their son expanded the palace to today's size. For 200 years, this was the Wittelsbach family's summer escape from Munich. (They still refer to themselves as princes and live in one wing of the palace.)

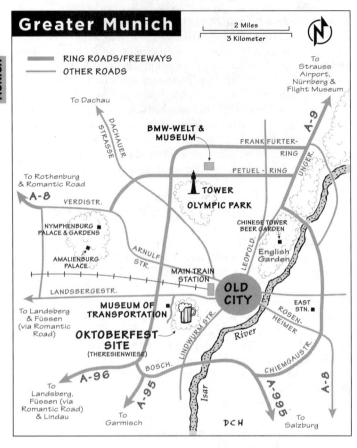

Greater Munich

2 Miles
3 Kilometer

RING ROADS/FREEWAYS
OTHER ROADS

To Dachau

To Strauss Airport, Nürnberg & Flight Museum

DACHAUER STRASSE

BMW-WELT & MUSEUM

FRANK FURTER-RING

PETUEL - RING

UNGER

A-9

To Rothenburg & Romantic Road

A-8

VERDISTR.

TOWER
OLYMPIC PARK

CHINESE TOWER BEER GARDEN

English Garden

NYMPHENBURG PALACE & GARDENS

AMALIENBURG PALACE

ARNULF STR.

LEOPOLD

MAIN TRAIN STATION

OLD CITY

EAST STN.

LANDSBERGESTR.

MUSEUM OF TRANSPORTATION

ROSEN-HEIMER

To Landsberg & Füssen (via Romantic Road)

OKTOBERFEST SITE
(THERESIENWIESE)

LINDWURM STR.

River

CHIEMGAUSTR.

BOSCH.

A-96

A-95

Isar

A-995

A-8

To Landsberg, Füssen (via Romantic Road) & Lindau

To Garmisch

DCH

To Salzburg

Your visit is limited to 16 main rooms on one floor: the Great Hall (where you start), the King's Wing (to the right as you approach the palace), and the Queen's Wing (to the left). The place is stingy on information—not even providing a map without charging—and the rooms only have meaning if you invest in the €3.50 audioguide.

○ Self-Guided Tour: The **Great Hall** in the middle was the dining hall, site of big Wittelsbach family festivals. One of the grandest Rococo rooms in Bavaria, it was decorated by Johann Baptist Zimmermann (of Wieskirche fame) and François de Cuvilliés in about 1760. The painting on the ceiling shows a pagan heavenly host of Olympian gods, a scene designed to help legitimize the supposedly divine rule of the Wittelsbachs. The windows connect you with the lavish gardens.

From here, the two wings (the King's and the Queen's) are mirror images of one another: antechamber, audience chamber, bedchamber, and private living quarters.

The **King's Wing** (north, right of entrance) has walls filled with Wittelsbach portraits and stories. In the second room straight ahead, notice the painting showing the huge palace grounds, with Munich (and the twin onion domes of the Frauenkirche) three miles in the distance. Imagine the logistics when the royal family—with their entourage of 200—decided to move out to the summer palace. The Wittelsbachs were high rollers; from 1624 until 1806, one of the seven electors of the Holy Roman Emperor was a Wittelsbach. In 1806, Napoleon ended that institution and made the Wittelsbachs kings. (Note: For simplicity, I often refer to the Wittelsbachs as kings and queens, even though before 1806, these rulers were technically dukes, duchesses, and electors—and some were even Holy Roman Emperors.)

In the **Queen's Wing** (south, left of entrance), head down the long hall. Near the end, you'll come to **King Ludwig I's Gallery of Beauties.** The gallery is decorated with portraits of 36 beautiful women—all of them painted by Joseph Stieler from 1827 to 1850. King Ludwig I was a consummate girl-watcher who prided himself on the ability to appreciate beauty regardless of social rank. He would pick the prettiest women from the general public and, with one of the most effective pickup lines of all time, invite them to the palace for a portrait. Who could refuse? He may not have been picky about status—the women range from royal princesses to a humble cobbler's daughter—but Ludwig sure seemed to prefer brunettes. (Find the cobbler's daughter, Helene Sedlmayr, in a dress way beyond her budget. She married the king's valet, had 10 kids, and lived until 1898.) The portraits reflect the modest Biedermeier style, as opposed to the more flamboyant Romanticism of the same period. If only these creaking floors could talk. Something about the place feels highly sexed, in a Prince Charles kind of way.

The next rooms are decorated in the Neoclassical style of the Napoleonic Era. At the rope, see the room where Ludwig II was born (August 25, 1845). Royal births were carefully witnessed, and the mirror allowed for a better view. While Ludwig's death was shrouded in mystery, his birth was well-documented.

Amalienburg Palace—Three hundred yards from the Nymphenburg Palace, hiding in the park (head into the sculpted garden and veer to the left, following signs), you'll find a fine little Rococo hunting palace. In 1734, Elector Karl Albrecht had this hunting lodge built for his wife, Maria Amalia. It was designed by François de Cuvilliés and decorated by Johann Baptist Zimmermann.

Touring the Palace: As you approach, notice its facade. Above the pink-and-white grand entryway, Diana, goddess of the chase, is surrounded by themes of the hunt and flanked by busts of satyrs. The queen would shoot from the perch atop the roof. Behind a wall in the garden, dogs would scare non-flying pheasants. When they jumped up in the air above the wall, the sporting queen—as if shooting skeet—would pick the birds off.

Tourists enter this tiny getaway through the back door. The first room has doghouses under gun cupboards. Next, in the fine yellow-and-silver bedroom, the bed is flanked by portraits of Karl Albrecht and Maria Amalia—decked out in hunting attire. She liked her dogs. The door under the portrait leads to stairs to the rooftop pheasant-shooting perch. The relief in the door shows Vulcan forging arrows for amorous cupids.

The mini-Hall of Mirrors is a blue-and-silver commotion of Rococo nymphs designed by Cuvilliés. In the next room, paintings depict court festivities, formal hunting parties, and no-contest kills (where the animal is put at an impossible disadvantage—like shooting fish in a barrel). Finally, the kitchen is decorated with Chinese picnics on blue Dutch tiles.

Royal Stables Museum (Marstallmuseum)—This huge garage is lined with gilded Cinderella coaches. The highlight is just inside the entrance: the 1742 Karl Albrecht coronation coach. When the Elector Karl Albrecht was chosen as Emperor, he rode in this coach, drawn by eight horses. Kings got only six.

Touring the Museum: Wandering through the collection, you can trace the evolution of 300 years of coaches—getting lighter and with better suspension as they were harnessed to faster horses. The carousel for the royal kids made development of dexterity fun—lopping off noses and heads and tossing balls through the snake. The glass case is filled with accessories.

In the room after the carousel, find the painting on the right of "Mad" King Ludwig on his sleigh at night. In his later years, Ludwig was a Howard Hughes-type recluse who stayed away from the public eye and only went out at night. (At his nearby Linderhof Palace, he actually had a hydraulic-powered dining table that would rise from the kitchen below, completely set for the meal—so he wouldn't be seen by his servants.) In the next room, you'll find Ludwig's actual sleighs. Ludwig's over-the-top coaches were Baroque. But this was 1870. The coaches, like the king, were in the wrong century. Notice the photos (c. 1865, in the glass case) of Ludwig and the Romantic composer Richard Wagner. Ludwig cried on the day Wagner was married. Hmmm.

Across the passage from the museum entrance, the second hall is filled with more practical coaches for everyday use. At the end of that hall, head upstairs to see a collection of **Nymphenburg porcelain** (described by an English loaner booklet at the entrance). Historically, royal families such as the Wittelsbachs liked to have their own porcelain plants to make fit-for-a-king plates, vases, and so on. The Nymphenburg Palace porcelain works is still in operation. Ludwig ordered the masterpieces of his royal collection (now at the Alte Pinakothek) to be copied in porcelain for safekeeping into the distant future. Take a close look—these are exquisite.

▲▲BMW-Welt and Museum

A brand with a rich heritage, an impressive display of futuristic architecture, and an enthusiastic welcome to the public combine to

make the headquarters of BMW ("bay-em-VAY" to Germans) one of the top sights in Munich. This vast complex—built on the site of Munich's first airstrip and home to the BMW factory since 1920—has four components: the headquarters (in the building nicknamed "the Four Cylinders"—not open to the public), the factory (tourable with advance reservations), the showroom (called BMW-Welt—"BMW World"), and the new BMW Museum.

The **BMW-Welt** building itself—a cloud-shaped, glass-and-steel architectural masterpiece—is reason enough to visit. It's free and filled with exhibits designed to enthuse car lovers so they'll find a way to afford a Bimmer. While the adjacent museum reviews the BMW past, BMW-Welt shows you the present and gives you a breathtaking look at the future. With interactive stations, high-powered videos, an inviting cafeteria, and lots of horsepower, this is where customers come to pick up their new Bimmers, and where hopeful customers-to-be come to nurture their automotive dreams.

In the futuristic **BMW Museum,** a bowl-shaped building encloses a world of floating walkways linking exhibits highlighting BMW motorcycle and car design and technology through the years. Employing seven themes and great English descriptions, the museum traces the Bavarian Motor Works' history since 1917, when the company began making airplane engines. Motorcycles came next, followed by the first BMW sedan in 1929. You'll see how design was celebrated here from the start. Exhibits showcase motorsports, roadsters, and luxury cars. Stand on an *E* for English to hear the chief designer talk about his favorite cars in the "treasure trove." The Info Bar lets you review 90 years of history with the touch of a finger. And the 1956 BMW 507 is enough to rev almost anyone's engine.

Cost and Hours: BMW-Welt is free and open daily (building open 9:00-24:00, exhibits open 9:00-18:00, www.bmw-welt.com). The museum costs €12 (Tue-Sun 10:00-18:00, closed Mon, www.bmw-museum.de). English tours are offered of both the Welt (€7, daily at 14:00, 80 minutes) and the museum (€3, 1.5 hours, call ahead for times). Factory tours are booked long in advance (€8, 2.5 hours, register online or call, tel. 0180-211-8822, www.bmw-werk-muenchen.de; ask at the BMW-Welt building about cancellations—released to the public a half-hour before each tour).

Getting There: It's very easy: Ride U-3 to Olympia-Zentrum; the stop faces the BMW-Welt entry. To reach the museum, walk through BMW-Welt and over the swoopy bridge.

Olympic Park (Olympiapark München)

Munich's great 1972 Olympic stadium and sports complex is now a lush park. You can get a good look at the center's striking

"cobweb" style of architecture while enjoying the park's picnic potential. In addition, there are several activities on offer at the park, including a tower (Olympiaturm) with a commanding but so-high-it's-boring view from 820 feet and an excellent swimming pool, the Olympia-Schwimmhalle. With the construction of Munich's Allianz Arena for the 2006 World Cup, Olympic Park has been left in the past, and has melted into the neighborhood as simply a fine park and swimming pool.

Cost and Hours: Tower—€4.50, daily 9:00-24:00, last trip 23:30, tel. 089/30670, www.olympiapark.de. Pool—€4, daily 7:00-23:00, last entry 22:00, tel. 01801-796-223, www.swm.de. The U-3 runs from Marienplatz directly to the Olympia-Zentrum stop.

▲Isar River Bike Ride

Munich's river, lined by a gorgeous park, leads bikers into the pristine countryside in just a few minutes. From downtown (easy access from the English Garden or Deutsches Museum), follow

the riverside bike path south (upstream) along the east (left) bank. You can't get lost. Just stay on the lovely bike path. It crosses the river after a while, passing tempting little *Biergartens* and lots of Bavarians having their brand of fun—including gangs enjoying Munich's famous river party rafts. Go as far as you like, then retrace your route to get home. The closest bike rental is at Munich Walk, near the Isartor, which also offers a guided bike tour along this route.

Near Munich

The following sights are a short train or bus ride away from Munich.

▲▲Dachau Concentration Camp Memorial (KZ-Gedenkstätte Dachau)

Dachau was the first Nazi concentration camp (1933). Today, it's

an easily accessible camp for travelers and an effective voice from our recent but grisly past, pleading "Never again." A visit here is a valuable experience and, when approached thoughtfully, well worth the trouble. After this powerful sightseeing experience, many people gain more respect for history and the dangers of mixing fear, blind patriotism, and an evil government. You'll likely see lots of students here, as all Bavarian schoolchildren are required to visit a concentration camp. It's interesting to think that little more than a couple of generations ago, people greeted each other with a robust *"Sieg Heil!"* Today, almost no Germans know the lyrics of their national anthem, and German flags are a rarity outside of major soccer matches.

Cost and Hours: Free, Tue-Sun 9:00-17:00, closed Mon except holidays, last entry 30 minutes before closing. Though the museum shuts down at 17:00, the grounds are unofficially open until about 17:30 or 18:00 (as it takes a while for people to walk back to the entrance). The museum discourages parents from bringing children under age 12.

Planning Your Time: Allow yourself about five hours here (four at a minimum), including your round-trip from central Munich. Giving yourself at least two and a half hours at the camp itself lets you see it at a comfortable pace (with just two hours, it's doable but rushed, and you'll have to skip the movie).

Getting There: The camp is a 45-minute trip from downtown Munich. Take the S-2 subway (direction: Petershausen) from any of the central S-Bahn stops in Munich to Dachau (3/hour, 20-minute trip from Hauptbahnhof). Then, at the Dachau station, go down the stairs and out to the bus platforms; find the one marked *KZ-Gedenkstätte*. Here, catch bus #726 and ride it seven minutes to the KZ-Gedenkstätte stop (3/hour; on Sundays, you can also take bus #724). The Munich XXL day pass covers the entire trip, both ways (€7.30/person, €12.80/partner ticket for up to 5 adults). If you've already invested in a three-day Munich transport pass (which covers only the white/inner zone), you can save a couple euros by buying and stamping single tickets (€2.50/person each way) to cover the part of the trip that's in the green zone. You can also take a guided tour from Munich.

Drivers follow Dachauer Strasse from downtown Munich to Dachau-Ost, then follow *KZ-Gedenkstätte* signs.

The Town: The town of Dachau is more pleasant than its unfortunate association with the camp on its outskirts, and tries hard to encourage you to visit its old town and castle (www.dachau.de). With 40,000 residents and quick access to downtown Munich, Dachau is now a high-priced and in-demand place to live.

Visitors Center: Coming from the bus stop or parking lot, you'll first see the visitors center, outside the camp wall. It doesn't have any exhibits, but does have some useful services: a café serving simple lunches (sandwiches and €5-6 pasta dishes), a bookstore with a modest selection of English-language books on Holocaust themes, and a small WC (there are larger ones in the

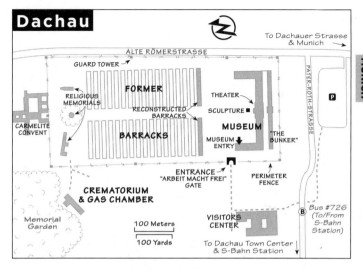

museum inside the camp). At the information desk, you can rent an audioguide or sign up for tours.

Tours: The €3.50 **audioguide** is informative and gives you a few extras (mainly short reminiscences by two camp survivors and three members of the Allied forces who liberated the camp), but isn't essential, since the camp is fully labeled in English. Two different free **guided walks** in English are offered, starting from the visitors center (daily at 11:00 and 13:00; limited to 30 people, so show up early, especially in summer; call or visit website to confirm times, tel. 08131/669-970, www.kz-gedenkstaette-dachau.de).

Background: While a relatively few 32,000 inmates died in Dachau between 1933 and 1945 (in comparison, more than a million were killed at Auschwitz in Poland), the camp is notorious because it was the Nazis' first. It was originally established to house political prisoners and opponents of the Nazi regime, and only later played a role in World War II. In the 1930s, the camp was located outside built-up areas, and was surrounded by a mile-wide restricted area. It was a work camp, where inmates were used for slave labor, including constructing the buildings that you see. A huge training center stood next to the camp. The people who ran the entire concentration-camp system during the war were trained here, and it was former Dachau officials who went on to manage the death camps farther east, mostly in Nazi-occupied Poland. For example, the first commandant at Auschwitz, Rudolf Höss, worked at Dachau from 1934 to 1938.

After war broke out, the regime found more purposes for Dachau: a departure point for people shipped east to the gas chambers, a special prison for priests, a center for barbaric medical experimentation on inmates, and finally—as the Nazis retreated—a transfer destination for prisoners from other camps. Oddly, Dachau actually housed people longer *after* the war than during the war. From 1945 to 1948, Nazi officials arrested by the Allies were interned here. After that (from 1948 to 1964), ethnic Germans expelled from Eastern Europe lived in the barracks, which were like a small town, with a cinema, shops, and so on. The last of the barracks was torn down in 1964, and the museum opened the following year.

○ Self-Guided Tour: Walking past the visitors center, turn right into the main compound. You enter, like the inmates did, through the infamous **iron gate** with the taunting slogan *Arbeit macht frei* ("Work makes you free"). The building around the gate, called the Jourhaus, was where new prisoners were processed. Inside are the four key experiences of the memorial: the museum, the bunker behind the museum, the restored barracks, and a pensive walk across the huge but now-empty camp to the

shrines and crematorium at the far end.

Museum: The large camp maintenance building to your right has been converted into a gripping museum. Walk toward the

forecourt of the building and you'll see the museum entrance. Just inside is a small bookshop that funds a nonprofit organization (founded by former prisoners) that researches and preserves the camp's history. Here you can pick up a €0.50 information sheet, or buy the excellent 200-page book with a CD (€15) that contains the same text and images that you'll see in the museum.

The museum is organized chronologically, focusing on three stages in the history of the camp: before the war (1933-1938), early in the war (1939-1942), and late in the war (1942-1945). Exhibits are thoughtfully and completely described in English, and computer touch-screens let you watch early newsreels.

In its first years, the camp was basically a political prison designed for opponents of the Nazi regime, and it could hold just under 3,000 inmates. Aside from political activists, these prisoners included homosexuals, Jehovah's Witnesses, Gypsies, so-called career criminals, and Germans who had been deported back home after trying to emigrate. As Nazi extremism increased, the camp operated with less and less regard for the rule of law, and after the Nazis whipped up domestic anti-Semitism, a number of German Jews were also sent to Dachau.

MUNICH

Prisoners had a regimented life, with lights out at 21:00, a wake-up call at 4:00 in the morning, and an 11-hour workday, plus standing for roll call at 5:15 and 19:00. In 1937 and 1938, the camp was expanded and the building that now houses the museum was built, as well as barracks intended to hold 6,000 prisoners.

Once Germany invaded Poland in 1939, fewer local detainees arrived at the camp, replaced by more and more prisoners from Poland and Czechoslovakia. Dachau was also the place of detention for almost 2,000 Polish Catholic clergymen and for former fighters in the Spanish Civil War. During these years, Dachau prisoners were used as convenient guinea pigs for war-related medical experiments of human tolerance for air pressure, hypothermia, and biological agents like malaria; the photos of these victims may be the most painful in the museum. After the Nazis put their plans for exterminating Europe's Jews in motion, Jewish prisoners at Dachau were typically sent east to the extermination camps in Poland and killed.

Once the tide of war started to turn in 1942 and 1943, both Nazi measures and camp conditions became more and more desperate. Inmates were now seen as a source of slave labor for the German war machine. Many were put to work in sub-camps (in nearby towns) making armaments. As the Allies closed in on both fronts, prisoners from concentration camps in France, the Low Countries, and Eastern Europe were transferred to Dachau, and the number of Jewish internees rose again. Disease broke out, and food ran short in the winter of 1944-1945. With coal for the crematorium running low, the corpses of those who died were buried in mass graves outside the camp site. Though the Nazis moved some camp inmates to the mountains of the Tirol in spring 1945, more than 30,000 people were jammed into Dachau's 34 barracks when the Allies arrived on April 29. Two thousand of them were so weak or sick that they died in the weeks after liberation.

In the middle of the museum building is a **theater,** which shows a powerful 22-minute documentary movie dating from the 1960s. Check the schedule for the next English-language showing.

• *Consider using the WC before leaving the museum building (there aren't any bathrooms elsewhere within the camp walls). Find the side door, at the end of the exhibition, which leads out to the long, low bunker behind the museum building.*

MUNICH

Bunker: This was a cellblock for prominent "special prisoners," such as failed Hitler assassins, German religious leaders, and politicians who challenged Nazism. Most of the 136 cells are empty, but exhibits in a few of them (near the entrance) profile the inmates and the SS guards who worked at Dachau, and allow you to listen to some inmates' testimonies. Look into cell #65, which was divided by partitions (now gone) into "standing cells,"

with less than three square feet of floor space. Inmates were tortured here by being forced to stay on their feet for days at a time.

• *Exit the bunker the way you came, and walk around past the* Arbeit macht frei *gate to the big square between the museum and the reconstructed barracks, which was used for roll call. Cross the square to the farther of the two reconstructed...*

Barracks: Take a quick look inside to get an idea of what sleeping and living conditions were like in the camp. There were

34 barracks, each measuring about 10 yards by 100 yards. When the camp was at its fullest, there was only about one square yard of living space per inmate.

• *Now walk between the two reconstructed barracks and down the tree-lined walk past the foundations of the other*

barracks. *At the end of the camp, in space that once housed the camp vegetable garden, rabbit farm, and brothel, there are now three places of meditation and worship (Jewish to your right, Catholic straight ahead, and Protestant to your left). Beyond them, just outside the camp, is a Carmelite convent. Turn left toward the corner of the camp and find the small bridge leading to the...*

Camp Crematorium: A memorial garden surrounds the two camp crematorium buildings, which were used to burn the bodies of prisoners who had died or been killed. The newer, larger, concrete crematorium was built to replace the smaller wooden one. One of its rooms is a **gas chamber,** which worked on the same

principles as the much larger one at Auschwitz, and was originally disguised as a shower room (the fittings are gone now). It was never put to use at Dachau for mass murder, but some historians suspect that a few people were killed in it experimentally. In the garden near the buildings is a Russian Orthodox shrine.

To end your visit, retrace your steps back to the visitors center and bus stop.

▲Andechs Monastery

This monastery crouches quietly with a big smile between two lakes just south of Munich. For a fine Baroque church in a rural Bavarian setting at a monastery that serves hearty cafeteria-quality food and perhaps the best beer in Germany, consider a short side-trip here. The cafeteria terrace offers first-class views and second-class prices. Don't miss the stroll up to the church, where you can sit peacefully and ponder the striking contrasts a trip through Germany offers.

Hours: *Biergarten* open daily 10:00-20:00, church open until 18:00, tel. 08152/3760, www.andechs.de.

Getting There: Reaching Andechs from Munich without a car is doable with a little planning. Bus #951 stops at the monastery on its run between Herrsching (at the end of the S-8 subway line) and Starnberg Nord (on the S-6 line). Use the online train schedule at www.bahn.com to find a convenient connection (put in Kloster Andechs as your destination, about an 80-minute trip, buy Munich *Gesamtnetz* day ticket for €10.80 single or €19.60 for up to 5 people). You can also take the S-8 train to Herrsching, then hike, bike, or catch a taxi for the 3 miles to the monastery.

More Day Trips from Munich

For day trips to many Bavarian destinations, including the first four listed here, consider traveling by train with the **Bayern-Ticket.** It covers up to five people from Munich to anywhere in Bavaria (plus Salzburg) and back for only €29 (€21 for one person, not valid before 9:00 Mon-Fri, valid only on slower "regional" trains—most of them labeled on schedules as either "RB," "RE," or "IRE"). The ticket is explained in *The Inside Track* newsletter and sold at EurAide.

▲▲▲**"Mad" King Ludwig's Castles**—The spectacular Neuschwanstein and Linderhof castles make a great day trip. Your easiest option is to take a tour (see "Tours in Munich," earlier). Without a tour, only Neuschwanstein is easy (2 hours by train to Füssen, then 10-minute bus ride to the castle). Or spend the night there.

▲▲**Nürnberg**—A handy but expensive ICE express train zips you to Nürnberg in about an hour (departures several times an hour), making this very historic city a viable day trip from Munich. Cheaper RE trains, covered by the Bayern-Ticket, take a little longer.

▲▲▲Salzburg—This Austrian city is an easy day trip and offers some exciting sightseeing (hourly trains from Munich get you there in less than 2 hours).

▲Berchtesgaden—This resort, near Hitler's Eagle's Nest getaway, is easier as a side-trip from Salzburg (just 12 miles from there).

Shopping in Munich

While the whole city is great for shopping, the most glamorous area is around Marienplatz. It's fun to window-shop, even if you have no plans to buy. Here are a few stores and streets to consider.

Department Stores: You'll see lots of modern department stores. Locals rate them this way: **C&A** (which sells only clothing) is considered cheap yet respected, **Kaufhof** (which sells everything) is mid-range, and **Karstadt** is upmarket. **Beck's,** an even more upscale department store at Marienplatz, has been a local institution since 1861. With six floors of expensive designer clothing (plus some music, stationery, and cosmetics), this is the place to go for a €200 pair of jeans. Beck's has long been to fabrics what Alois Dallmayr is to fine food—too expensive to actually buy anything in, but fun to browse (Mon-Sat 10:00-20:00, closed Sun).

Also on Marienplatz is the big **Hugendubel bookstore.** Their English selection is paltry—you'll find more at their English-language store on Salvatorplatz, behind Fünf Höfe.

Weinstrasse/Theatinerstrasse: Shoppers will want to stroll from Marienplatz down the pedestrianized Weinstrasse (it begins to the left as you face New Town Hall). After a few short blocks, the street name changes to Theatinerstrasse; look for **Fünf Höfe** on your left, a delightful mall filled with Germany's top shops (open until 20:00, www.fuenfhoefe.de). Named for its five courtyards, this is where tradition meets modern. Note how its Swiss architects (who also designed Munich's grand Allianz soccer stadium for the 2006 World Cup) play with light and color. Even if you're not a shopper, wander through the **Kunsthalle** to appreciate the architecture, the elegant window displays, and the sight of Bavarians living very well.

For fine-quality (and very expensive) traditional clothing, detour a block west along Maffeistrasse to **Loden-Frey Verkaufshaus.** The third floor of this fine department store is dedicated to classic Bavarian wear for men and women (Mon-Sat 10:00-

20:00, closed Sun, Maffeistrasse 7, tel. 089/210-390, www.loden -frey.com).

Theatinerstrasse spills out onto Odeonsplatz, where you'll find the **Nymphenburg Porcelain Store** (Mon-Fri 10:00-18:30, Sat 10:00-18:00, closed Sun, Odeonsplatz 1, tel. 089/282-428, www .nymphenburg.com).

Maximilianstrasse: Built by Maximilian II in the 1850s, this street was designed for shoppers. Today it's home to Munich's most exclusive shops.

Lowbrow Tips: For that beer stein you promised to take home to your uncle, try the shops on the pedestrian zone by St. Michael's Church and the gift shops that surround the Hofbräuhaus. If you're looking for a used cell phone or exotic groceries, the area south of the train station is a lot of fun.

Sleeping in Munich

Unless you hit Munich during a fair, convention, or big holiday, you can sleep reasonably here. Lots of student hotels around the station house anyone who's young at heart for €20, and it's easy to find a fine double with breakfast in a good basic hotel for €80. I've listed accommodations in two neighborhoods: within a few blocks of the central train station (Hauptbahnhof), and in the old center, between Marienplatz and Sendlinger Tor. Many of these places have complicated, slippery pricing schemes. I've listed the normal non-convention, non-festival prices. There are major conventions about 30 nights a year—prices increase from 20 percent to as much as 300 percent during Oktoberfest (Sept 22-Oct 7 in 2012; reserve well in advance). On the other hand, during slow times, you may be able to do better than the rates listed here— always ask. Sunday is very slow and usually comes with a huge discount if you ask.

Near the Train Station

Good budget hotels cluster in the multicultural area immediately south of the station. It feels seedy after dark (erotic cinemas and men with moustaches loitering in the shadows), but it's dangerous only for those in search of trouble. Still, hotels in the old center (listed later) might feel more comfortable to some.

$$ Hotel Royal is perhaps the best value in its price range (as long as you can look past the strip joints flanking the entry). While a bit institutional, it's clean, entirely non-smoking, and plenty comfortable. Most importantly, it's energetically run by Pasha and Changiz. Each of its 40 rooms is fresh and bright (Sb-€54-69, Db-€74-89, Tb-€94-109, Qb-€99-129, lower prices generally Nov-March, book direct for a 10 percent discount off the prevailing

Sleep Code

(€1 = about $1.40, country code: 49, area code: 089)

S = Single, **D** = Double/Twin, **T** = Triple, **Q** = Quad, **b** = bathroom, **s** = shower only. Unless otherwise noted, credit cards are accepted, a buffet breakfast is included, there is an elevator but no air-conditioning, and English is spoken.

To help you sort easily through these listings, I've divided the accommodations into three categories based on the price for a standard double room with bath:

$$$ Higher Priced—Most rooms €100 or more.
$$ Moderately Priced—Most rooms between €70-100.
$ Lower Priced—Most rooms €70 or less.

Prices can change without notice; verify the hotel's current rates online or by email. For other updates, see www.ricksteves.com/update.

price with this book, ask for a room on the quiet side—especially in summer when you'll want the window open, free Internet access and Wi-Fi, Schillerstrasse 11a, tel. 089/5998-8160, fax 089/5998-81616, www.hotel-royal.de, info@hotel-royal.de).

$$ Hotel Uhland is a stately mansion that rents 29 delightful rooms in a safe-feeling, less-seedy residential neighborhood a slightly longer walk from the station than the others in this section (toward the Theresienwiese Oktoberfest grounds). It's been in the Hauzenberger family for 50 years (Sb-€75-80, small Db-€88, big Db-€98-108, Tb-€123-130, price depends on room size, great family rooms, online deals, non-smoking floor, free Wi-Fi, limited free parking; from station, take bus #58 to Georg-Hirth-Platz, or walk 15 minutes: go up Goethestrasse and turn right on Pettenkoferstrasse, cross Georg-Hirth-Platz to Uhlandstrasse and find #1; tel. 089/543-350, fax 089/5433-5250, www.hotel-uhland.de, info@hotel-uhland.de).

$$ Hotel Monaco is a delightful and welcoming little hideaway, tucked inside the fifth floor of a giant nondescript building two blocks from the station. Emerging from the elevator, you're warmly welcomed by Christine and her staff into a flowery, cherub-filled oasis. It's homey, with 24 clean and fresh rooms (S-€53, Sb-€73, D-€75, Db-€91-96, Tb-€134, €8/person less without breakfast, free Wi-Fi, Schillerstrasse 9, entrance on Adolf-Kolping-Strasse, tel. 089/545-9940, fax 089/550-3709, www.hotel-monaco.de, info@hotel-monaco.de).

$$ Hotel Eckelmann has 65 sunny rooms in a practical, concrete shell (Sb-€62, Db-€91, Tb-€120, €9/person less without breakfast, parking-€13, non-smoking rooms, free Wi-Fi, Adolf-Kolping-Strasse 11, tel. 089/5999-3902, fax 089/5999-3994, www.hotel-eckelmann.de, info@hotel-eckelmann.de).

$$ Hotel Bristol has 57 comfortable, business-class rooms. While a longer walk from the station, it's bright, efficient, and pleasantly located just across the street from the Sendlinger Tor U-Bahn stop, one stop from the train station on the U-1 or U-2 (Sb-€89, Db-€99, non-smoking rooms, free Internet access and Wi-Fi, air-con in lobby, Pettenkoferstrasse 2, tel. 089/5434-8880, fax 089/5434-888111, www.bristol-munich.de, info@bristol-munich.de).

$$ Litty's Hotel is a basic hotel with 37 small rooms run by Verena and Bernd Litty (S-€46, Sb-€58, D-€66, Ds-€74, Db-€82, T-€84, free Wi-Fi at reception reaches lower floors, near Schillerstrasse at Landwehrstrasse 32c, tel. 089/5434-4211, fax 089/5434-4212, www.littyshotel.de, info@littyshotel.de).

$$ Hotel Deutsches Theater is a brass-and-marble-filled place with 27 tight, modern three-star rooms. The back rooms face the courtyard of a neighboring theater—when there's a show, there can be some street noise (Sb-€68, Db-€97, Tb-€136, pricier suites, €9/person less without breakfast, non-smoking floors, free Wi-Fi, Landwehrstrasse 18, tel. 089/5999-3903, fax 089/5999-3995, www.hoteldeutschestheater.de, info@hoteldeutschestheater.de).

$$ Hotel Europäischer Hof, across from the station, is a huge, impersonal business hotel with 150 decent rooms. Official rates are sky-high, but actual rates are usually lower (close to S-€50, Sb-€85, smaller "tourist class" D with head-to-toe twin beds-€57, Db-€92; 10 percent discount on prevailing rate with this book and advance reservation, *or* if you pay cash—no double discounts; no discounts during conventions, major events, and Oktoberfest weekends; check website for other discounts, non-smoking rooms, family rooms, free Internet access, expensive Wi-Fi and cable Internet, Bayerstrasse 31, tel. 089/551-510, fax 089/5515-11444, www.heh.de, info@heh.de). They also run **$$ Hotel Mark** around the corner, with a large lobby, dim hallways, 92 fine rooms, and a similar institutional 1970s ambience (Sb-€75, basic Db-€82, ask for 10 percent discount described above, free Internet access, expensive Wi-Fi and cable Internet, Senefelderstrasse 12, tel. 089/559-820, fax 089/5598-22444, www.hotel-mark.de, mark@heh.de).

$ The **CVJM (YMCA),** open to all ages, rents 85 beds in clean, slightly worn rooms with sinks in the rooms and showers and toilets down the hall. Doubles are head-to-head; triples are like doubles with a bunk over one of the beds (S-€36, D-€61, T-€83, €28/bed in a shared triple, guests over 26 pay €3/person more, cheaper for 3 nights or more and in winter, only €10/night per person more during Oktoberfest—reserve at least a year ahead;

MUNICH

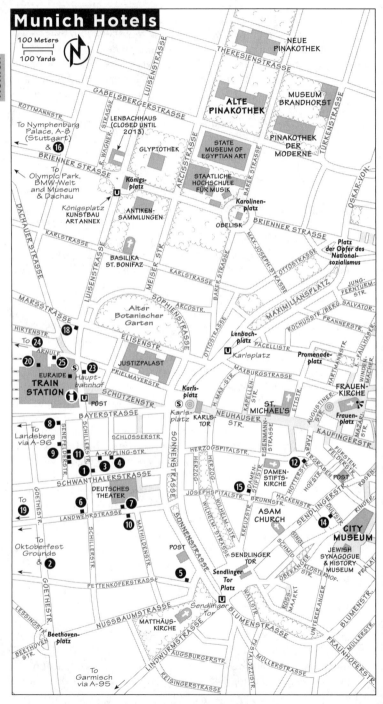

Munich Hotels

100 Meters
100 Yards

THERESIENSTRASSE

NEUE PINAKOTHEK

GABELSBERGERSTRASSE

ALTE PINAKOTHEK

MUSEUM BRANDHORST

ROTTMANNSTR.

To Nymphenburg Palace, A-8 (Stuttgart) & 16

LENBACHHAUS (CLOSED UNTIL 2013)

GLYPTOTHEK

STATE MUSEUM OF EGYPTIAN ART

PINAKOTHEK DER MODERNE

BRIENNER STRASSE

To Olympic Park, BMW-Welt and Museum & Dachau

Königsplatz

STAATLICHE HOCHSCHULE FÜR MUSIK

Königsplatz KUNSTBAU ART ANNEX

ANTIKEN-SAMMLUNGEN

Karolinenplatz

OBELISK

BRIENNER STRASSE

Platz der Opfer des National-sozialismus

KARLSTRASSE

BASILIKA ST. BONIFAZ

KARLSTRASSE

MARSSTRASSE

Alter Botanischer Garten

Lenbach-platz

Promenadeplatz

HIRTENSTR.

To 24

ELISENSTR.

Karlsplatz

FRAUEN-KIRCHE

18

JUSTIZPALAST

20 25 23

EURAIDE TRAIN STATION

Haupt-bahnhof

Karls-platz

ST. MICHAEL'S

Frauen-platz

POST

SCHÜTZENSTR.

Karls-platz

KARLS-TOR

NEUHAUSER STR.

KAUFINGERSTR.

BAYERSTRASSE

8

To Landsberg via A-96

9

11

1 3 4

SCHLOSSERSTR.

A.-KOPLING-STR.

HERZOGSPITALSTR.

12

SCHWANTHALERSTRASSE

DEUTSCHES THEATER

DAMEN-STIFTS-KIRCHE

POST

6

7

To 19

LANDWEHRSTRASSE

15

10

JOSEPHSPITALSTR.

ASAM CHURCH

14

CITY MUSEUM

To Oktoberfest Grounds & 2

POST

5

SENDLINGER TOR

JEWISH SYNAGOGUE & HISTORY MUSEUM

Sendlinger Tor Platz

PETTENKOFERSTR.

NUSSBAUMSTRASSE

Sendlinger Tor

MATTHÄUS-KIRCHE

Beethoven-platz

To Garmisch via A-95

LINDWURMSTR.

AUGSBURGERSTR.

REISINGERSTR.

MUNICH

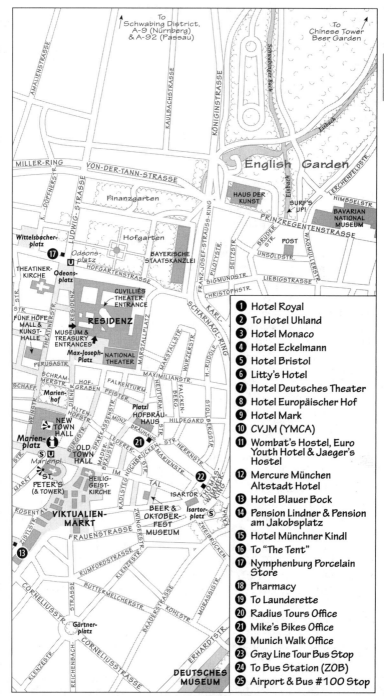

To Schwabing District,
A-9 (Nürnberg)
& A-92 (Passau)

To
Chinese Tower
Beer Garden

AMALIENSTRASSE

KAULBACHSTRASSE

KÖNIGINSTRASSE

Schwabinger Bach

English Garden

MILLER-RING

VON-DER-TANN-STRASSE

Finanzgarten

K. DOPPNERSTR.

LUDWIGSTRASSE

HAUS DER
KUNST

Eisbach

SURF'S
UP!

TERCHENFELDSTR.

HIMBELSTR.

BAVARIAN
NATIONAL
MUSEUM

PRINZREGENTENSTRASSE

Wittelsbacher-
platz

Hofgarten

Odeons-
platz

17

BRUDER
STR.

POST

WAGMÜLLERSTR.

UNSÖLDSTR.

THEATINER-
KIRCHE

Odeons-
platz

BAYERISCHE
STAATSKANZLEI

HOFGARTENSTRASSE

FRANZ-JOSEF-STRAUSS-RING

PILOTYSTR.

SEITZSTR.

SIGMUNDSTR.

LIEBIGSTRASSE

CHRISTOPHSTR.

THEATINERSTR.

FÜNF HÖFE
MALL &
KUNST-
HALLE

CUVILLIÉS
THEATER
ENTRANCE

RESIDENZ

MUSEUM &
TREASURY
ENTRANCES

PERUSASTR.

Max-Joseph-
Platz

NATIONAL
THEATER

MARSTALLPLATZ

SCHARNAGL-RING

KARL-

H.-RUDLE

MARSTALLSTR.

WURZER-STR.

SCHAFF...

SCHRAM-
MERSTR.

HOF-
GRABEN

FALKENTURM

MAXIMILIANSTR.

NEUTURM-

FALCKEN-
BERG

Marien-
hof

PFISTER-

DIENER-

ALTEN-
HOFSTR.

MÜNZ

PLATZL

LEDERER-

HILDEGARD

1 Hotel Royal

2 To Hotel Uhland

3 Hotel Monaco

4 Hotel Eckelmann

5 Hotel Bristol

6 Litty's Hotel

7 Hotel Deutsches Theater

8 Hotel Europäischer Hof

9 Hotel Mark

10 CVJM (YMCA)

NEW
TOWN
HALL

Marien-
platz

Marienpl.

OLD
TOWN
HALL

BURGSTR.

WEINSTR.

STARK-

MADER-
BRÄUSTR.

KADLSTEG

HOCHBRÜCKEN

MARIENSTR.

21

HOFBRÄU-
HAUS

BRAUNAU

STR.-HERRNSTR.

BERG-

GEORG.STR.

ST.
PETER'S
(& TOWER)

HEILIG-
GEIST-
KIRCHE

IM

TAL

22

ISARTOR

THOMAS-

Isartor-
platz

S

ROSENTA...

VIKTUALIEN-
MARKT

13

FRAUENSTRASSE

BEER &
OKTOBER-
FEST
MUSEUM

ZWINGERSTR.

RING

KANAL-

ZWEIBRÜCKEN

11 Wombat's Hostel, Euro
    Youth Hotel & Jaeger's
    Hostel

12 Mercure München
    Altstadt Hotel

13 Hotel Blauer Bock

14 Pension Lindner & Pension
    am Jakobsplatz

15 Hotel Münchner Kindl

16 To "The Tent"

17 Nymphenburg Porcelain
    Store

18 Pharmacy

19 To Launderette

20 Radius Tours Office

21 Mike's Bikes Office

22 Munich Walk Office

23 Gray Line Tour Bus Stop

24 To Bus Station (ZOB)

25 Airport & Bus #100 Stop

RUMFORDSTRASSE

KLENZESTR.

BAADERSTR.

KOHLSTR.

MORASSISTR.

CORNELIUSSTR.

BUTTERMELCHERSTR.

ZEISTLSTR.

Gärtner-
platz

REICHENBACH...

KLENZESTR.

CORNELIUSSTR.

ERHARDTSTR.

DEUTSCHES
MUSEUM

includes sheets, breakfast, and Internet access, but no lockers; pay Wi-Fi by reception, Landwehrstrasse 13, tel. 089/552-1410, fax 089/550-4282, www.cvjm-muenchen.org/hotel, hotel@cvjm -muenchen.org).

"Hostel Row" on Senefelderstrasse, a Block from the Station

All three of the following hostels are casual and well-run, with friendly and creative management, and all cater expertly to the needs of young beer-drinking backpackers enjoying Munich on a shoestring. With 900 cheap dorm beds, this is a spirited street. There's no curfew at any of these places, and each one has a lively bar that rages until the wee hours (Euro Youth's is open the latest—until 4:00 in the morning), along with staff who speak English as the primary language. All have 24-hour receptions, pay Internet access, free Wi-Fi laundry facilities, lockers, and included linens; none has a kitchen, but each offers a buffet breakfast for €4-5. Sleep cheap in big dorms, or spend a little more for a two-, three-, or four-bed room. Prices vary with demand, and can range a little higher than the rates listed here in summer—and quite a bit lower in the off-season.

$ Wombat's Hostel, perhaps the most hip and colorful, rents cheap doubles and six- to eight-bed dorms with lockers. Each bedroom is fresh and modern, with its own bathroom, and there's a relaxing and peaceful winter garden (300 beds, 8-bed dorms-€20/bed, 6-bed dorms-€25/bed, Db-€76, Senefelderstrasse 1, tel. 089/5998-9180, www.wombats-hostels.eu, office@wombats -munich.de).

$ Euro Youth Hotel fills a classy and rare pre-WWII building (200 beds, 10- to 12-bed dorms-€19/bed, 3- to 5-bed dorms-€25/bed; D-€59, Db-€70, breakfast included for private rooms; bike rental-€10/day, Senefelderstrasse 5, tel. 089/5990-8811, www .euro-youth-hotel.de, info@euro-youth-hotel.de, run by Alfio).

$ Jaeger's Hostel rounds out this trio, with 300 cheap beds and all the fun and efficiency you'd hope for in a hostel—plus the only air-conditioning on the street. If you're not looking to party, this is your hostel—it seems to be the quietest (40-bed dorm-€19/bed, 8-bed dorm-€23/bed, 3- to 6-bed rooms-€27/bed, hotel-quality Db-€78, towel-€1/day, Senefelderstrasse 3, tel. 089/555-281, fax 089/592-598, www.jaegershostel.de, info@jaegershostel.de).

In the Old Center

A few good deals remain in the area south of Marienplatz, going toward the Sendlinger Tor.

$$$ Mercure München Altstadt Hotel is a huge, impersonal, basic business-class hotel with all the modern comforts on a boring street very close to the Marienplatz action. If you want an American-style hotel room buried deep in Munich for a decent price, this place has 75 of them (typically Sb-€114, Db-€156, better rates sometimes available online, parking-€17, non-smoking floors, air-con, inexpensive Wi-Fi, a block south of the pedestrian zone at Hotterstrasse 4, tel. 089/232-590, fax 089/2325-9127, www .mercure.com, h3709@accor.com).

$$$ Hotel Blauer Bock, formerly a dormitory for Benedictine monks, has been on the same corner near the Munich City Museum since 1841. Recently remodeled, it's a little spartan for the price, but offers 69 clean, decent rooms, a straightforward pricing system (the same rates every day, except during fairs and Oktoberfest), and a great location (S-€55, Sb-€75-99, D-€90, Db-€119, fancy premium Db-€153, extra bed-€40, €10 more if paying with credit card, free Wi-Fi with this book, parking-€19, Sebastiansplatz 9, tel. 089/231-780, fax 089/2317-8200, www.hotelblauerbock.de, info@hotelblauerbock.de).

$$ Pension Lindner is clean and quiet, with nine pleasant pastel-bouquet rooms off a bare stairway (S-€39, D-€60, Ds-€70, Db-€80, these prices with this book and cash payment, tiny elevator, free Wi-Fi, Dultstrasse 1, tel. 089/263-413, fax 089/268-760, www.pension-lindner.com, info@pension-lindner.com, Marion Sinzinger).

$$ Pension am Jakobsplatz, downstairs from Pension Lindner, has four basic but pleasant rooms. Two have fully private facilities, and the other two have a sink and shower but share a toilet. Showers here are in-room (Ss-€60-80, Sb-€70-90, Ds-€70-90, Db-€80-100, non-smoking, free Internet access and Wi-Fi, Dultstrasse 1, tel. 089/2323-1556, mobile 0173-973-4598, fax 089/2323-1564, www.pension-jakobsplatz.de, info@pension -jakobsplatz.de).

$$ Hotel Münchner Kindl is a no-frills place with 22 decent rooms above a friendly neighborhood bar (S-€50, D-€75, Db-€92, Tb-€115, Qb-€130, €8/person less without breakfast, lower rates possible in summer—ask, no elevator, pay Wi-Fi, night noises travel up central courtyard, no air circulation in courtyard-facing rooms so they can get hot in summer—request a fan, Damenstiftstrasse 16, tel. 089/264-349, fax 089/264-526, www .hotel-muenchner-kindl.de, reservierung@hotel-muenchner-kindl .de, Gunter and Renate).

Away from the Center

$ The Tent—a venerable Munich institution officially known as the International Youth Camp Kapuzinerhölzl—offers 400 spots in three huge circus tents near Nymphenburg Palace. It never fills up, though you are encouraged to reserve online. Choose a mattress

MUNICH

on a wooden floor (€7.50) or a bunk bed (€10.50), or pitch your own tent (€5.50/tent plus €5.50/person). Blankets, hot showers, lockers (bring or buy a lock), a kitchen, and Wi-Fi are all included; breakfast is a few euros extra. It can be a fun but noisy experience—kind of a cross between a slumber party and Woodstock. It feels quite wholesome, but I wouldn't bring kids—it's really for young adults. There's a cool table-tennis-and-Frisbee atmosphere through-

out the day, nightly campfires, and no curfew, though silence is requested after 1:00 (open early June-mid-Oct only, prices a little higher during Oktoberfest, cash only, pay Internet access, self-service laundry, bikes-€9/day, catch tram #17 from train station for 18 minutes to Botanischer Garten, direction Amalienburgstrasse, then go right down Franz-Schrank-Strasse—it's behind the trees at the end of the street, tel. 089/141-4300, www.the-tent.com, cu @the-tent.com).

Eating in Munich

Munich cuisine is traditionally seasoned with beer. In beer halls, beer gardens, or at the Viktualienmarkt, try the most typical meal in town: *Weisswurst* (white-colored veal sausage—peel off the skin before eating, often available only until noon) with *süsser Senf* (sweet mustard), a salty *Brezel* (pretzel), and *Weissbier* ("white" wheat beer). Another traditional favorite is *Obatzda* (a.k.a. *Obatzter*), a mix of soft cheeses and butter with paprika and raw onions that's spread on bread. *Brotzeit*, literally "bread time," gets you a wooden platter of cold cuts, cheese, and pickles and is a good option for a light dinner. Also unique and memorable is a *Steckerlfisch*—fish on a stick (great with a pretzel and a big beer).

I'm here for the beer-hall and beer-garden fun (my first several listings). But when the *Wurst und Kraut* get to be too much for you, Munich has plenty of good alternatives; I've listed my favorites later in this section.

Bavarian restaurants are now smoke-free. The only ashtrays you'll see throughout Bavaria are outside.

Beer Halls, Beer Gardens, and Bavarian Food

For a boisterous cliché of the beer hall, nothing beats the Hofbräuhaus (the only place in town where you'll find oompah music). Locals prefer their innumerable beer gardens. On a warm day, when you're looking for the authentic outdoor beer-garden experience, your best options are the Augustiner (near the train station), the small beer garden at the Viktualienmarkt (near Marienplatz), or the thousands of tables in the Englischer Garten.

Near Marienplatz
The **Hofbräuhaus** (HOAF-broy-howze) is the world's most famous beer hall. While it's grotesquely touristy and filled with sloppy backpackers and tour groups, it's still a lot of fun—a Munich must. Even if you don't eat here, check it out to see 200 Japanese people drinking beer in a German beer hall...across from a Hard Rock Café. Germans go for the entertainment—to sing "Country Roads," see how Texas girls party, and watch tourists try to chug beer. You can drop by anytime for a large or light meal (my favorite: €7 for *Schweinswurst mit Kraut*—pork sausages with sauerkraut), or for just a drink. Except for Weissbier, they only sell beer by the *Mass* (one-liter mug, €7.30)—and they claim to sell 10,000 of these liters every day. The Hofbräuhaus is the only beer hall in town offering regular live oompah music. This music-every-night atmosphere is thick, and the fat, shiny-leather bands even get church mice to stand up and conduct three-quarter time with breadsticks (daily 9:00-23:30, music during lunch and dinner, 5-minute walk from Marienplatz at Platzl 6, tel. 089/2901-3610, www.hofbraeuhaus.de).

The small beer garden at the center of the **Viktualienmarkt** taps you into about the best budget eating in town just steps from Marienplatz (closed Sun). There's table service wherever you see a tablecloth; to picnic, choose a table without one. Buy your drinks from the counter. Countless stalls surround the beer garden and sell wurst, sandwiches, produce, and so on. This B.Y.O.F. tradition goes back to the days when monastery beer gardens served beer but not food. This is a good spot to grab a typical Munich *Weisswurst*—and some beer.

Jodlerwirt ("Yodeling Innkeeper") is a tiny, cramped, and smart-alecky pub. The food is great, and the ambience is as Bavarian as you'll find. Avoid the basic ground-floor bar and climb the stairs into the action. Even if it's just you and the accordionist, it's fun. Good food and lots of belly laughs...completely incomprehensible to the average tourist (€8-16 main courses, Tue-Sat 19:00-3:00 in the morning, food until 23:00, closed Mon except Sept-Dec, always closed Sun, accordion act nightly 20:00-2:00 in the morning, between Hofbräuhaus and Marienplatz at Altenhofstrasse 4, tel. 089/221-249).

The trendy **Andechser am Dom,** at the rear of the twin-domed Frauenkirche on a breezy square, serves Andechs beer and great food to appreciative regulars. Münchners favor the dark beer

Munich's Beer Scene

In Munich's beer halls *(Brauhäuser)* and beer gardens *(Biergartens)*, meals are inexpensive, white radishes are salted and cut in delicate spirals, and surly beer maids pull mustard packets from their cleavage. Unlike with wine, spending more money on beer doesn't get you a better drink. Beer is truly a people's drink, and you'll get the very best here in Munich. The big question among connoisseurs (local and foreign) is, "Which brew today?"

Beer gardens go back to the days when monks brewed their beer and were allowed to sell it directly to the thirsty public. They stored their beer in cellars under courtyards kept cool by the shade of bushy chestnut trees. Eventually, tables were set up, and these convivial eateries evolved. The tradition (complete with chestnut trees) survives, and any real beer garden will keep a few tables (those without tablecloths) available for customers who buy only beer and bring their own food.

Huge liter beers (called *ein Mass* in German, or "*ein* pitcher" in English) cost about €7. You can order your beer *helles* (light but not "lite"—which is what you'll get if you say "*ein* beer"), *dunkles* (dark), or *Radler* (half lemon soda, half beer). Most beer gardens have a deposit *(Pfand)* system for their big glass steins: You pay €1 extra, and when you're finished, you can take the mug to the return man *(Pfandrückgabe)* for your refund, or leave it on the table and lose your money. (Men's rooms come with vomitoriums.)

Many beer halls have a cafeteria system. Eating outside is made more pleasant by the *Föhn* (warm winds that come over the Alps from Italy), which gives this part of Germany 30 more days of sunshine than the North—and sometimes even an Italian ambience. (Many natives attribute the city's huge increase in outdoor dining to global warming.)

Beer halls take care of their regular customers. You'll notice many tables marked *Stammtisch* (reserved for regulars and small groups, such as the "Happy Saturday Club"). These have a long tradition of being launch pads for grassroots action. In the days before radio and television, aspiring leaders used beer halls to connect with the public. Hitler hosted numerous political rallies in beer halls, and the Hofbräuhaus was the first place he talked to a big crowd.

(ask for *dunkles*), but I love the light *(helles)*. The €11.50 *Gourmetteller* is a great sampler of their specialties, and the *Rostbratwurst* with kraut (€6.90) gives you the virtual *Nürnberger* bratwurst experience (see next) with the better Andechs beer (€7-15 main courses, daily 10:00-24:00, Weinstrasse 7a, reserve during peak times, tel. 089/298-481).

Nürnberger Bratwurst Glöckl am Dom, just across from Andechser am Dom, is popular with tourists and offers a classier, fiercely Bavarian evening. Dine outside under the trees or in the dark, medieval, cozy interior—patrolled by wenches and spiked with antlers. I come here to enjoy the tasty little *Nürnberger* sausages with kraut (€8-19 main courses, Mon-Sat 10:00-24:00, Sun 11:00-23:00, Frauenplatz 9, tel. 089/291-9450).

Altes Hackerhaus is popular with locals for its traditional *Bayerisch* (Bavarian) fare served with a slightly fancier feel in one of the oldest buildings in town. It offers a small courtyard and a fun forest of characteristic nooks festooned with old-time paintings, ads, and posters. This place is much-appreciated for its Hacker-Pschorr beer (€7-10 wurst dishes, €9-25 main courses, daily 10:00-24:00, Sendlinger Strasse 14, tel. 089/260-5026).

Der Pschorr, an upscale beer hall occupying a former slaughterhouse, has a terrace overlooking the Viktualienmarkt and serves a special premium version of what many consider Munich's finest beer. With organic "slow food" and chilled glasses, this place mixes modern concepts—no candles, industrial-strength conviviality—with traditional, quality, classic dishes. They tap classic wooden kegs every few minutes with gusto. The sound of the hammer lets patrons know they're getting it good and fresh (€11-23 main courses, €8-9 lunch specials, daily 10:00-24:00, Viktualienmarkt 15, at end of Schrannenhalle, tel. 089/5181-8500).

Spatenhaus is the opera-goers' beer hall, serving more elegant food in a woodsy, traditional setting since 1896—maybe it's not even right to call it a "beer hall." You can also eat outside, on the square facing the opera and palace. It's pricey, but you won't find better-quality Bavarian cuisine (€13-25 main courses, daily 9:30-24:00, on Max-Joseph-Platz opposite opera, Residenzstrasse 12, tel. 089/290-7050, www.kuffler.de).

Heilig-Geist-Stüberl ("Holy Ghost Pub") is a funky, retro little hole-in-the-wall where you are sure to meet locals (the German cousins of those who go to Reno because it's cheaper than Vegas, and who consider karaoke high culture). The interior, a 1980s time warp, makes you feel like you're stepping into an alcoholic cuckoo clock. There's no food—just drink here (daily 9:00-22:00, just off the Viktualienmarkt at Heiliggeiststrasse 1, tel. 089/297-233).

MUNICH

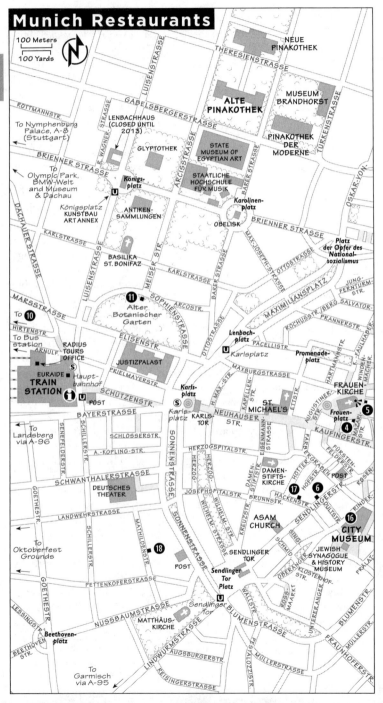

Munich Restaurants

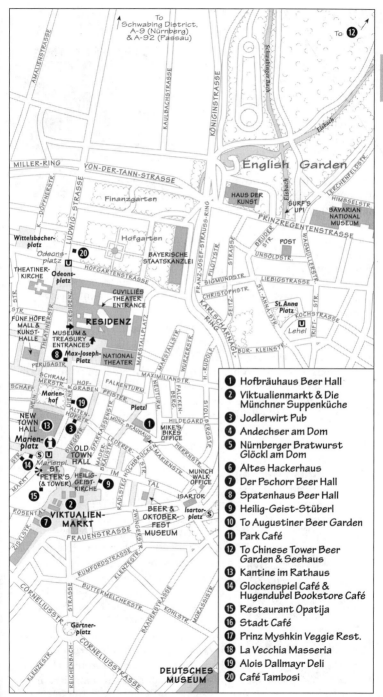

1 Hofbräuhaus Beer Hall
2 Viktualienmarkt & Die Münchner Suppenküche
3 Jodlerwirt Pub
4 Andechser am Dom
5 Nürnberger Bratwurst Glöckl am Dom
6 Altes Hackerhaus
7 Der Pschorr Beer Hall
8 Spatenhaus Beer Hall
9 Heilig-Geist-Stüberl
10 To Augustiner Beer Garden
11 Park Café
12 To Chinese Tower Beer Garden & Seehaus
13 Kantine im Rathaus
14 Glockenspiel Café & Hugendubel Bookstore Café
15 Restaurant Opatija
16 Stadt Café
17 Prinz Myshkin Veggie Rest.
18 La Vecchia Masseria
19 Alois Dallmayr Deli
20 Café Tambosi

MUNICH

Near the Train Station

Augustiner Beer Garden is a sprawling haven for well-established local beer-lovers on a balmy evening. For a true under-the-leaves beer garden packed with Münchners, this is a delight. In fact, most Münchners consider Augustiner the best beer garden in town. There's no music, it's away from the tourist hordes, and it serves up great beer, good traditional food, huge portions, reasonable prices, and the perfect conviviality. The outdoor self-service ambience is

best, making this place ideal on a nice summer evening (figure €12 for a main course and a drink). There's also indoor and outdoor seating at a more expensive restaurant with table service (€11-18 main courses) by the entrance (daily 10:00-23:00, self-service food outside until 22:00, Arnulfstrasse 52, 3 loooong blocks from station going away from the center—or take tram #16/#17 one stop to Hopfenstrasse, taxis always waiting at the gate, tel. 089/594-393, www.augustinerkeller.de).

Park Café, though in a park, is much more than a café. The indoor section is big and bold, with clean yet rustic ambience, DJs or live music in the late evening, few tourists, and quality food (€9-15 main courses). When it's hot, everyone decamps to the beer garden out back in the Alter Botanischer Garden, where you can order off the menu or from the self-service counters. Don't forget to reclaim the deposit for your plate and mug when you leave (daily 10:00-24:00, a short walk north of the train station at Sophienstrasse 7, tel. 089/5161-7980).

In the English Garden

For outdoor ambience and a cheap meal, spend an evening at the

English Garden's **Chinese Tower Beer Garden** *(Chinesischer Turm Biergarten).* You're welcome to B.Y.O. food and grab a table, or buy from the picnic stall *(Brotzeit)* right there. Don't bother to phone ahead—they have 6,000 seats. This is a fine opportunity to try a *Steckerlfisch,* sold for €9 at a separate kiosk (daily, long hours in good weather, usually live music, tel. 089/383-8730, www.chinaturm.de; take tram #17 from main train station or Sendlinger Tor to Tivolistrasse, or

U-3 or U-6 to Universität).

Seehaus im Englischen Garten is famous among Münchners for its idyllic lakeside setting and excellent Mediterranean and traditional cooking. It's dressy and a bit snobbish, and understandably filled with locals who fit the same description. Choose from classy indoor or lakeside seating (€20-25 main courses, daily 10:00-late, a pleasant 15-minute hike into the English Garden—located on all the city maps—or take tram #44 or a taxi to the doorstep, Kleinhesselohe 3, tel. 089/381-6130).

Seehaus Beer Garden, adjacent to the fancy Seehaus restaurant, is a less expensive, more casual beer garden with all the normal wurst, kraut, pretzels, and fine beer at typical prices. What makes this spot special: You're buried in the English Garden, enjoying the fine lakeside setting (daily, long hours from 11:00 when the weather's fine).

Non-Beer Hall Restaurants

Man does not live by beer alone. Well, maybe some do. But for the rest of us, I recommend the following alternatives to the beer-and-wurst circuit.

On Marienplatz

Kantine im Rathaus is your solid, fast, economical, and no-nonsense standby in the center. The entrance is just behind the New Town Hall tower—go through the arch under the tower into the courtyard and look for the sign on the right. There's seating in the courtyard or inside (€5-10 main courses, Mon-Fri 11:00-18:30, Sat 12:00-16:00, closed Sun).

Glockenspiel Café is good for a coffee or a meal with a bird's-eye view down on the Marienplatz action—I'd come for the view more than the food. Locals like the sunroof, but regardless of the weather, I grab a seat overlooking Marienplatz (Mon-Sat 10:00-24:00, Sun 10:00-19:00, ride elevator from Rosenstrasse entrance, opposite glockenspiel at Marienplatz 28, tel. 089/264-256).

The **Hugendubel bookstore** has a Starbucks-style café on the top floor. It's quicker and less crowded than the Glockenspiel Café, and comes with the same great view (self-serve, take the glass elevator, Mon-Sat 9:30-20:00, closed Sun).

Around the Viktualienmarkt

The area south of Marienplatz—especially **Sebastiansplatz,** a long, pedestrianized square between the synagogue and Viktualienmarkt—is becoming a kind of SoHo, with lots of fun shops, wine bars, and bistros handy for a healthy and quick lunch. The options range from French to Italian, Asian to vegetarian, and all serve €10 plates on the busy cobbled square or inside. You can just survey the scene and choose; I've listed a few reliable options below.

Restaurant Opatija, in the Viktualienmarktpassage a few steps from Marienplatz, brings the Adriatic to Munich with a big, eclectic Italian and Balkan menu, plus traditional German favorites. Choose between the comfortable indoor section and the outdoor seating in a quiet, narrow courtyard. Prices are low, it's family-friendly, and they do takeout (€7 pizzas, €7-10 pastas, €9 salad plates, €9-12 main courses, daily 11:30-22:30, kitchen closes at 21:30, enter the passage at Viktualienmarkt 6 or Rindermarkt 2, tel. 089/2323-1995).

Die Münchner Suppenküche ("Munich Soup Kitchen"), a self-service soup joint at the Viktualienmarkt, is fine for a small, cozy sit-down lunch at picnic tables under a closed-in awning (€4-6 soup meals, Mon-Fri 10:00-18:00, Sat 9:00-18:00, closed Sun, near corner of Reichenbachstrasse and Frauenstrasse, tel. 089/260-9599).

Stadt Café is a lively café serving healthy fare, with great daily specials (€7-10) and an inventive menu of Italian, German, salads, and vegetarian dishes. This informal, no-frills restaurant draws newspaper-readers, stroller moms, and tourists, too. Dine in the quiet cobbled courtyard, inside, or outside facing the new synagogue (blackboard has today's specials, daily 10:00-24:00, in Munich City Museum, St.-Jakobs-Platz 1, tel. 089/266-949).

Prinz Myshkin Vegetarian Restaurant is everybody's favorite upscale vegetarian eatery in the old center. The menu is totally meatless and dictated by the season. You'll find a clever, appetizing selection of €10-15 main courses. The decor is modern, the arched ceilings are cool, the outside seating is on a quiet street, and the clientele is entirely local. Don't miss the enticing appetizer selection on display as you enter (they do a fine €11 mixed-appetizer plate). They also have vegetarian sushi, pastas, Indian dishes, and their own baker, so they're proud of their sweets (€6 lunch specials, daily 11:30-23:00, Hackenstrasse 2, tel. 089/265-596).

Near the Train Station

La Vecchia Masseria, between Sendlinger Tor and the train station hotels, serves simple Italian food inside amid a cozy Tuscan farmhouse decor, or outside in a beautiful flowery courtyard. Try the €24 tasting *menu* (€6-8 pizza or pasta, €15 main courses, daily 11:30-23:30, reservations smart, Mathildenstrasse 3, tel. 089/550-9090).

Picnics

For a truly elegant picnic, **Alois Dallmayr's** is the place to shop. The crown in their emblem reflects that no less than the royal fam-

MUNICH

ily assembled its picnics at this historic and expensive delicatessen. Pretend you're a Bavarian aristocrat—King Ludwig himself, even—and put together a royal spread to munch in the nearby Hofgarten. Or visit the classy but pricey cafés that serve light meals on the ground floor and first floor (Mon-Sat 9:30-19:00, closed Sun, behind New Town Hall, Dienerstrasse 13-15).

A Budget Picnic: To save money, browse at Dallmayr's but buy in the **supermarkets** that hide in the basements of department stores: the **Kaufhof** stores at Marienplatz and Karlsplatz (Mon-Sat 9:30-20:00, closed Sun), the more upmarket **Karstadt** across from the train station (same hours), or the **REWE** at Fünf Höfe (Mon-Sat 7:00-20:00, closed Sun, entrance is in Viscardihof).

Munich Connections

Munich is a super transportation hub (one reason it was the target of so many WWII bombs), with easy train and bus connections to most Bavarian destinations, as well as international trains.

Trains

For quick help at the main train station, stop by the service counter in front of track 18. For better English and more patience, drop by the EurAide desk at counter #1 in the *Reisezentrum*. Train info: tel. 0180-599-6633, www.bahn.com.

From Munich by Train to: Füssen (hourly, 2 hours, some direct but most with easy transfer in Buchloe; for a Neuschwanstein Castle day trip, leave as early as possible and no later than 9:00), **Reutte,** Austria (every 2 hours, 2.5 hours, change in Garmisch), **Oberammergau** (nearly hourly, 1.75 hours, change in Murnau), **Salzburg,** Austria (2/hour, 1.5-2 hours), **Berchtesgaden** (at least hourly, 2.5-3 hours, change in Freilassing), **Nürnberg** (2-3/hour, 1-1.25 hours), **Köln** (2/hour, 4.5 hours, some with 1 change), **Würzburg** (1-2/hour, 2 hours), **Rothenburg** (hourly, 2.5-3.5 hours, 2-3 changes), **Frankfurt** (hourly, 3.25 hours), **Frankfurt Airport** (1-2/hour, 3.5 hours), **Leipzig** (every 2 hours direct, 5.5 hours; also every 2 hours with change in Nürnberg or Naumburg, 4.75-5 hours), **Erfurt** (about 2/hour, 4.5-4.75 hours, change in Würzburg or Fulda), **Dresden** (every 2 hours, 6 hours, change in Nürnberg), **Hamburg** (hourly, 6-6.5 hours), **Berlin** (1-2/hour, 6-6.75 hours, every 2 hours direct, otherwise a change in Göttingen), **Vienna** (direct trains every 2 hours, 4.25 hours), **Venice** (every 2 hours, 7-7.5 hours, change in Verona, 1 direct night train, 9.5 hours), **Paris** (4/day, 6 hours, usually with 1 change), **Prague** (2/day direct, 6.25 hours; 6 more/day with change in Nürnberg then express bus, 5.25 hours; no night trains), **Zürich** (4/day direct, 4.25 hours). Trains run nightly to Berlin, Vienna, Venice, Florence, Rome, Paris, Amsterdam, Budapest, and Copenhagen (at least 6 hours to each city). To use a railpass for a night train to Italy, your pass must include all countries on the train route (i.e., Austria or Switzerland), or you'll have to buy the segment that's not included.

Buses

Romantic Road Bus: The **Romantic Road bus** (mid-April-late Oct only) connects Munich's Central Bus Station to Füssen, Dinkelsbühl, Rothenburg, Würzburg, Frankfurt, and other destinations en route. This slower but more scenic alternative to the train allows a glimpse of towns such as Augsburg, Nördlingen, and Dinkelsbühl (no advance reservations needed, northbound bus departs Munich at 10:50, arrives Rothenburg at 15:50; southbound bus departs Munich at 17:50, arrives Füssen at 19:55).

Munich Airport

Munich's airport (code: MUC) is an easy 40-minute ride on the S-1 or S-8 **subway,** each of which runs every 20 minutes (starting at 4:00 in the morning and continuing until almost 2:00 in the morning) between the airport and Marienplatz and the train station. While you can buy a single ticket for €10, the €10.80 Munich *Gesamtnetz* day pass, which covers public transportation all day, is worth getting if you'll be making just one more public transport journey that same day. Groups of two or more should buy the €19.60 Munich *Gesamtnetz* partner day pass, which gives up to five adults the run of the system for the day (for more info on Munich transport passes). The trip is also free with a validated and dated railpass. The S-8 is a bit quicker and easier, as the S-1 line has two branches and some trains split—if on the S-1 to the airport, be certain your train is going to the *Flughafen*. Another alternative is the Lufthansa **airport bus,** which links the airport with the main train station (€10.50, €17 round-trip, 3/hour, 45 minutes, buses depart train station 5:10-19:50, buy tickets on bus; from inside the station, exit near track 26 and look for yellow *Airport Bus* signs; www.auto busoberbayern.de). If you're traveling alone, going round-trip, and not using other public transport the same day, the bus saves a few euros. Avoid taking a **taxi** from the airport, as it's a long, expensive drive; it's better to take public transport and then switch to a taxi if needed. Airport info: tel. 089/97500, www.munich-airport.de.

BAVARIA and TIROL

*Füssen • King's Castles • Wieskirche • Oberammergau •
Linderhof Castle • Ettal Monastery • Zugspitze •
Reutte, Austria*

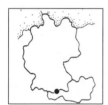

Two hours south of Munich, in Germany's Bavaria and Austria's Tirol, is a timeless land of fairy-tale castles, painted buildings shared by cows and farmers, and locals who still yodel when they're happy.

In Germany's Bavaria, tour "Mad" King Ludwig II's ornate Neuschwanstein Castle, Europe's most spectacular. Stop by the Wieskirche, a textbook example of Bavarian Rococo bursting with curlicues, and browse through Oberammergau, Germany's woodcarving capital and home of the famous Passion Play (next performed in 2020). Then, just over the border in Austria's Tirol, explore the ruined Ehrenberg Castle and scream down the mountain on an oversized skateboard.

In this chapter, I'll cover Bavaria first, then Tirol. My favorite home base for exploring Bavaria's castles is actually in Austria, in the Tirolean town of Reutte. Reutte's hotels offer better value to those with a car. Füssen, in Germany, is more touristy, but a handier home base for train travelers.

Planning Your Time and Getting Around Bavaria

While Germans and Austrians vacation here for a week or two at a time, the typical speedy American traveler will find two days' worth of sightseeing. With a car and more time, you could enjoy three or four days, but the basic visit ranges anywhere from a long day trip from Munich to a three-night, two-day stay. If the weather's good and you're not going to Switzerland on your trip, be sure to ride a lift to an alpine peak.

By Car

This region is best by car, and all the sights are within an easy 60-mile loop from Reutte or Füssen. Even if you're doing the rest of your trip by train, consider renting a car for your time here.

Here's a good one-day circular drive from Reutte (or from Füssen, starting half an hour later):

7:00	Breakfast
7:30	Depart hotel
8:00	Arrive at Neuschwanstein to pick up tickets for the two castles (Neuschwanstein and Hohenschwangau)
9:00	Tour Hohenschwangau
11:00	Tour Neuschwanstein
13:00	Drive to Oberammergau, and spend an hour there browsing the carving shops
15:00	Drive to Ettal Monastery for a half-hour stop (if you're not otherwise seeing the Wieskirche), then on to Linderhof Castle
16:00	Tour Linderhof
18:00	Drive along scenic Plansee lake back into Austria (or return to Füssen)
19:00	Back at hotel
20:00	Dinner at hotel

Off-season (Oct-March), start your day an hour later, since Neuschwanstein and Hohenschwangau don't open until 10:00; and skip Linderhof, as it closes an hour early.

The next morning, you could stroll through Reutte, hike to the Ehrenberg ruins, and ride the luge on your way to Munich, Innsbruck, Switzerland, Venice, or wherever.

By Public Transportation

Where you stay determines which sights you can see most easily. Train travelers use **Füssen** as a base, and bus or bike the three miles to Neuschwanstein and the Tegelberg luge or gondola. Staying in **Oberammergau** gives you easy access to Linderhof and Ettal Monastery, and you can day-trip to the top of the Zugspitze via Garmisch. Although **Reutte** is the least convenient base if you're carless, travelers staying there can easily bike or hike to the Ehrenberg ruins, and can reach Neuschwanstein by bus (via Füssen), bike (1.5 hours), or taxi (€35 one-way); if you stay at the recommended Gutshof zum Schluxen hotel (between Reutte and Füssen, in Pinswang, Austria) it's a one-hour hike through the

Füssen & Reutte Area

To Munich
via Buchloe

Romantic Road
to Rothenburg

ECHELSBACHER
BRIDGE
(GORGE)

Steingaden

To
Kempten

WIESKIRCHE

Saulgrub

Forggensee

A-7

17

23

See King's Castles map

LUGE

STECKENBERG
LUGE

Oberammergau

Tegelberg

LINDERHOF

Kofel

To
Munich

Füssen

Schwangau

NEUSCHWANSTEIN

HOHENSCHWANGAU

Ettal

Pinswang

GERMANY

HAHNEN-
KAMMBAHN

See Reutte map

Reutte

Garmisch-
Partenkirchen

Eibsee

187

198

Plansee

EHRENBERG
RUINS

AUSTRIA

Grainau

Lech River

Bichlbach

179

Zugspitze
9718'

Stanzach

Lermoos

Ehrwald

LUGE

Blindsee

Namlos

NARROW
ROAD

Fernpass

Biberwier

Fallerschein

REST STOP

N

5 Kilometers

5 Miles

Nassereith

Telfs

179

To Zürich

A-12

Stams

To
Innsbruck

BAVARIA AND TIROL

woods to Neuschwanstein.

Visiting sights farther from your home base is not impossible by local bus, but requires planning. The German Railway website (www.bahn.com) does a great job of finding bus connections that work, on both sides of the border. (Schedules for each route are available at www.rvo-bus.de, but only in German.) Those staying in **Füssen** can day-trip by bus to Reutte and the Ehrenberg ruins, to the Wieskirche, or, with some effort, to Linderhof via Oberammergau. From **Oberammergau,** you can reach Neuschwanstein and Füssen by bus. From **Reutte,** you can take the train to Ehrwald to reach the Zugspitze from the Austrian side, but side-trips from Reutte to Oberammergau and Linderhof are impractical. More transport details are provided later, under each individual destination.

Hitchhiking, though always risky, is a slow-but-possible way to connect the public-transportation gaps. For example, even reluctant hitchhikers can catch a ride from Linderhof back to Oberammergau, as virtually everyone leaving there is a tourist like you and heading that way.

Bavarian Craftsmanship

The scenes you'll see painted on the sides of houses in Bavaria are called *Lüftlmalerei*. The term came from the name of the house ("Zum Lüftl") owned by a man from Oberammergau who pioneered the practice in the 18th century. As the paintings became popular during the Counter-Reformation Baroque age, themes tended to involve Christian symbols, saints, and stories (such as scenes from the life of Jesus), to reinforce the Catholic Church's authority in the region. Some scenes also depicted an important historical event that took place in that house or town.

Especially in the northern part of this region, you'll see *Fachwerkhäuser*—half-timbered houses. *Fachwerk* means "craftsmanship," as this type of home required a highly skilled master craftsman to create. They are most often found inside fortified cities (such as Rothenberg, Nürnberg, and Dinkelsbühl) that were once strong and semi-independent.

Staying overnight in this region is magical, but travelers in a hurry can make it a day trip from **Munich.** If you can postpone leaving Munich until after 9:00 on weekday mornings, the **Bayern-Ticket** is a great deal for getting to Füssen or Oberammergau (covers buses and slower regional trains throughout Bavaria for €21/day, or €29/day for up to 5 people). If you're interested only in Ludwig's castles, consider an all-day organized bus tour of the Bavarian biggies as a side-trip from Munich.

By Bike

This is great biking country. Many hotels loan bikes to guests, and shops in Reutte and at the Füssen train station rent bikes for €8-15 per day. The ride from Reutte to Neuschwanstein and the Tegelberg luge (1.5 hours) is a natural.

Helpful Hints

Sightseeing Pass: The Bavarian Palace Department offers a 14-day **Bavarian Castles Pass** that covers admission to Neuschwanstein (but not Hohenschwangau) and Linderhof; the Residenz, Nymphenburg Palace, and Amalienburg Palace in Munich; the Imperial Palace in Nürnberg; the Residenz and Marienberg Fortress in Würzburg; and many other castles and palaces not mentioned in this book. The one-person pass costs €24, and the family/partner version (up to two adults plus children) costs €40. If you are planning to visit at least three of these sights within a two-week period, the pass will likely pay for itself. (For longer stays, there's also an annual pass available—€45/single, €65/family.) The pass is sold at all covered castles and online. For more information, see www .schloesser.bayern.de.

Local Guest Tax: Hotels and B&Bs in the region are usually required to collect a local tax (called a *Kurtax*) of about €1.50 per person per night, which is not included in the rates listed here and will be added to your bill.

Visiting Churches: At any type of church, if you'd like to attend a service, look for the *Gottesdienst* schedule. In every small German town in the very Catholic south, when you pass the big town church, look for a sign that says *Heilige Messe*. This is the schedule for holy Mass, usually on Saturday *(Sa.)* or Sunday *(So.).*

Füssen

Dramatically situated under a renovated castle on the lively Lech River, Füssen (FEW-sehn) is a handy home base for exploring the region. This town has been a strategic stop since ancient times. Its

main street sits on the Via Claudia Augusta, which crossed the Alps (over the Brenner Pass) in Roman times. Going north, early traders could follow the Lech River downstream to the Danube, and then cross over to the Main and Rhine valleys—a route now known to modern travelers as the "Romantic Road." Today, while Füssen is overrun by tourists in the summer, few venture to the back streets...which is where you'll find the real charm. Apart from my self-guided walk and the Füssen Heritage Museum, there's little to do here. It's just a pleasant small town with a big history and lots of hardworking people in the tourist business.

Halfway between Füssen and the border (as you drive, or a woodsy walk from the town) is the **Lechfall,** a thunderous water-fall (with a handy WC).

Orientation to Füssen

(area code: 08362)
Füssen's train station is a few blocks from the TI, the town center (a cobbled shopping mall), and all my hotel listings.

Tourist Information

The TI is in the center of town (July-mid-Sept Mon-Fri 9:00-18:00, Sat 10:00-14:00, Sun 10:00-12:00; mid-Sept-June Mon-Fri 9:00-17:00, Sat 10:00-14:00, closed Sun; one free Internet terminal, 3 blocks down Bahnhofstrasse from station at Kaiser-Maximilian-Platz 1, tel. 08362/93850, www.fuessen.de). If necessary, the TI can help you find a room. After hours, the little self-service info pavilion near the front of the TI features an automated room-finding service with a phone to call hotels.

Arrival in Füssen

From the train station (lockers available, €2-3), exit to the left and walk a few blocks to reach the center of town and the TI. Buses to Neuschwanstein, Reutte, and elsewhere leave from a parking lot next to the station.

Helpful Hints

Internet Access: Beans & Bytes is the best place to get online, with fast terminals and good drink service (€2/2 hours, Wi-Fi, Skype, disc-burning, Mon-Sat 10:00-20:00, closed Sun except July-Aug, down the pedestrian alley off the main drag at Reichenstrasse 33, tel. 08362/926-8960).

Bike Rental: Bike Station, sitting right where the train tracks end, outfits sightseers with good bikes and tips on two-wheeled fun in the area (€8-10/24 hours, March-Oct Mon-Fri 9:00-12:00 & 14:00-18:00, Sat 9:00-13:00, Sun in good weather 9:00-12:00, closed Nov-Feb, tel. 08362/983-651, mobile 0176-2205-3080, www.ski-sport-luggi.de).

Car Rental: Peter Schlichtling, in the town center, rents cars for reasonable prices (€62/day, includes insurance, Mon-Fri 8:00-18:00, Sat 9:00-12:00, closed Sun, Kemptener Strasse 26, tel. 08362/922-122, www.schlichtling.de). **Auto Osterried/Europcar** rents at similar prices, but is an €8 taxi ride away from the train station. Their cheapest car goes for about €59 per day (daily 8:00-19:00, past waterfall on road to Austria, Tiroler Strasse 65, tel. 08362/6381).

Local Guide: Silvia Beyer speaks English, knows the region very well, and can even drive you to sights that are hard to reach by train (€30/hour, silliby@web.de, mobile 0160-901-13431).

Self-Guided Walk

Welcome to Füssen

For most, Füssen is just a home base for visiting Ludwig's famous castles. But the town has a rich history and hides some evocative corners, as you'll see when you follow this short orientation walk.

Throughout the town, "City Tour" information plaques explain points of interest in English. Use them to supplement the information I've provided.

• *Begin at the square in front of the TI, three blocks from the train station.*

❶ Kaiser-Maximilian-Platz: The entertaining "Seven Stones" fountain on this square, by sculptor Christian Tobin, was built in 1995 to celebrate Füssen's 700th birthday. The stones symbolize community, groups of people gathering, conviviality...each is different, with "heads" nodding and talking. It's granite on granite. The moving heads are not connected, and nod only with waterpower. While frozen in winter, it's a popular and splashy play zone for kids on hot summer days.

• *Just half a block down the busy street stands...*

❷ Hotel Hirsch and Medieval Towers: Recent renovations have restored some of the original Art Nouveau flavor to Hotel Hirsch, which opened in 1904. In those days, aristocratic tour-

ists came here to appreciate the castles and natural wonders of the Alps. Across the busy street stands one of two surviving towers from Füssen's medieval town wall (c. 1515), and next to it is a passageway into the old town.

• *Walk 50 yards farther down the street to another tower. Just before it, you'll see an information plaque and an archway where a small street called Klosterstrasse emerges through a surviving piece of the old town wall. Step through the smaller pedestrian archway,* walk along Klosterstrasse for a few yards, and turn left through the gate into the...

❸ Historic Cemetery of St. Sebastian (Alter Friedhof): This peaceful oasis of Füssen history, established in the 16th century, fills a corner between the town wall and the Franciscan monastery. It's technically full, and only members of great and venerable Füssen families (who already own plots here) can join those who are buried (free, daily April-Sept 7:30-19:00, Oct-March 8:00-17:00).

Just inside the gate (on the right) is the tomb of Dominic Quaglio, who painted the Romantic scenes decorating the walls

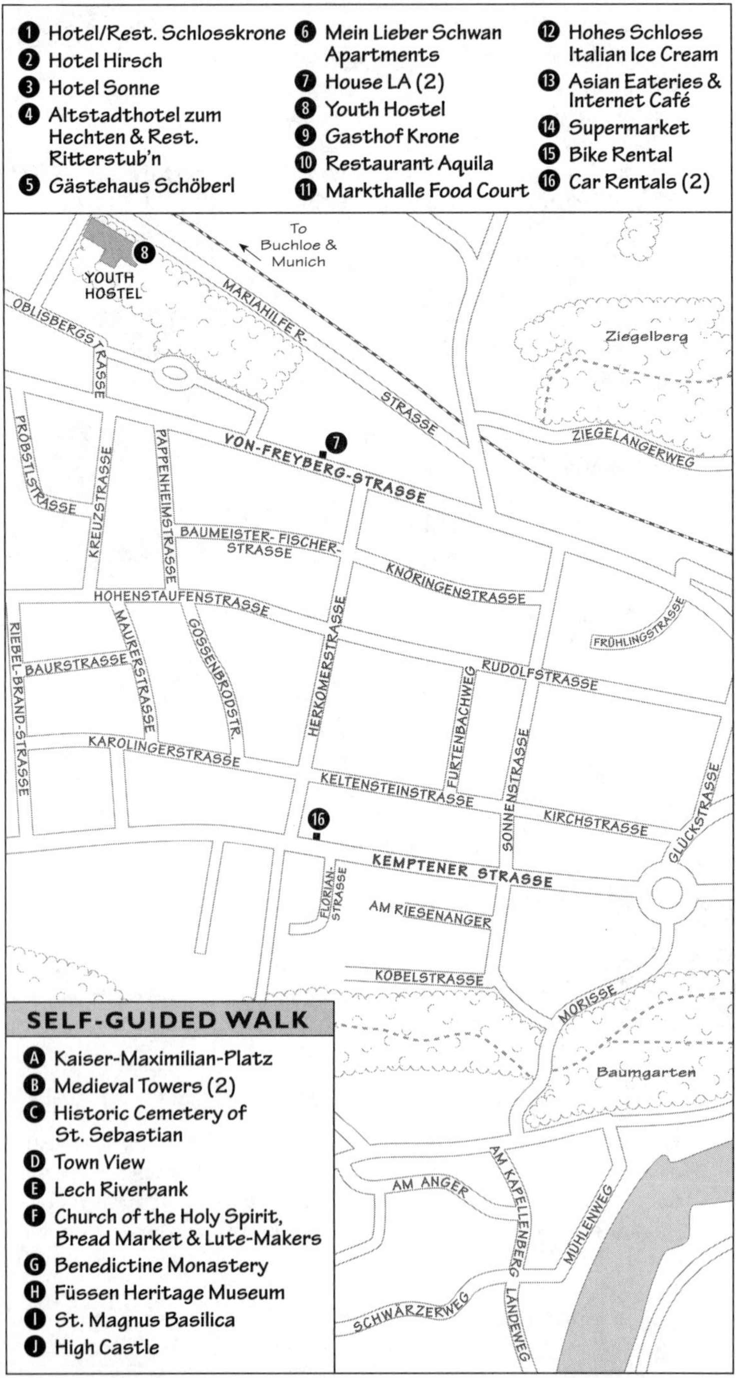

BAVARIA AND TIROL

1 Hotel/Rest. Schlosskrone
2 Hotel Hirsch
3 Hotel Sonne
4 Altstadthotel zum Hechten & Rest. Ritterstub'n
5 Gästehaus Schöberl
6 Mein Lieber Schwan Apartments
7 House LA (2)
8 Youth Hostel
9 Gasthof Krone
10 Restaurant Aquila
11 Markthalle Food Court
12 Hohes Schloss Italian Ice Cream
13 Asian Eateries & Internet Café
14 Supermarket
15 Bike Rental
16 Car Rentals (2)

To Buchloe & Munich

YOUTH HOSTEL

Ziegelberg

OBLISBERGSTRASSE
MARIAHILFER-
STRASSE
ZIEGELANGERWEG
PROBSTLSTRASSE
KREUZSTRASSE
PAPPENHEIMSTRASSE
VON-FREYBERG-STRASSE
BAUMEISTER-FISCHER-STRASSE
KNÖRINGENSTRASSE
FRÜHLINGSTRASSE
RIEBEL-BRAND-STRASSE
BAURSTRASSE
HOHENSTAUFENSTRASSE
MAURERSTRASSE
GOSSENBRODSTR.
HERKOMERSTRASSE
RUDOLFSTRASSE
KAROLINGERSTRASSE
FURTENBACHWEG
KELTENSTEINSTRASSE
SONNENSTRASSE
KIRCHSTRASSE
GLÜCKSTRASSE
KEMPTENER STRASSE
FLORIAN-STRASSE
AM RIESENANGER
KOBELSTRASSE
MORISSE
Baumgarten
AM ANGER
AM KAPELLENBERG
MÜHLENWEG
LANDEWEG
SCHWÄRZERWEG

SELF-GUIDED WALK

A Kaiser-Maximilian-Platz
B Medieval Towers (2)
C Historic Cemetery of St. Sebastian
D Town View
E Lech Riverbank
F Church of the Holy Spirit, Bread Market & Lute-Makers
G Benedictine Monastery
H Füssen Heritage Museum
I St. Magnus Basilica
J High Castle

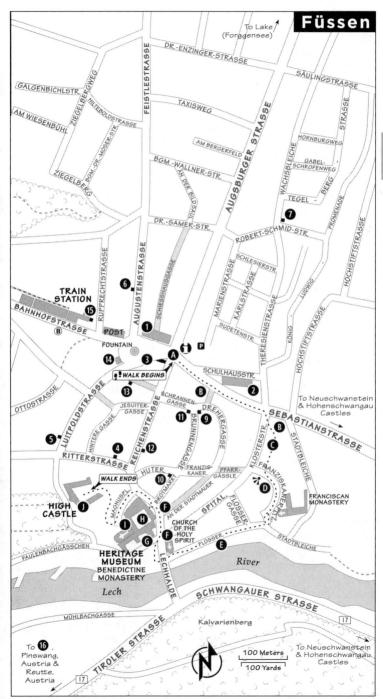

Füssen

To Lake (Forggensee)

DR.-ENZINGER-STRASSE

SÄULINGSTRASSE

GALGENBICHLSTR.

AM WIESENBÜHL

ZIEGELBERGWEG

HILTEBOLDSTRASSE

BGM.-DR.-MOSER-STR.

FEISTLESTRASSE

TAXISWEG

AM BERGERFELD

AUGSBURGER STRASSE

HORNBURGWEG

GABEL-SCHROFENWEG

WACHSBLEICHE

TEGEL-BERG

ZIEGELBERG

BGM.-WALLNER-STR.

AN DER BILDSÄULE

DR.-SAMER-STR.

ROBERT-SCHMID-STR.

MARIENSTRASSE

SCHLESIERSTR.

KARLSTRASSE

SUDETENSTR.

THERESIENSTRASSE

PROMENADE

LUDWIG

KÖNIG

HOCHSTIFTSTRASSE

7

BAVARIA AND TIROL

RUPPRECHTSTRASSE

AUGUSTENSTRASSE

SCHIESSHAUSGASSE

TRAIN STATION

BAHNHOFSTRASSE

B

15

POST

6

1

FOUNTAIN

14

3

A

P

SCHULHAUSSTR.

2

SEBASTIANSTRASSE

To Neuschwanstein & Hohenschwangau Castles

! WALK BEGINS

13

OTTOSTRASSE

LUITPOLDSTRASSE

JESUITER-GASSE

SCHRANNEN-GASSE

B

DREHERGASSE

11

9

BRUNNENGASSE

KLOSTERSTR.

STADTBLEICHE

B

HINTERE GASSE

REICHENSTRASSE

FRANZISKANERGASSE

C

5

RITTERSTRASSE

4

12

FRANZIS-KANER-GÄSSLE

PFARR-GÄSSLE

D

FRANCISCAN MONASTERY

WALK ENDS

HUTER

10

BROTMARKT

AN DER STADTMAUER

SPITAL-GASSE

FLOSSER-GASSE

J

HIGH CASTLE

MAGNUSPL.

I

H

F

STADTBLEICHE

FAULENBACHGÄSSCHEN

G

F

CHURCH OF THE HOLY SPIRIT

FLOSSER

E

HERITAGE MUSEUM BENEDICTINE MONASTERY

LECHHALDE

River

Lech

MÜHLBACHGASSE

SCHWANGAUER STRASSE

TIROLER STRASSE

Kalvarienberg

17

To **16**, Pinswang, Austria & Reutte, Austria

17

100 Meters

100 Yards

N

To Neuschwanstein & Hohenschwangau Castles

of Hohenschwangau Castle in 1835. Over on the old city wall is the World War I memorial, listing all the names of men from this small town killed in that devastating conflict (along with each one's rank and place of death). A bit to the right, also along the old wall, is a statue of the hand of God holding a fetus—a place to remember babies who died before being born. And in the corner, farther to the right, are the simple wooden crosses of Franciscans who lived just over the wall in the monastery. Note the fine tomb art from many ages collected here, and the loving care this community gives its cemetery.

• *Exit on the far side, just past the dead Franciscans, and continue toward the big church.*

❿ Town View from Franciscan Monastery (Franziskanerkloster): From the Franciscan Monastery (which still has big responsibilities, but only a handful of monks in residence), there's a fine view over the medieval town. The Church of St. Magnus and the High Castle (the summer residence of the Bishops of Augsburg) break the horizon. The chimney (c. 1886) and workers' housing on the left are reminders that when Ludwig built Neuschwanstein, the textile industry (linen and flax) was very big here. Walk all the way to the far end of the monastery chapel and peek around the corner, where you'll see a gate that proclaims the *Ende der romantischen Strasse* (end of the Romantic Road).

• *Now go down the stairway and turn left, through the medieval "Bleachers' Gate," to the riverbank.*

❺ Lech Riverbank: This low end of town, the flood zone, was the home of those whose work depended on the river—bleachers, rafters, and fishermen. In its heyday, the Lech River was an expressway to Augsburg (about 70 miles to the north). Around the year 1500, the rafters established the first professional guild in Füssen. As Füssen was on the Via Claudia, cargo from Italy passed here en route to big German cities farther north. Rafters would assemble rafts and pile them high with goods—or with people needing a lift. If the water was high, they could float all the way to Augsburg in as little as one day. There they'd disassemble their raft and sell off the lumber along with the goods they'd carried, then make their way home to raft again. Today you'll see no modern-day rafters here, as there's a hydroelectric plant just downstream.

• *Walk upstream a bit, and head inland immediately after crossing under the bridge.*

❻ Church of the Holy Spirit, Bread Market, and Lute-Makers: Climbing uphill, you pass the colorful Church of the

Holy Spirit (Heilig-Geist-Spitalkirche) on the right. As this was the church of the rafters, their patron, St. Christopher, is prominent on the facade. Today it's the church of Füssen's old folks' home (it's adjacent—notice the easy-access skyway).

Farther up the hill on the right (almost opposite an archway into a big courtyard) is Bread Market Square (Brotmarkt), with a fountain honoring the famous 16th-century lute-making family, the Tieffenbruckers. In its day, Füssen was a huge center of violin- and lute-making, with about 200 workshops. Today only two survive.

• *Backtrack and go through the archway into the courtyard of the former...*

❼ Benedictine Monastery (Kloster St. Mang): From 1717 until secularization in 1802, this was the powerful center of town. Today the courtyard is popular for concerts, and the building houses the City Hall and Füssen Heritage Museum (and a public WC).

❽ Füssen Heritage Museum: This is Füssen's one mustsee sight (€6, €7 combo-ticket includes painting gallery and castle tower; April-Oct Tue-Sun 11:00-17:00, closed Mon; Nov-March Fri-Sun 13:00-16:00, closed Mon-Thu; tel. 08362/903-146, www .fuessen.de). Pick up the loaner English translations and follow the one-way route. In the St. Anna Chapel, you'll see the famous *Dance of Death*. This was painted shortly after a plague devastated the community in 1590. It shows 20 social classes, each dancing with the Grim Reaper—starting with the pope and  the emperor. The words above say, essentially, "You can say yes or you can say no, but you must ultimately dance with death."

Leaving the chapel, you walk over the metal lid of the crypt. Upstairs, exhibits illustrate the rafting trade and violin- and lutemaking (with a complete workshop). The museum also includes an exquisite *Festsaal* (main festival hall), an old library, an exhibition on textile production, and a King Ludwig-style "castle dream room."

• *Leaving the courtyard, hook left around the old monastery and go uphill. The square tower marks...*

❾ St. Magnus Basilica (Basilika St. Mang): St. Mang (or Magnus) is Füssen's favorite saint. In the eighth century, he worked miracles all over the area with his holy rod. For centuries, pilgrims came from far and wide to enjoy art depicting the great works of St. Magnus. Above the altar dangles a glass cross containing his relics (including that holy stick). Just inside the door is a chapel remembering a much more modern saint—Franz Seelos (1819-1867), the local boy who went to America (Pittsburgh and New Orleans) and lived such a righteous life that in 2000 he was beatified by Pope John Paul II. If you're in need of a miracle, fill out a request card next to the candles.

• *From the church, a lane leads high above, into the courtyard of the...*

❶ **High Castle (Hohes Schloss):** This castle, long the summer residence of the Bishop of Augsburg, houses a painting gallery (the

upper floor is labeled in English) and a tower with a view over the town and lake (included in the €7 Füssen Heritage Museum combo-ticket, otherwise €6, same hours as museum). Its courtyard is interesting for the striking perspective tricks painted onto its flat walls. From below the castle, the city's main drag (once the Roman Via Claudia, and now Reichenstrasse) leads from a grand statue of St. Magnus past lots of shops, cafés, and strolling people to Kaiser-Maximilian-Platz and the TI...where you began.

Sleeping in Füssen

(country code: 49, area code: 08362)
Though I prefer sleeping in Reutte, convenient Füssen is just three miles from Ludwig's castles and offers a cobbled, riverside retreat. It's fairly touristy, but it has plenty of rooms, and is the region's best base for those traveling by train. All recommended accommodations are within a few handy blocks of the train station and the town center. Parking is easy at the station, and some hotels also have their own lot or garage. Prices listed are for one-night stays; most hotels give about 5-10 percent off for two-night stays—always request this discount. Competition is fierce, and off-season prices are soft. High season is mid-June-September. Rooms are generally 10-15 percent less in shoulder season and much cheaper in off-season.

Big, Fancy Hotels in the Center of Town

$$$ Hotel Schlosskrone, with 62 rooms and all the amenities, is just a block from the station. It also runs a fine pastry shop—you'll notice at breakfast—and restaurant (Sb-€99-109, standard Db-€119-139, bigger Db-€129-165, Tb-€145-165, Qb-€159-179, 4-person suite-€199-255, lower prices are for Oct-April, you'll likely

Sleep Code

(€1 = about $1.40, Germany country code: 49, Austria country code: 43)

S = Single, **D** = Double/Twin, **T** = Triple, **Q** = Quad, **b** = bathroom, **s** = shower only. Unless otherwise noted, credit cards are accepted, English is spoken, and breakfast is included.

To help you sort easily through these listings, I've divided the accommodations into three categories, based on the price for a standard double room with bath:

$$$ Higher Priced—Most rooms €100 or more.
$$ Moderately Priced—Most rooms between €60-100.
$ Lower Priced—Most rooms €60 or less.

Prices can change without notice; verify the hotel's current rates online or by email. For other updates, see www .ricksteves.com/update.

save money by booking via their website, air-con in some rooms, elevator, free Wi-Fi and cable Internet, free sauna and fitness center, parking-€9/day, Prinzregentenplatz 2-4, tel. 08362/930-180, fax 08362/930-1850, www.schlosskrone.com, info@schlosskrone .com, Norbert Schöll and family).

$$$ Hotel Hirsch is a romantic, well-maintained, 53-room, old-style hotel on the main street two blocks from the station. Their standard rooms are fine, and their rooms with historical and landscape themes are a fun splurge (Sb-€70-95, standard Db-€120-140, theme Db-€150-180, lower prices are for Nov-March and during slow times, family rooms, elevator, expensive Internet access, free Wi-Fi, free parking, Kaiser-Maximilian-Platz 7, tel. 08362/93980, fax 08362/939-877, www.hotelfuessen.de, info@hotelhirsch.de).

$$$ Hotel Sonne, in the heart of town, has a modern lobby and takes pride in decorating (some would say over-decorating) its 50 stylish rooms (Sb-€89-111, Db-€111-129, bigger Db-€149-165, Tb-€139-149, bigger Tb-€169-193, Qb-€189-205, lower prices are for Nov-March, 5 percent discount if you book on their website, elevator, free Internet access and Wi-Fi, free sauna and fitness center, parking-€5-7, kitty-corner from TI at Prinzregentenplatz 1, tel. 08362/9080, fax 08362/908-100, www.hotel-sonne.de, info @hotel-sonne.de).

Smaller, Mid-Priced Hotels and Pensions

$$ Altstadthotel zum Hechten offers 35 modern rooms in a friendly, traditional building right under Füssen Castle in the old-town pedestrian zone (Sb-€59-69, Db-€94-108, Tb-€125,

Qb-€156, ask when you reserve for 5 percent off these prices with this book, also mention if you're very tall as most beds can be short, non-smoking, lots of stairs, free Internet access in lounge, free Wi-Fi, and parking-€3, laundry-€10-15/load, fun miniature bowling alley in basement, electrobike rental-€20/day; from TI, walk down pedestrian street and take second right to Ritterstrasse 6; tel. 08362/91600, fax 08362/916-099, www.hotel-hechten.com, info@hotel-hechten.com, Pfeiffer and Tramp families).

$$ Gästehaus Schöberl, run by the head cook at Altstadthotel zum Hechten, rents six attentively furnished, modern rooms a five-minute walk from the train station. One room is in the owners' house, and the rest are in the building next door (Sb-€40-50, Db-€65-75, Tb-€85-95, Qb-€100-120, lower prices are for Jan-Feb and Nov or for longer stays, cash only, free Wi-Fi, free parking, Luitpoldstrasse 14-16, tel. 08362/922-411, www.schoeberl-fuessen .de, info@schoeberl-fuessen.de, Pia and Georg Schöberl).

$$ Mein Lieber Schwan, a block from the train station, is a former private house with four superbly outfitted apartments, each with a double bed, sofa bed, and kitchen. The catch is the three-night minimum stay (Sb-€68-79, Db-€78-89, Tb-€88-99, Qb-€98-109, price depends on apartment size, slightly cheaper off-season, cash or PayPal only, no breakfast, free Wi-Fi, free parking, laundry facilities, garden, from station turn left at traffic circle to Augustenstrasse 3, tel. 08362/509-980, fax 08362/509-914, www.meinlieberschwan.de, fewo@meinlieberschwan.de, Herr Bletschacher).

Budget Beds

$ House LA, run by energetic mason Lahdo Algül and hardworking Agata, has two branches. The backpacker house has 11 basic, clean four-bed dorm rooms at rock-bottom prices about a 10-minute walk from the station (€18/bed, D-€42, breakfast-€2.50, free Internet access and Wi-Fi, free parking, Wachsbleiche 2). A second building has five family apartments with kitchen and bath, each sleeping 4-6 people (apartment-€60-90, breakfast-€2.50, free Wi-Fi, free parking, 6-minute walk back along tracks from station to von Freybergstrasse 26; contact info for both: tel. 08362/607-366, mobile 0170-624-8610, fax 08362/925-1909, www.housela .de, info@housela.de). Both branches rent bikes (€8/day) and have laundry facilities (€7/load).

$ Füssen Youth Hostel occupies a pleasant modern building in a grassy setting an easy walk from the center. There are ping-pong tables and a basketball net out front (bed in 2- to 6-bed dorm rooms-€21, D-€50, €3 more for nonmembers, includes breakfast and sheets, guests over age 26 without kids in tow pay €4 penalty for being so old, laundry-€3.20/load, dinner-€5, office open

7:00-12:00 & 17:00-23:00, Nov-March until 22:00, free Wi-Fi, free parking, from station backtrack 10 minutes along tracks, Mariahilfer Strasse 5, tel. 08362/7754, fax 08362/2770, www .fuessen.jugendherberge.de, jhfuessen@djh-bayern.de).

$ Gasthof Krone, a rare bit of pre-glitz Füssen in the pedestrian zone, has dumpy halls and stairs and 12 big, worn, time-warp rooms—left unrenovated by the building's owner. Still, the location makes it worth considering as an alternative to the youth hostel (S-€26, D-€46, T-€69, €3 less per person for 2-night stays, no breakfast but bakeries across the street, closed Nov-early June; from TI, head down pedestrian street and take first left to Schrannengasse 17; tel. 08362/7824, fax 08362/37505, www.krone -fuessen.de, info@krone-fuessen.de).

Eating in Füssen

Restaurant Aquila serves modern international dishes in a simple, traditional *Gasthaus* setting with great seating outside on the delightful little Brotmarkt Square (€10-16 main courses, serious €9-10 salads, Wed-Mon 11:30-14:30 & 17:30-22:00, closed Tue, Brotmarkt 9, tel. 08362/6253).

Restaurant Ritterstub'n offers delicious, reasonably priced fish, salads, veggie plates, and a fun kids' menu. They have three eating zones: modern decor in front, traditional Bavarian in back, and a courtyard. Demure Gabi serves while her husband cooks standard Bavarian fare (€8-15 main courses, €5.50 lunch specials, €19 three-course fixed-price dinners, Tue-Sun 11:30-14:30 & 17:30-23:00, closed Mon, Ritterstrasse 4, tel. 08362/7759).

Schenke & Wirtshaus (inside the recommended Altstadthotel zum Hechten) dishes up hearty, traditional Bavarian fare. They specialize in pike *(Hecht)* pulled from the Lech River, served with a tasty fresh-herb sauce (€8-14 main courses, salad bar, cafeteria ambience, daily 10:00-22:00, Ritterstrasse 6, tel. 0836/91600).

Hotel Schlosskrone's fine restaurant, right on Füssen's main traffic circle, has good weekly specials and live Bavarian zither music most Fridays and Saturdays during dinner. Choose between a traditional dining room and a pastel winter garden. If your pension doesn't offer breakfast, consider their €10 "American-style" breakfast or huge €14.50 Sunday spread (open daily 7:30-10:30 & 11:30-14:30 & 18:00-22:00, Prinzregentenplatz 2-4, tel. 08362/930-180).

The **Markthalle,** just across the street from Gasthof Krone, is a fun food court offering a wide selection of reasonably priced, wurst-free food. Located in an old warehouse from 1483, it's now home to a fishmonger, deli counters, a fruit stand, a bakery, and a wine bar. Buy your food from one of the vendors, park yourself at any one of the tables, then look up and admire the Renaissance ceiling (Mon-Fri 7:30-18:30, Sat 7:30-14:30, closed Sun, corner of Schrannengasse and Brunnengasse).

Gelato: **Hohes Schloss Italian Ice Cream** is a good *gelateria* on the main drag and has an inviting people-watching perch for coffee or dessert (Reichenstrasse 14).

Asian Food: You'll find inexpensive Thai, Indian, and Chinese restaurants in the Luitpold-Passage at Reichenstrasse 33.

Picnic Supplies: Bakeries and *Metzger*s (butcher shops) abound and frequently have ready-made sandwiches. For groceries, try the underground **Netto** supermarket at Prinzregentenplatz, the roundabout on your way into town from the train station (Mon-Sat 7:00-20:00, closed Sun).

Füssen Connections

From Füssen to: Neuschwanstein (bus #73 or #78, departs from train station, most continue to Tegelberg lift station after castles, 1-2/hour, 10 minutes, €1.90 one-way, €3.80 round-trip; taxis cost €10 one-way); **Oberammergau** (bus #73 to Echelsbacher Brücke, change there to bus #9622—often marked *Garmisch,* confirm with driver that bus will stop in Oberammergau; in summer 4-6/day Mon-Sat, 2/day Sun, 1.5 hours total, bus continues to **Garmisch/Zugspitze**)—from Oberammergau, you can connect to **Linderhof Castle** or **Ettal Monastery; Reutte** (bus #74, Mon-Fri almost hourly, last bus 19:00, Sat-Sun every 2 hours, last bus 18:00, 45 minutes, €3.90 one-way; taxis cost €35 one-way); **Wieskirche** (4-5/day, 40-50 minutes each way, more frequently with a transfer in Steingaden; or take Romantic Road bus—see next); **Munich** (hourly trains, 2 hours, some change in Buchloe); **Innsbruck** (take bus #74 to Reutte, then train from Reutte to Innsbruck via Garmisch, 5/day, 3.5 hours); **Salzburg** (hourly via Munich, 4 hours, 1-2 changes); **Rothenburg ob der Tauber** (hourly, 5 hours, look for connections with only 2-3 changes—often in Augsburg, Treuchtlingen, and Steinach); **Frankfurt** (hourly, 5-6 hours, 1-2 changes). Train info: tel. 0180-599-6633, www.bahn.com.

Romantic Road Buses: The northbound Romantic Road bus departs Füssen at 8:00; the southbound bus arrives in Füssen at 19:55 (daily, mid-April-late Oct only, bus stop is at train station, www.romanticroadcoach.de). A railpass gets you a 20 percent discount on the Romantic Road bus (without using up a day of a flexipass). The northbound bus arrives in Munich at 10:50 and in Rothenburg at 15:50. The bus is much slower than the train, especially to Rothenburg; the only reason to take the bus is that it gives you the briefest glimpse of the Wieskirche, Ettal, Oberammergau, and other sights along the way, and requires no changes. Note that the northbound bus stops at the **Wieskirche** for 20 minutes, but the southbound bus stops there for just 10 minutes after the church is closed.

The Best of Bavaria

Within a short drive of Füssen and Reutte, you'll find some of the most enjoyable—and most tourist-filled—sights in Germany. The otherworldly "King's Castles" of Neuschwanstein and Hohenschwangau capture romantics' imaginations, the ornately decorated Wieskirche puts the faithful in a heavenly mood, and the little town of Oberammergau overwhelms visitors with cuteness. Yet another impressive castle (Linderhof), another fancy church (Ettal), and a sky-high viewpoint (the Zugspitze) round out Bavaria's top attractions.

The King's Castles: Neuschwanstein and Hohenschwangau

The most popular tourist destinations in Bavaria are the "King's Castles" (Königsschlösser). The older Hohenschwangau, King Ludwig's boyhood home, is less touristy but more historic. The more dramatic Neuschwanstein, which inspired Walt Disney, is the one everyone visits. I'd recommend visiting both, and planning some time to hike above Neuschwanstein to Mary's Bridge— and, if you enjoy romantic hikes, down through the gorge below. Reservations are a magic wand to smooth out your visit. With fairy-tale turrets in a fairy-tale alpine setting built by a fairy-tale king, these castles are understandably a huge hit.

Getting There

If arriving by **car,** note that road signs in the region refer to the sight as *Königsschlösser,* not Neuschwanstein. There's plenty of parking (all lots-€5). The first lots require more walking. Drive right through Touristville and past the ticket center, and park in lot #4 by the lake for the same price.

From **Füssen,** those without cars can catch **bus #73 or #78** (1-2/hour, €1.90 one-way, €3.80 round-trip, 10 minutes, catch bus at train station, extra buses often run when crowded), take a **taxi** (€10 one-way), or ride a rental **bike** (two level miles). The bus drops you at the tourist office; it's a one-minute walk from there to the ticket office.

From **Reutte,** take bus #74 to the Füssen train station, then hop on bus #73 or #78 to the castles. Or pay €35 for a taxi right to the castles.

Orientation to the King's Castles

Cost: Neuschwanstein costs €12, Hohenschwangau costs €10.50, a *Königsticket* for both castles costs €21.50, and children under 18 (accompanied by an adult) are admitted free. Neuschwanstein, but not Hohenschwangau, is covered by the Bavarian Castles Pass. If you have the pass, note this in the "message" field when making an online reservation.

Hours: The ticket center, located at street level between the two castles, is open daily April-Sept 8:00-17:00, Oct-March 9:00-15:00. The first and last castle tours of the day depart an hour after the ticket office opens and closes: April-Sept at 9:00 and 18:00, Oct-March at 10:00 and 16:00.

Getting Tickets for the Castles: Every tour bus in Bavaria converges on Neuschwanstein, and tourists flush in each morning from Munich. A handy reservation system sorts out the chaos for smart travelers. Tickets, whether reserved in advance or bought on the spot, come with admission times. If you miss your appointed tour time, you can't get in. To tour both castles, you must do Hohenschwangau first (logical, since this gives a better introduction to Ludwig's short life). You'll get two tour times: Hohenschwangau and then, two hours later, Neuschwanstein.

Arrival: Make the **ticket center** your first stop. If you have a reservation, there's a short line for picking up tickets. If you don't have a reservation...welcome to the very long line. Arrive by 8:00 in summer, and you'll likely be touring at 9:00. During August, the busiest month, tickets for English tours usually run out between 16:00 and 17:00.

Reservations: It's smart to reserve in peak season (June-early Oct, especially July-Aug). Reservations cost €1.80 per person per castle, and must be made no later than 17:00 on the previous day, ideally online (www.ticket-center-hohenschwangau .de); it's also possible to reserve by phone (tel. 08362/930-830) or email (info@ticket-center-hohenschwangau.de). You must pick up reserved tickets an hour before the appointed entry time, as it takes a while to walk up to the castles. (It doesn't usually take an hour, though—so this might be a good time to pull out a sandwich or a snack.) Show up late and they may have given your slot to someone else (but then they'll likely help you make another reservation). Better yet, if you know a couple of hours in advance that you're running late and can call the office, they'll normally rebook you at no charge.

Tips for Day-Tripping from Munich: If coming by train, make a castle tour reservation and take a train leaving at least four hours before your reserved castle entry. (The train to Füssen takes over two hours, getting from Füssen to the castle ticket office by bus takes another half-hour, and you must be there an hour before your tour.) Trains from Munich leave hourly at :51 past the hour. So, if you take the 9:51 train, you can make a 14:00 castle tour. If you reserve a castle tour for 11:00, you'll need to pack breakfast and take the 6:51 train.

Getting Up to the Castles: From the ticket booth, Hohenschwangau is an easy 10-minute climb, while Neuschwanstein is a steep 30-minute hike in the other direction. To minimize hiking to Neuschwanstein, you can take a shuttle bus (leaves every few minutes from in front of Hotel Lisl, just above ticket office and to the left) or a horse-drawn carriage (in front of Hotel Müller, just above ticket office and to the right), but neither gets you to the castle doorstep. The shuttle bus drops you off near Mary's Bridge (Marienbrücke), leaving you a steep, 10-minute downhill walk to the castle—so be sure to see the view from Mary's Bridge *before* hiking down (€1.80 one-way, the €2.60 round-trip is not worth it since you have to hike uphill to the bus stop for your return trip). Carriages (€6 up, €3 down) are slower than walking and stop below Neuschwanstein, leaving you a five-minute uphill hike. Here's the most economic and least strenuous plan: Ride the bus to Mary's Bridge for the view, hike down to Neuschwanstein, and then catch the horse carriage from the castle back down to the parking lot. Carriages also run to Hohenschwangau (€4 up, €2 down).

Entry Procedure: For each castle, tourists jumble at the entry, waiting for their ticket number to light up on the board. When it does, power through the mob (most waiting there are holding higher numbers) and go to the turnstile. Warning: You must use your ticket while your number is still on the board. If you space out while waiting for a polite welcome, you'll miss your entry window and never get in.

Services: A helpful TI, bus stop, ATM, WC (€0.50), and telephones cluster around the main intersection a couple hundred yards before you get to the ticket office (TI open daily April-Sept 10:00-18:00, Oct-March 11:00-17:00, tel. 08362/81980, www.schwangau.de).

Eating: Bring a packed lunch. The park by the Alpsee (the nearby lake) is ideal for a picnic, although you're not allowed to sit on the grass—only on the benches (you could also eat out on the lake in one of the old-fashioned rowboats, rented by

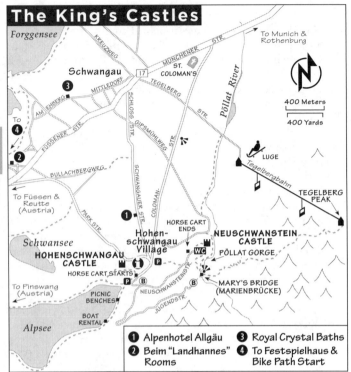

The King's Castles

Forggensee

KREUZWEG

Schwangau

ST. COLOMAN'S

MÜNCHENER STR.

To Munich & Rothenburg

MITTELDORF

Pöllat River

17

TEGELBERG

SCHLOSS STR.

GIPSMÜHLWEG

AM EHBERG

To 4

FÜSSENER STR.

STR.

400 Meters

400 Yards

BULLACHBERGWEG

LUGE

Tegelbergbahn

TEGELBERG PEAK

To Füssen & Reutte (Austria)

PARK STR.

SCHWANGAUER STR.

COLOMAN STR.

HORSE CART ENDS

Hohen-schwangau Village

NEUSCHWANSTEIN CASTLE

Schwansee

HOHENSCHWANGAU CASTLE

WC

PÖLLAT GORGE

HORSE CART STARTS

P

To Pinswang (Austria)

P   B

B

MARY'S BRIDGE (MARIENBRÜCKE)

PICNIC BENCHES

NEUSCHWANSTEINSTR.

JUGENDSTR.

BOAT RENTAL

Alpsee

❶ Alpenhotel Allgäu   ❸ Royal Crystal Baths
❷ Beim "Landhannes"   ❹ To Festspielhaus &
   Rooms   Bike Path Start

BAVARIA AND TIROL

the hour in summer). There are no grocery shops by the castles, but you can buy sandwiches and hot dogs across from the TI and at the Hotel Alpenstuben. The restaurants in the "village" at the foot of Europe's Disney castle are mediocre, feeding off the endless droves of hungry, shop-happy tourists. The **Bräustüberl cafeteria** serves the cheapest grub, but isn't likely to be a highlight of your visit (€6-7 gut-bomb grill meals, often with live folk music, daily 10:00-18:00, close to end of road and lake).

Sights at the King's Castles

▲▲▲Hohenschwangau Castle

Standing quietly below Neuschwanstein, the big, yellow Hohenschwangau Castle was Ludwig's boyhood home. Originally built in the 12th century, it was ruined by Napoleon. Ludwig's father, King Maximilian II, rebuilt it in 1830. Hohenschwangau (hoh-en-SHVAHN-gow, loosely translated as "High Swanland") was used by the royal family as a summer hunting lodge until 1912.

"Mad" King Ludwig
(1845-1886)

A tragic figure, Ludwig II (a.k.a. "Mad" King Ludwig) ruled Bavaria for 22 years until his death in 1886 at the age of 40. Bavaria was weak. Politically, Ludwig's reality was to "rule" either as a pawn of Prussia or a pawn of Austria. Rather than deal with politics in Bavaria's capital, Munich, Ludwig frittered away most of his time at his family's hunting palace, Hohenschwangau. He spent much of his adult life constructing his fanciful Neuschwanstein Castle—like a kid builds a tree house—on a neighboring hill upon the scant ruins of a medieval castle. Although Ludwig spent 17 years building Neuschwanstein, he lived in it only 172 days.

Ludwig was a true romantic living in a Romantic age. His best friends were artists, poets, and composers such as Richard Wagner. His palaces are wallpapered with misty medieval themes—especially those from Wagnerian operas. Eventually he was declared mentally unfit to rule Bavaria and taken away from Neuschwanstein. Two days after this eviction, Ludwig was found dead in a lake. To this day, people debate whether the king was murdered or committed suicide.

The interior decor is harmonious, cohesive, and original—

all done in 1835, with paintings inspired by Romantic themes. The Wittelsbach family (which ruled Bavaria for nearly seven centuries) still owns the place (and lived in the annex—today's shop—until the 1970s). As you tour the castle, imagine how the paintings must have inspired young Ludwig. For 17 years, he lived here at his dad's place and followed the construction of his dream castle across the way—you'll see the telescope still set up and directed at Neuschwanstein.

The excellent 30-minute tours give a better glimpse of Ludwig's life than the more-visited and famous Neuschwanstein Castle tour. Tours here are smaller (35 people rather than 60) and more relaxed.

▲▲▲Neuschwanstein Castle

Imagine "Mad" King Ludwig as a boy, climbing the hills above his dad's castle, Hohenschwangau, dreaming up the ultimate fairy-tale castle. Inheriting the throne at the young age of 18, he

had the power to make his dream concrete and stucco. Neuschwanstein (noy-SHVAHN-shtine, roughly "New Swanstone") was designed first by a theater-set designer...then by an architect. It looks medieval, but it's modern iron-and-brick construction with a sandstone veneer—only about as old as the Eiffel Tower. It feels like something you'd see at a home show for 19th-century royalty. Built from 1869 to 1886, it's the epitome of the Romanticism popular in 19th-century Europe. Construction stopped with Ludwig's death (only a third of the interior was finished), and within six weeks, tourists were paying to go through it.

During WWII, the castle took on a sinister role. The Nazis used Neuschwanstein as one of their primary secret storehouses for stolen art. After the war, Allied authorities spent a year sorting through and redistributing the art, which filled 49 rail cars from this one location alone. It was the only time the unfinished rooms were put to use.

Today, guides herd groups of 60 through the castle, giving an interesting—if rushed—30-minute tour. You'll go up and down more than 300 steps, through lavish rooms based on Wagnerian opera themes, the king's gilded-lily bedroom, and his extravagant throne room. You'll visit 15 rooms with their original furnishings and fanciful wall paintings. After the tour, before you descend to the king's kitchen, see the 20-minute video about the king's life and passions accompanied by Wagner's music (next to the café, alternates between English and German, schedule board at the entry says what's playing and what's on deck). After the kitchen (state of the art for this high-tech king in its day), you'll see a room lined with fascinating drawings (described in English) of the castle plans, construction, and drawings from 1883 of Falkenstein—a whimsical, over-the-top, never-built castle that makes Neuschwanstein look stubby. Falkenstein occupied Ludwig's fantasies the year he died.

Near the Castles

Mary's Bridge (Marienbrücke)—Before or after the Neuschwanstein tour, climb up to Mary's Bridge to marvel at Ludwig's castle, just as Ludwig did. This bridge was quite an engineering accomplishment 100 years ago. From the bridge, the frisky can hike even higher to the *Beware—Danger of Death* signs and an even more glorious castle view. (Access to the bridge is closed in bad winter weather, but many travelers walk around the barriers to get there—at their own risk, of course.) The most scenic way to descend from Neuschwanstein is to walk up to Mary's Bridge and then follow the signs down the Pöllat Gorge to the TI *(Pöllatschlucht,* 15 minutes longer than walking down the road but worth it, especially with new steel walkways and railings that make this slippery area safer).

▲**Tegelberg Gondola**—Just north of Neuschwanstein is a fun play zone around the mighty Tegelberg Gondola, a scenic ride to the mountain's 5,500-foot summit. On a clear day, you get great views of the Alps and Bavaria and the vicarious thrill of watching hang gliders and paragliders leap into airborne ecstasy. Weather

permitting, scores of adventurous Germans line up and leap from the launch ramp at the top of the lift. With someone leaving every two or three minutes, it's great for spectators. Thrill-seekers with exceptional social skills may talk themselves into a tandem ride with a paraglider. From the top of Tegelberg, it's a steep

and demanding 2.5-hour hike down to Ludwig's castle. (Avoid the treacherous trail directly below the gondola.) At the base of the gondola, you'll find a playground, a cheery eatery, the stubby remains of an ancient Roman villa, and a luge ride.

Cost and Hours: €17.50 round-trip, €11 one-way, daily 9:00-17:00, closed Nov, 4/hour, last ride at 16:30, in bad weather call first to confirm, tel. 08362/98360, www.tegelbergbahn.de. Most buses #73 and #78 from Füssen continue from the castles to Tegelberg.

▲**Tegelberg Luge**—Next to the Tegelberg Gondola is a luge course. A luge is like a bobsled on wheels. This stainless-steel track is heated, so it's often dry and open even when drizzly weather shuts down the concrete luges. A funky cable system pulls riders (in their sleds) to the top without a ski lift. It's not as long, fast, or scenic as Austria's Biberwier luge, but it's handy, harder to get hurt on, and half the price.

Cost and Hours: €3/ride, 6-ride shareable card-€11, July-Sept daily 10:00-18:00, otherwise same hours as gondola, in winter sometimes opens late due to wet track, in bad weather call first to confirm, waits can be long in good weather, no children under 3, ages 3-8 may ride with an adult, tel. 08362/98360, www.tegelberg bahn.de.

▲**Royal Crystal Baths (Königliche Kristall-Therme)**—This pool/sauna complex just outside Füssen is the perfect way to relax on a rainy day, or to cool off on a hot one. The downstairs contains two heated indoor pools and a café; outside you'll find a shallow kiddie pool, a lap pool, a heated *Kristallbad* with massage jets and a whirlpool, and a salty mineral bath. The extensive saunas upstairs are well worth the few extra euros, as long as you're OK with nudity. (Swimsuits are required in the downstairs pools, but *verboten* in the upstairs saunas.) You'll see pool and sauna rules in German all over, but don't worry—just follow the locals' lead.

To enter the baths, first choose the length of your visit and your focus (big outdoor pool only, all ground-floor pools but not the saunas, or the whole enchilada—a flier explains all the prices in English). You'll get a wristband and a credit-card-sized ticket with a bar code. Insert that ticket into the entry gate, and keep it—you'll need it to get out. Enter through the yellow changing stalls—where you'll change into your bathing suit—then choose a storage locker (€1 coin deposit). When it's time to leave, reinsert your ticket in the gate—if you've gone over the time limit, feed extra euros into the machine.

Cost and Hours: €9.90/2 hours, €14.20/4 hours, €17.80/day, saunas-€5, towel rental-€2.50, bathing suit rental-€3, Sun-Thu 9:00-22:00, Fri-Sat until 23:00, nude swimming everywhere Tue and Fri after 19:00; from Füssen, drive, bike, or walk across the river, turn left toward Schwangau, and then, about a mile later, turn left at signs for *Kristall-Therme*, Am Ehberg 16; tel. 08362/819-630, www.kristalltherme-schwangau.de.

Bike Ride Around the Forggensee—On a beautiful day, nothing beats a bike ride around the bright turquoise Forggensee, a nearby lake. This 20-mile ride is almost exclusively on bike paths, with just a few stretches on country roads. Locals swear that going clockwise is less work, but either way has a couple of strenuous uphill parts. Still, the amazing views of the surrounding Alps will distract you from your churning legs—so this is still a great way to spend the afternoon. Rent a bike, pack a picnic lunch, and figure about a three-hour round-trip. From Füssen, follow *Festspielhaus* signs; once you reach the theater, follow *Forggensee Rundweg* signs.

From the theater, you can also take a **boat ride** on the Forggensee (€8/50-minute cruise, 6/day; €11/2-hour cruise, 3/day; or buy a one-way ticket and bike back, fewer departures Oct-May, tel. 08362/921-363, www.schifffahrt.fuessen.de).

Sleeping near the King's Castles

(€1 = about $1.40, country code: 49, area code: 08362)
Inexpensive farmhouse B&Bs abound in the Bavarian countryside
around Neuschwanstein, offering drivers a decent value. Look for
Zimmer Frei signs ("room free"/vacancy). The going rate is about
€50-65 for a double, including breakfast. Though a bit inconve-
nient for those without a car, my listings here are a quick taxi ride
from the Füssen train station and also close to local bus stops.

$$ **Alpenhotel Allgäu** is a small, family-run hotel with 18
rooms in a bucolic setting. It's a 15-minute walk from the castle
ticket office, not far beyond the humongous parking lot (small Sb
without balcony-€48, Sb-€58, perfectly fine older Db-€80, newer
Db-€88, Tb-€120, these are book-direct prices, ask about discount
with cash and this book, all rooms except one single have porches
or balconies—some with castle views, family rooms, free Wi-Fi,
elevator, free parking, just before tennis courts at Schwangauer
Strasse 37 in the town of Schwangau—don't let your GPS take
you to Schwangauer Strasse 37 in Füssen, tel. 08362/81152, fax
08362/987-028, www.alpenhotel-allgaeu.de, info@alpenhotel-
allgaeu.de, Frau Reiss).

$ **Beim "Landhannes,"** a 200-year-old working dairy farm
run by Conny Schön, rents three creaky but sunny rooms, and
keeps flowers on the balconies, big bells and antlers in the halls,
and cows in the yard (Sb-€30, Db-€60, €5 less per person for 3
or more nights, also rents apartments with kitchen with a 5-night
minimum, cash only, free Wi-Fi, nearby bike rental, poorly signed
in the village of Horn on the Füssen side of Schwangau, look for
the farm down a tiny lane through the grass 100 yards in front
of Hotel Kleiner König, Am Lechrain 22, tel. 08362/8349, www
.landhannes.de, info@landhannes.de).

Wieskirche

Germany's greatest Rococo-style church, this recently restored
"Church in the Meadow"—worth ▲▲—looks as brilliant as the

day it floated down from
heaven. Overripe with deco-
ration but bright and burst-
ing with beauty, this church
is a divine droplet, a curly
curlicue, the final flowering
of the Baroque movement.

Cost and Hours: Dona-
tion requested, daily April-Oct 8:00-19:00, Nov-March 8:00-
17:00, tel. 08862/932-930, www.wieskirche.de.

Getting There: The Wieskirche is a 30-minute drive north of Neuschwanstein. The Romantic Road bus tour stops here for 20 minutes on the northbound route to Frankfurt. Southbound buses stop here for 10 minutes, but it's after the church has closed for the day. By car, head north from Füssen, turn right at Steingaden, and follow the signs. Take a commune-with-nature-and-smell-the-farm detour back through the meadow to the parking lot (€1/hour).

⊖ Self-Guided Tour: This pilgrimage church is built around the much-venerated statue of a scourged (or whipped) Christ, which supposedly wept in 1738. The carving—too graphic to be accepted by that generation's Church—was the focus of worship in a peasant's barn. Miraculously, it shed tears—empathizing with all those who suffer. Pilgrims came from all around. A tiny and humble chapel was built to house the statue in 1739. (You can see it where the lane to the church leaves the parking lot.) Bigger and bigger crowds came. Two of Bavaria's top Rococo architects, the Zimmermann brothers (Johann Baptist and Dominikus), were commissioned to build the Wieskirche that stands here today.

Follow the theological sweep from the altar to the ceiling: Jesus whipped, chained, and then killed (notice the pelican above the altar—recalling a pre-Christian story of a bird that opened its breast to feed its young with its own blood);

the painting of a baby Jesus posed as if on the cross; the sacrificial lamb; and finally, high on the ceiling, the resurrected Christ before the Last Judgment. This is the most positive depiction of the Last Judgment around. Jesus, rather than sitting on the throne to judge, rides high on a rainbow—a symbol of forgiveness—giving any sinner the feeling that there is still time to repent, with plenty of mercy on hand. In the back, above the pipe organ, notice the empty throne—waiting for Judgment Day—and the closed door to paradise.

Above the entrances to both side aisles are murky glass cases with 18th-century handkerchiefs. People wept, came here, were healed, and no longer needed their hankies. Walk up either aisle flanking the high altar to see votives—requests and thanks to God (for happy, healthy babies, and so on). Notice how the kneelers are positioned so that worshippers can meditate on scenes of biblical miracles painted high on the ceiling and visible through the ornate tunnel frames. A priest here once told me that faith, architecture, light, and music all combine to create the harmony of the Wieskirche.

Two paintings flank the door at the rear of the church. One shows the ceremonial parade in 1749 when the white-clad monks of Steingaden carried the carved statue of Christ from the tiny church to its new big one. The second painting, from 1757, is a votive from one of the Zimmermann brothers, the artists and architects who built this church. He is giving thanks for the successful construction of the new church.

If you can't visit the Wieskirche, visit one of the other churches that came out of the same heavenly spray can: Oberammergau's church, Munich's Asamkirche, Würzburg's Hofkirche Chapel (at the Residenz), the splendid Ettal Monastery (free and near Oberammergau), and, on a lesser scale, Füssen's basilica.

Route Tips for Drivers: If you're driving from Wieskirche to Oberammergau, you'll cross the **Echelsbacher Bridge,** which arches 230 feet over the Pöllat Gorge. Thoughtful drivers let their passengers walk across to enjoy the views, then meet them at the other side. Any kayakers? Notice the painting of the traditional village woodcarver (who used to walk from town to town with his art on his back) on the first big house on the Oberammergau side. It holds the Almdorf Ammertal shop, with a huge selection of overpriced carvings and commission-hungry tour guides.

Oberammergau

The Shirley Temple of Bavarian villages, and exploited to the hilt by the tourist trade, Oberammergau wears way too much makeup. During its famous Passion Play (every 10 years, next in 2020), the crush is unbearable—and the prices at the hotels and restaurants

can be as well. The village has about 1,200 beds for the 5,000 playgoers coming daily. If you're passing through, Oberammergau is a ▲ sight—worth a wander among the half-timbered *Lüftl-malerei* houses frescoed with biblical scenes and famous fairy-tale characters. It's also a relatively convenient home base for visiting Linderhof Castle, Ettal Monastery, and the Zugspitze (via Garmisch). A day trip to Neuschwanstein from Oberammergau is manageable if you have a car, but train travelers do better to stay in Füssen.

Tourist Information: The TI is at Eugen-Papst-Strasse 9A (Mon-Fri 9:00-18:00, Sat 10:00-14:00, closed Sun, tel. 08822/922-740, www.ammergauer-alpen.de).

BAVARIA AND TIROL

Oberammergau

- ❶ Gasthof zur Rose & Gästehaus Magold
- ❷ Hotel Garni Fux
- ❸ Pension Anton Zwink
- ❹ Youth Hostel
- ❺ Hotel Maximilian (Beer Garden)
- ❻ To Sommerrodelbahn Steckenberg

Getting There

Trains run from Munich to Oberammergau (nearly hourly, 1.75 hours, change in Murnau). From Füssen to Oberammergau, **buses** run daily (in summer 4-6/day Mon-Sat, 2/day Sun, 1.5 hours, most change at Echelsbacher Brücke). **Drivers** entering the town from the north should cross the bridge, take the second right, and park in the free lot a block beyond the TI. Leaving town (to Linderhof or Reutte), head out past the church and turn toward Ettal on Road 23. You're 20 miles from Reutte via the scenic Plansee. If heading to Munich, Road 23 takes you to the autobahn, which gets you there in less than an hour.

Sights in Oberammergau

Oberammergau Church—Visit the town church, which is typically Bavarian Baroque—but a poor cousin of the one at Wies. Being in a woodcarving center, it's only logical that all the statues are made of wood, and then stuccoed and gilded to look like marble or gold. Saints Peter and Paul flank the altar, where the central painting can be raised to reveal a small stage decorated to celebrate special times during the church calendar. In the central dome, a touching painting shows Peter and Paul bidding each other fare-

Woodcarving in Oberammergau

The Ammergau region is relatively poor, with no appreciable industry and no agriculture, save for some dairy farming. What they *do* have is wood. Carving religious and secular themes became a lucrative way for the locals to make some money, especially when confined to the house during the long, cold winter. Carvers from Oberammergau peddled their wares across Europe, carrying them on their backs as far away as Rome. Today, the Oberammergau Carving School is a famous institution that takes only 20 students per year out of 450 applicants. Their graduates do important restoration work throughout Europe. For example, much of the work on Dresden's Frauenkirche was done by these artists.

well (with the city of Rome as a backdrop) on the day of their execution—the same day, in the year A.D. 67. On the left, Peter is crucified upside-down. On the right, Paul is beheaded with a sword. (A fine little €3 booklet explains it all.) Wander through the lovingly maintained graveyard. A stone WWI and WWII memorial at the gate reads, "We honor and remember the victims of the violence that our land gave the world."

Local Arts and Crafts—The town's best sights are its wood-carving shops. Browse through these small art galleries filled with very expensive whittled works. The beautifully frescoed **Pilatus House** at Ludwig-Thoma-Strasse 10 has an open workshop where you can watch woodcarvers and painters at work (free; mid-May-mid-Oct Tue-Sat 13:00-18:00, closed Sun-Mon; open two weeks after Christmas 11:00-17:00; closed rest of year, tel. 08822/949-511).

Oberammergau Museum—The museum's main branch at Dorfstrasse 8 showcases local woodcarving. A museum ticket also lets you into the lobby of the Passion Play theater, which houses a modest exhibition on the history of the performances, and into a small gallery of "reverse glass" paintings in the Pilatus House. The museum also organizes guided tours of the theater (see next).

Cost and Hours: €6; museum and theater lobby open April-Oct and Dec-mid-Jan Tue-Sun 10:00-17:00; Pilatus House exhibit open same days 15:00-17:00; all three closed Mon, in Nov and mid-Jan-March; tel. 08822/94136, www.oberammergaumuseum.de.

Passion Play—Back in 1633, in the midst of the bloody Thirty Years' War and with horrifying plagues devastating entire cities, the people of Oberammergau promised God that if they were spared from extinction, they'd "perform a play depicting the suffering, death, and resurrection of our Lord Jesus Christ" every decade thereafter. The town survived, and, heading into its 41st decade, the people of Oberammergau are still making good on the deal. For 100 days every 10 years (most recently in 2010), about half of the town's population (a cast of 2,000) are involved in the production of this extravagant five-hour Passion Play—telling the story of Jesus' entry into Jerusalem, Crucifixion, and Resurrection.

Until the next show in 2020, you'll have to settle for reading the book, seeing Nicodemus tool around town in his VW, or taking a quick look at the **Passion Play theater,** a block from the center of town. The only way to see the theater hall itself is on a twice-weekly 45-minute guided tour organized by the Oberammergau Museum (€6, April-Oct Wed and Sat at 14:00, in German and—on request—English, no tours off-season, tel. 08822/94136, www.oberammergaumuseum.de).

Sommerrodelbahn Steckenberg—This stainless-steel luge track (near Oberammergau) is faster than the Tegelberg luge, but not quite as wicked as the one in Biberwier.

Cost and Hours: €2.50/ride, €11/6 rides, May-Oct daily 8:30-17:00, closed when wet, Liftweg 1 in Unterammergau, clearly marked and easy 2.5-mile bike ride to Unterammergau along Bahnhofstrasse/Rottenbucherstrasse, take the first left when entering Unterammergau, tel. 08822/4027, www.steckenberg.de.

Sleeping in Oberammergau

(€1 = about $1.40, country code: 49, area code: 08822)

$$ Gasthof zur Rose is a big, central, classic, family-run place with 21 straightforward rooms. At the reception desk, look at the several decades of photos showing the family performing in the Passion Play (Sb-€50, Db-€80, Tb-€90, Qb-€100, free Internet access and Wi-Fi, Dedlerstrasse 9, tel. 08822/4706, fax 08822/6753, www.rose-oberammergau.de, info@rose-oberammergau.de, Frank family).

$$ Hotel Garni Fux, quiet and romantic and a little fancier than the Rose, rents eight large rooms and six apartments decorated in the Bavarian *Landhaus* style (Sb-€65, Db-€84; apartment prices without breakfast: Sb-€68, Db-€78, larger apartments-€89-120; cheaper Nov-April, free Internet access and Wi-Fi, Mannagasse 2a, tel. 08822/93093, www.firmafux.de, info@firmafux.de).

$ Pension Anton Zwink offers 10 small, quiet, no-frills rooms in a neighborhood adjacent to the town center (Sb-€33,

Db-€56, cash only, free Wi-Fi, behind Gasthof zur Rose at Daisenbergerstrasse 10, tel. 08822/6334, www.pension-zwink.de, info@pension-zwink.de).

$ Gästehaus Magold is a homey, grandmotherly place with three bright and spacious rooms—twice as nice as the cheap hotel rooms in town, and for much less money (Db-€50, cash only, non-smoking, free cable Internet, also has two family apartments, immediately behind Gasthof zur Rose at Kleppergasse 1, tel. 08822/4340, www.gaestehaus-magold.de, info@gaestehaus -magold.de, Christine).

$ Oberammergau Youth Hostel, on the river, is a short walk from the center (€17/bed, includes breakfast and sheets, €3 extra for nonmembers, €4 extra if over 26, closed mid-Nov-Dec, Malensteinweg 10, tel. 08822/4114, fax 08822/1695, www.ober ammergau.jugendherberge.de, oberammergau@jugendherberge.de).

Eating in Oberammergau

Locals won't be caught dead inside the chic, five-star **Hotel Maximilian.** But they fill its serene beer garden to enjoy the hotel's home-brewed beer and summertime grill, which cooks up delicious chicken, sausage, and spareribs. On summer Wednesdays after 18:00, they offer all-you-can-eat from the grill for €17.50 (daily 11:00-23:00, right behind the church, Ettaler Strasse 5, tel. 08822/948-740).

Oberammergau Connections

From Oberammergau to: Linderhof Castle (bus #9622, 6/day Mon-Fri, 4/day Sat-Sun, 30 minutes; many of these also stop at **Ettal Monastery**), **Füssen** (in summer 4-6 buses/day Mon-Sat, 2/day Sun, most transfer at Echelsbacher Brücke and stop also at **Hohenschwangau** for Neuschwanstein, 1.5 hours total), **Garmisch** (nearly hourly buses, 40 minutes; also possible by train with a transfer in Murnau, 1.5 hours; from Garmisch, you can ascend the **Zugspitze**), **Munich** (nearly hourly trains, 1.75 hours, change in Murnau). Train info: tel. 0180-599-6633, www.bahn.com.

Linderhof Castle

This homiest of "Mad" King Ludwig's castles is small and comfortably exquisite—good enough for a minor god, and worth ▲▲.. Set in the woods 15 minutes from Oberammergau and surrounded by fountains and sculpted, Italian-style gardens, it's the only palace I've toured that actually had me feeling envious.

Ludwig was king for 22 of his 40 years. He lived much of

his last 8 years here—the only one of his castles that was finished in his lifetime. Frustrated by the limits of being a "constitutional monarch," he retreated to Linderhof, inhabiting a private fantasy world where extravagant castles glorified his otherwise weakened kingship. He lived here as a royal hermit; his dinner table—pre-set with dishes and food—rose from the kitchen below into his dining room, so he could eat alone.

Beyond the palace is Ludwig's **grotto.** Inspired by Wagner's *Tannhäuser* opera, this performance space is 300 feet long and 70 feet tall. Its rocky walls are actually made of cement poured over an iron frame. The grotto provided a private theater for the reclusive king to enjoy his beloved Wagnerian operas—he was usually the sole member of the audience. The grotto features a waterfall, fake stalactites, and a swan boat floating on an artificial lake (which could be heated for swimming). The first electricity in Bavaria was generated here, to change the colors of the stage lights and to power Ludwig's fountain and wave machine.

Cost and Hours: €8.50, covered by Bavarian Castles Pass, €3.50 for grotto only, daily April–mid-Oct 9:00-18:00, mid-Oct–March 10:00-16:00, last tour 30 minutes before closing, fountains often erupt on the half-hour, tel. 08822/92030, www.linderhof.de.

Getting There: Without a car, getting to (and back from) Linderhof is a royal headache, unless you're staying in Oberammergau. Buses from Oberammergau take 30 minutes (6/day Mon-Fri, 4/day Sat-Sun). If you're driving, park near the ticket office (obligatory €2.50). Driving from Reutte, take the scenic Plansee route.

Visiting the Castle: The complex sits isolated in natural splendor. Plan for lots of walking and a two-hour stop to fully enjoy this royal park. Bring raingear in iffy weather. Your ticket comes with an entry time to tour the palace, which is a five-minute hike from the ticket office. At the palace entrance, wait in line at the turnstile listed on your ticket (A through D) to take the required 30-minute English tour. Afterwards, hike 10 minutes uphill to the grotto (take the brief but interesting free tour in English, no reservations necessary). Then see the other royal buildings dotting the king's playground if you like. You can eat lunch at a café across from the ticket office.

Crowd-Beating Tips: July and August crowds can mean an hour's wait between when you buy your ticket and when you start your tour. During this period, you're wise to arrive after 15:00. Any other time of year, you should get your palace tour time shortly after you arrive. Unlike Neuschwanstein, Linderhof doesn't take advance reservations online.

Ettal Monastery and Pilgrimage Church

In 1328, the Holy Roman Emperor was returning from Rome with what was considered a miraculous statue of Mary and Jesus. He was in political and financial trouble, so to please God, he founded a

monastery with this statue as its centerpiece. The monastery was located here because it was suitably off the beaten path, but today Ettal is on one of the most-traveled tourist routes in Bavaria. Stopping here (free and easy for drivers) offers a convenient peek at a splendid Baroque church. Restaurants across the road serve lunch.

Cost and Hours: Free, daily 8:00-19:45 in summer, until 18:00 off-season, tel. 08822/740, www.kloster-ettal.de. If you're moved to make a donation, there are self-serve credit-card machines for doing so to the right as you enter.

Getting There: The Ettal Monastery is a few minutes' **drive** (or a delightful **bike** ride) from Oberammergau. Just park for free and wander in. Some Oberammergau-to-Linderhof **buses** stop here (see "Oberammergau Connections," earlier).

❷ Self-Guided Tour: As you enter the more than 1,000-square-foot **courtyard,** imagine the 14th-century Benedictine abbey, an independent religious community. It produced everything it needed right here. In the late Middle Ages, abbeys like this had jurisdiction over the legal system, administration, and taxation of their district. Since then, the monastery has had its ups and downs. Secularized during the French Revolution and Napoleonic age, the

Benedictines' property was confiscated by the state and sold. Religious life returned a century later. Today the abbey survives, with 50 or 60 monks. It remains a self-contained community, with living quarters for the monks, workshops, and guests' quarters. Along with their religious responsibilities, the brothers make their famous liqueur, brew beer, run a hotel, and educate 380 students

20 + C + M + B + 12

All over Germany (and much of Catholic Europe), you'll likely see written on doorways a mysterious message: "20 + C + M + B + 12." This is marked in chalk on Epiphany (Jan 6), the Christian holiday celebrating the arrival of the Magi to adore the newborn Baby Jesus. In addition to being the initials of the three wise men (Caspar, Melchior, and Balthazar), the letters also stand for the Latin phrase *Christus mansionem benedicat*—"May

Christ bless the house." The little crosses separating the letters remind all who enter that the house has been blessed in this year (20+12). Epiphany is a bigger deal in Catholic Europe than in the US. The holiday includes gift-giving, feasting, and caroling door to door—often collecting for a charity organization. Those who donate get their doors chalked up in thanks, and these marks are left on the door through the year.

in their private high school. The monks' wares are for sale at two shops (look for the *Klosterladen* by the courtyard or the *Kloster-Markt* across the street).

At the front of the church, you pass a **tympanum** over the door dating from 1350. It shows the founding couple, Emperor Louis the Bavarian and his wife Margaret, directing our attention to the crucified Lord and inviting us to enter the church contemplatively.

Stepping inside, the light draws our eyes to the **dome** (it's a double-shell design 230 feet high) rather than to the high altar. Illusions—with the dome opening right to the sky—merge heaven and earth. The dome fresco shows hundreds of Benedictines worshipping the Holy Trinity...the glory of the Benedictine Order. This is classic "south-German Baroque."

Statues of the **saints** on the altars are either engaged in a holy conversation with each other or singing the praises of God. Broken shell-style patterns seem to create constant movement, with cherubs adding to the energy. Side altars and confessionals seem to grow out of the architectural structure; its decorations and furnishings become part of an organic whole. Imagine how 18th-century farmers and woodcutters, who never traveled, would step in here on Sunday and be inspired to praise their God.

The origin of the monastery is shown over the **choir arch:** An angel wearing the robe of a Benedictine monk presents the emperor with a marble Madonna and commissions him to found this monastery. (In reality, the statue was made in Pisa, circa 1300, and given to the emperor in Italy.)

Dwarfed by all the magnificence and framed by a monumental tabernacle is that tiny, most precious statue of the abbey—the miraculous **statue of Mary and the Baby Jesus.**

Zugspitze

The tallest point in Germany, worth ▲▲, is also a border crossing. Lifts from both Austria and Germany meet at the 9,700-foot sum-

mit of the Zugspitze (TSOOG-shpit-seh). You can straddle the border between two great nations while enjoying an incredible view. Restaurants, shops, and telescopes await you at the summit.

German Approach: First, head to Garmisch. From Garmisch, there are two ways to ascend the Zugspitze: the whole way by cogwheel train (1.25 hours one-way), or a faster cogwheel train-plus-cable car option (about 45 minutes one-way). Both cost the same (€48 round-trip). Although the train ride takes longer, many travelers enjoy the more involved cog-railway experience. The train departs from Garmisch, stops at Eibsee for the cable-car connection, and then continues up—and through—the mountain (hourly departures daily 8:15-14:15). The cable car simply zips you to the top in five minutes from the Eibsee station. Cable cars go up daily 8:00-14:15. The last cable car down departs at about 16:15 (tel. 08821/7970, www.zugspitze .de). Allow plenty of time for afternoon descents: If bad weather hits in the late afternoon, cable cars can be delayed at the summit, causing tourists to miss their train connection from Eibsee back to Garmisch.

Drivers can park for €3 at the cable-car station at Eibsee. Hikers can enjoy the easy six-mile walk around the lovely Eibsee (start 5 minutes downhill from cable-car station).

Austrian Approach: The Tiroler Zugspitzbahn ascent is less crowded and cheaper. Departing from above the village of Ehrwald (a 30-minute train trip from Reutte, runs almost hourly), the lift zips you to the top in 10 minutes (€35.50 round-trip, departures in each direction

at :00, :20, and :40 past the hour, daily 8:40-16:40 except closed late April-mid-May and most of Nov, last ascent at 16:00, drivers follow signs for *Tiroler Zugspitzbahn*, free parking, Austrian tel. 05673/2309, www.zugspitze.at). While the German ascent from Garmisch is easier for those without a car, buses connect the Ehrwald train station and the Austrian lift nearly every hour (or pay €8 for the 5-minute taxi ride from Ehrwald train station).

❷ Self-Guided Tour: Whether you ascended from the Austrian or German side, you're high enough now to enjoy a little tour of the summit. The two terraces—Bavarian and Tirolean—are connected by a narrow walkway, which was the border station before Germany and Austria opened their borders. The Austrian (Tirolean) side was higher until the Germans blew its top off in World War II to make a flak tower, so let's start there.

Tirolean Terrace: Before you stretches the Zugspitzplatt glacier. Each summer, a 65,000-square-foot reflector is spread over the ice to try to slow the shrinking. Since metal ski lift towers collect heat, they, too, are wrapped to try to save the glacier. Many ski lifts fan out here, as if reaching for a ridge that defines the border between Germany and Austria. The circular metal building is the top of the cog-railway line that the Germans cut through the mountains in 1931. Just above that, find a small square building— the wedding chapel (Hochzeitskapelle) consecrated in 1981 by Cardinal Joseph Ratzinger (now Pope Benedict XVI).

Both Germany and Austria use this rocky pinnacle for communication purposes. The square box on the Tirolean Terrace provides the Innsbruck airport with air-traffic control, and a tower nearby is for the German *Kathastrophenfunk* (civil defense network).

This highest point in Germany (there are many higher points in Austria) was first climbed in 1820. The Austrians built a cable car that nearly reached the summit in 1926. (You can see it just over the ridge on the Austrian side—look for the ghostly, abandoned concrete station.) In 1964, the final leg, a new lift, was built connecting that 1926 station to the actual summit, where you stand now. Before then, people needed to hike the last 650 feet to the top. Today's lift dates from 1980, but was renovated after a 2003 fire. The Austrian station, which is much nicer than the German station, has a fine little museum—free with Austrian ticket, €2.50 if you came up from Germany—that shows three interesting videos (6-minute 3-D mountain show, 30-minute making-of-the-lift documentary, and 45-minute look at the nature, sport, and culture of the region).

Looking up the valley from the Tirolean Terrace, you can see the towns of Ehrwald and Lermoos in the distance, and the valley that leads to Reutte. Looking farther clockwise, you'll see the Eibsee lake below. Hell's Valley, stretching to the right of Eibsee, seems to merit its name.

Bavarian Terrace: The narrow passage connecting the two terraces used to be a big deal—you'd show your passport here at the little blue house and shift from Austrian shillings to German marks. Notice the regional pride here: no German or Austrian banners, but regional ones instead—*Freistaat Bayern* (Bavaria) and *Land Tirol*.

The German side features a golden cross marking the summit...the highest point in Germany. A priest and his friends hauled it up in 1851. The historic original was shot up by American soldiers using it for target practice in the late 1940s, so what you see today is a modern replacement. In the summer, it's easy to "summit" the Zugspitze, as there are steps and handholds all the way to the top. Or you can just stay behind and feed the birds. The yellow-beaked ravens get chummy with those who share a little pretzel or bread.

The oldest building up here is the rustic tin-and-wood weather tower, erected in 1900 by the *Deutscher Wetterdienst* (German weather service). The first mountaineers' hut, built in 1897, didn't last. The existing one—entwined with mighty cables that cinch it down—dates from 1914. In 1985, observers clocked 200-mph winds up here—those cables were necessary. Step inside the restaurant to enjoy museum-like photos and paintings on the wall (including a look at the team who hiked up with the golden cross in 1851).

Reutte, Austria

Reutte (ROY-teh, with a rolled *r*), a relaxed Austrian town of 5,700, is located 20 minutes across the border from Füssen. While overlooked by the international tourist crowd, it's popular with Germans and Austrians for its climate. Doctors recommend its "grade 1" air. I like Reutte for the opportunity to simply be in a real community. As an example of how the town is committed to its character, real estate can be sold only to those using it as a primary residence. (Many formerly vibrant alpine towns made a pile of money but lost their sense of community by becoming resorts. They allowed wealthy foreigners—who just drop in for a week or two a year—to buy up all the land, and are now shuttered up and dead most of the time.)

Reutte has one claim to fame among Americans: As Nazi Germany was falling in 1945, Hitler's top rocket scientist, Werner von Braun, joined the Americans (rather than the Russians) in

Reutte. You could say that the American space program began here.

Reutte isn't featured in any other American guidebook. While its generous sidewalks are filled with smart boutiques and lazy coffeehouses, its charms are subtle. It was never rich or important. Its castle is ruined, its buildings have painted-on "carvings," its churches are full, its men yodel for each other on birthdays, and its energy is spent soaking its Austrian and German guests in *Gemütlichkeit*. Most guests stay for a week, so the town's attractions are more time-consuming than thrilling.

Orientation to Reutte

(country code: 43, area code: 05672)
Remember, Reutte is in a different country. While Austrians use the same euro currency the Germans do, postage stamps and phone cards only work in the country where you buy them.

To **telephone** from Germany to Austria, dial 00-43 and then the number listed in this section (omitting the initial zero). To call from Austria to Germany, dial 00-49 and then the number (again, omitting the initial zero).

Tourist Information
Reutte's TI is a block in front of the train station (Mon-Fri 8:00-12:00 & 14:00-17:00, no midday break July-Aug, Sat 8:30-12:00, closed Sun, Untermarkt 34, tel. 05672/62336, www.reutte.com). Go over your sightseeing plans, ask about a folk evening, pick up city and biking maps and the *Sommerprogramm* events schedule (in German only), and ask about discounts with the hotel guest cards. Their free informational booklet has a good self-guided town walk.

Ask your hotel to give you an **Aktiv-Card,** which gives free travel on local buses (including the Reutte-Füssen route) as well as small discounts on sights and activities.

Arrival in Reutte
If you're coming by car from Germany, skip the north *(Nord)* exit and take the south *(Süd)* exit into town. For parking in town, blue lines denote pay-and-display spots. There is a free lot (P-1) near the train station on Muhlerstrasse.

While Austria requires a **toll sticker** *(Vignette)* for driving on its expressways (€8/10 days, buy at the border, gas stations, car-rental agencies, or *Tabak* shops), those just dipping into Tirol from Bavaria do not need one—even on the expressway-like bypass around Reutte.

Helpful Hints

Internet Access: Café Alte Post has one expensive terminal in a back room (€7.20/hour, Mon-Fri 7:00-19:00, Sat-Sun 9:00-18:00, Untermarkt 15).

Laundry: There isn't an actual launderette in town, but the recommended Hotel Maximilian lets non-guests use its laundry service (wash, dry, and fold-€16/load).

Bike Rental: Try **Intersport** (€15/day, Mon-Fri 9:00-18:00, Sat 9:00-17:00, closed Sun, Lindenstrasse 25, tel. 05672/62352), or check at the recommended Hotel Maximilian.

Taxi: STM Shuttle Service promises 24-hour service (mobile tel. 0664-113-3277).

Car Rental: Autoreisen Köck rents cars at Mühlerstrasse 12 (tel. 05672/62233, www.koeck-tours.com, koeck@koeck-tours .com).

"Nightlife": Reutte is pretty quiet. For any action at all, there's a strip of bars, dance clubs, and Italian restaurants on Lindenstrasse.

Sights in and near Reutte

▲▲Ehrenberg Castle Ensemble (Festungsensemble Ehrenberg)

If Neuschwanstein was the medieval castle dream, Ehrenburg is the medieval castle reality. Once the largest fortification in Tirol,

its brooding ruins lie about two miles outside Reutte. Ehrenburg is actually an "ensemble" of four castles, built to defend against the Bavarians and to bottle up the strategic Via Claudia trade route, which cut through the Alps as it connected Italy and Germany. Today, these castles have become a European "castle museum," showing off 500 years of military architecture in one swoop. The European Union is helping fund the project (paying a third of its €9 million cost) because it promotes the heritage of a multinational region—Tirol—rather than a country.

The four parts of the complex are the fortified Klause toll booth on the valley floor, the oldest castle on the first hill above (Ehrenberg), a mighty and more modern castle high above

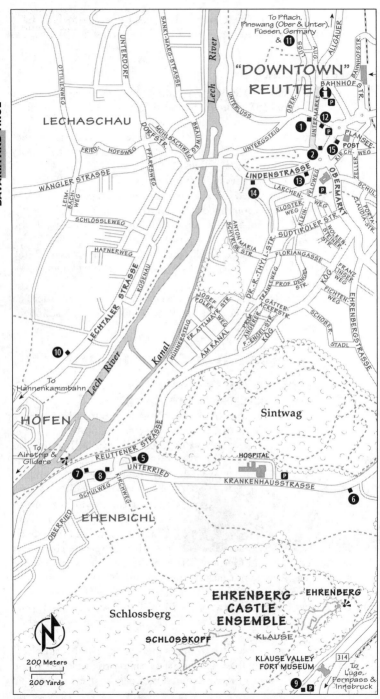

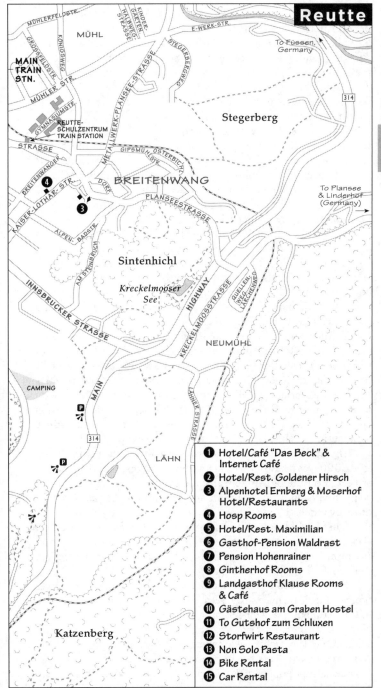

Reutte

1. Hotel/Café "Das Beck" & Internet Café
2. Hotel/Rest. Goldener Hirsch
3. Alpenhotel Ernberg & Moserhof Hotel/Restaurants
4. Hosp Rooms
5. Hotel/Rest. Maximilian
6. Gasthof-Pension Waldrast
7. Pension Hohenrainer
8. Gintherhof Rooms
9. Landgasthof Klause Rooms & Café
10. Gästehaus am Graben Hostel
11. To Gutshof zum Schluxen
12. Storfwirt Restaurant
13. Non Solo Pasta
14. Bike Rental
15. Car Rental

(Schlosskopf, built in the age when cannon positioned there made the original castle vulnerable), and a smaller fourth castle across the valley (Fort Claudia, an hour's hike away). All four were once a single complex connected by walls. Signs posted throughout the site help visitors find their way and explain some background on the region's history, geology, geography, culture, flora, and fauna. (While the castles are free and open all the time, the museum and multimedia show at the fort's parking lot charge admission.)

Getting to the Castle Ensemble: The Klause, Ehrenberg, and Schlosskopf castles are on the road to Lermoos and Innsbruck. These are a pleasant 30- to 45-minute walk or a short bike ride from Reutte; bikers can use the *Radwanderweg* along the Lech River (the TI has a good map). Local buses run from Reutte to Ehrenberg several times a day (see www.vvt.at for schedules—the stop name is "Ehrenberger Klause").

▲**Klause Valley Fort Museum**—Historians estimate that about 10,000 tons of precious salt passed through this valley (along the route of Rome's Via Claudia) each year in medieval times, so it's no wonder the locals built this complex of fortresses and castles. Beginning in the 14th century, the fort controlled traffic and levied tolls on all who passed. Today, these scant remains hold a museum and a theater with a multimedia show.

While there are no real artifacts here (other than the sword used in A.D. 2008 to make me the honorary First Knight of Ehrenberg), the clever, kid-friendly **museum** takes one 14th-century decade (1360-1370) and attempts to bring it to life. It's a hands-on experience, well-described in English. You can try on a set of armor (and then weigh yourself), see the limited vision knights had to put up with when wearing their helmet, empathize with victims of the plague, and join a Crusade.

The **multimedia show** takes you on a 30-minute spin through the 2,000-year history of this valley's fortresses, with images projected on the old stone walls and modern screens (50-minute English version at 13:00 with a minimum of 5 people, or sometimes by request).

Cost and Hours: €7.50 for museum, €10.50 combo-ticket also includes multimedia show, €17.80 family pass for 2 adults and any number of kids, daily 10:00-17:00, closed Nov-mid-Dec, tel. 05672/62007, www.ehrenberg.at.

Eating: Next to the museum, the **Landgasthof Klause** serves typical Tirolean meals (€9-15 main courses, officially Tue-Sun 10:00-18:00 but likely longer hours in summer, closed Mon, closed Nov and Jan-Feb, tel. 05672/62213). They also rent a few rooms if you'd like to stay right at Ehrenberg.

▲▲**Ehrenberg Ruins**—Ehrenberg, a 13th-century rock pile, provides a super opportunity to let your imagination off its leash.

Hike up 30 minutes from the parking lot of the Klause Valley Fort Museum for a great view from your own private ruins. Ehrenberg (which means "Mountain of Honor") was the first castle here, built in 1296. Thirteenth-century castles were designed to stand boastfully tall. With the advent of gunpowder, castles dug in. (Notice the 18th-century **ramparts** around you.)

Approaching Ehrenberg Castle, look for the small **door** to the left. It's the night entrance (tight and awkward, and therefore safer against a surprise attack). Entering this castle, you go through two doors. Castles allowed step-by-step retreat, giving defenders time to regroup and fight back against invading forces.

Before climbing to the top of the castle, follow the path around to the right to a big, grassy courtyard with commanding views and a fat, newly restored **turret.** This stored gunpowder and held a big cannon that enjoyed a clear view of the valley below. In medieval times, all the trees approaching the castle were cleared to keep an unobstructed view.

Look out over the valley. The pointy spire marks **Breitenwang,** which was a stop on the ancient Via Claudia. In A.D. 46, there was a Roman camp there. In 1489, after the Reutte bridge crossed the Lech River, Reutte (marked by the onion-domed church) was made a market town and eclipsed Breitenwang in importance. Any gliders circling? They launch from just over the river in Höfen.

For centuries, this castle was the seat of government—ruling an area called the "judgment of Ehrenberg" (roughly the same as today's "district of Reutte"). When the emperor came by, he stayed here. In 1604, the ruler moved downtown into more comfortable quarters, and the castle was no longer a palace.

Now climb to the top of Ehrenberg Castle. Take the high ground. There was no water supply here—just kegs of wine, beer, and a cistern to collect rain.

Ehrenberg repelled 16,000 Swedish soldiers in the defense of Catholicism in 1632. Ehrenberg saw three or four other battles, but its end was not glorious. In the 1780s, a local businessman bought the castle in order to sell off its parts. Later, in the late 19th century, when vagabonds moved in, the roof was removed to make squatting miserable. With the roof gone, deterioration quickened, leaving only this evocative shell and a whiff of history.

▲**Schlosskopf**—From Ehrenberg, you can hike up another 30 minutes to the mighty Schlosskopf ("Castle Head"). When the Bavarians captured Ehrenberg in 1703, the Tiroleans climbed up to the bluff above it to rain cannonballs down on their former fortress. In 1740, a mighty new castle—designed to defend against modern artillery—was built on this sky-high strategic location. By the end of the 20th century, the castle was completely overgrown with trees—you literally couldn't see it from Reutte. But today the trees are shaved away, and the castle has been excavated. In 2008, the Castle Ensemble project, led by local architect Armin Walch, opened the site with English descriptions and view platforms. One spot gives spectacular views of the strategic valley. The other looks down on the older Ehrenberg Castle ruins, illustrating the strategic problems presented with the advent of cannon.

In the Town

Reutte Museum (Museum Grünes Haus)—Reutte's cute city museum, offering a quick look at the local folk culture and the story of the castles, was recently redone. There are exhibits on Ehrenberg and the Via Claudia, local painters, and more—ask to borrow the English translations.

Cost and Hours: €3; May-Oct Tue-Sat 13:00-17:00, closed Sun-Mon; early Dec-Easter Wed-Sat 14:00-17:00, closed Sun-Tue; closed Easter-April and Nov-early Dec; in the bright-green building at Untermarkt 25, around corner from Hotel Goldener Hirsch, tel. 05672/72304, www.museum-reutte.at.

▲▲Tirolean Folk Evening—Ask the TI or your hotel if there's a Tirolean folk evening scheduled. During the summer (July-Aug), nearby towns (such as Höfen on Tuesdays) occasionally put on an evening of yodeling, slap dancing, and Tirolean frolic. These are generally free and worth the short drive. Off-season, you'll have to do your own yodeling. There are also weekly folk concerts featuring the local choir or brass band in Reutte's Zeiller Platz (free, July-Aug only, ask at TI). For listings of these and other local events, pick up a copy of the German-only *Sommerprogramm* schedule at the TI.

▲Flying—For a major thrill on a sunny day, drop by the tiny airport in Höfen (across the river from downtown) and fly. You have two options: prop planes and gliders. Small single-prop planes, which take three passengers, can buzz the Zugspitze and Ludwig's castles and give you a bird's-eye peek at Reutte's Ehrenberg ruins.

Cost and Hours: €110/30 minutes, €220/1 hour, ask at Fliegerklause café, tel. 05672/63207, www.flugsportverein-reutte .at. The phone is rarely answered (and then not in English), so your best bet is to show up at the Höfen airport on good-weather afternoons.

▲Gliding—To try something more angelic, how about gliding (*Segelfliegen*)? For a relatively modest price, you and a pilot get 30 minutes in a two-seat glider. Just watching the towrope launch

Luge Lesson

Taking a wild ride on a luge (pronounced "loozh") is a quintessential alpine experience. It's also called a *Sommerrodelbahn,* or "summer toboggan run." To try

one of Europe's great accessible thrills (€3-7), take the lift up to the top of a mountain, grab a wheeled sled-like go-cart, and scream back down the mountainside on a banked course. Then take the lift back up and start all over again.

Luge courses are highly weather-dependent, and can close at the slightest hint of rain. If the weather's questionable, call ahead to confirm that your preferred luge is open. Stainless-steel courses are more likely than concrete ones to stay open in drizzly weather.

Operating the sled is simple: Push the stick forward to go faster, pull back to apply brakes. Even a novice can go very, very fast. Most are cautious on their first run, speed demons on their second...and bruised and bloody on their third. A woman once showed me her travel journal illustrated with her husband's dried five-inch-long luge scab. He had disobeyed the only essential rule of luging: Keep both hands on your stick. To avoid getting into a bumper-to-bumper traffic jam, let the person in front of you get way ahead before you start. You'll emerge from the course with a windblown hairdo and a smile-creased face.

Here are a few key luge terms:

Lenkstange	lever
drücken / schneller fahren	push / go faster
ziehen / bremsen	pull / brake
Schürfwunde	scrape
Schorf	scab

the graceful glider like a giant slow-motion rubber-band gun is exhilarating.

Cost and Hours: €40/30 minutes, €65/1 hour, May-mid-Sept 12:00-19:00 in good but breezy weather only, find someone in the know at the airport's "Thermik Ranch" café, English not always spoken, tel. 05672/64010, mobile 0676-945-1288, www.segelflug verein-ausserfern.at.

Hahnenkammbahn—This mountain lift swoops you high above the tree line to an attractive restaurant and starting point for several hikes. In the alpine flower park, special paths lead you past countless varieties of local flora. Unique to this lift is a barefoot hiking trail *(Barfusswanderweg)*, designed to be walked without shoes—no joke.

Cost and Hours: €10 one-way, €14.50 round-trip, flowers best in late July, runs mid-June–Sept daily 9:00-16:30, also in good weather late May–mid-June and through late Oct, base station across the river in Höfen, tel. 05672/62420, www.reuttener-seilbahnen.at.

Near Reutte

Bird Lookout Tower—Between Reutte and Füssen is a pristine (once you get past the small local industrial park) nature preserve with an impressive wooden tower from which to appreciate the vibrant bird life in the wetlands along the Lech River. Look for *Vogel-Erlebnispfad* signs as you're driving through the village of Pflach (on the road between Reutte and Füssen). The EU gave half the money needed to enjoy the nature preserve—home to 110 different species of birds that nest here. The best action is early in the day. Be quiet, as eggs are being laid.

▲▲Biberwier Luge Course—Near Lermoos, on the road toward Innsbruck, you'll find the Biberwier *Sommerrodelbahn*. At 4,250 feet, it's the longest luge in Tirol. The only drawbacks are its brief season, short hours, and a proclivity for shutting down sporadically—even at the slightest bit of rain. But if you don't have a car, this is not worth the trouble; consider the luge near Neuschwanstein instead. The ugly cube-shaped building marring the countryside near the luge course is a hotel for outdoor adventure enthusiasts. You can ride your mountain bike right into your room, or skip the elevator by using its indoor climbing wall.

Cost and Hours: €7.20/ride, less for 3-, 5-, and 10-ride tickets, June–early Oct daily 9:00-16:30, closed early Oct–May, tel. 05673/2323, www.bergbahnen-langes.at. It's 20 minutes from Reutte on the main road toward Innsbruck; Biberwier is the first exit after a long tunnel.

▲Fallerschein—Easy for drivers and a special treat for those who may have been Kit Carson in a previous life, this extremely remote log-cabin village is a 4,000-foot-high flower-speckled world of serene slopes and cowbells. Thunderstorms roll down the valley like it's God's bowling alley, but the pint-size church on the high ground, blissfully simple in a land of Baroque, seems to promise that this huddle of houses will survive, and the river and breeze will just keep flowing. The couples sitting on benches are mostly Austrian vacationers who've rented cabins here. Some of them, appreciating the remoteness of Fallerschein, are having affairs.

Getting to Fallerschein: From Reutte, it's a 45-minute drive. Take road 198 to Stanzach (passing Weisenbach am Loch, then Forchach), then turn left toward Namlos. Follow the L-21 Berwang road for about five miles to a parking lot. From there, it's a two-mile walk down a drivable but technically closed one-lane road. Those driving in do so at their own risk.

Sleeping in Fallerschein: $ **Michl's Fallerscheiner Stube** is a family-friendly mountain-hut restaurant with a low-ceilinged attic space that has basic beds for up to 17 sleepy hikers. The accommodations aren't fancy, but if you're looking for remote, this is it (dorm bed-€19, €11 cheaper without breakfast, dinner-€11, sheets-€4, open May-Oct only, wildlife viewing deck, mobile 0676-727-9681, www.alpe-fallerschein.at, michaelknitel@mountainmichl.at, Knitel family).

Sleeping in and near Reutte

(€1 = about $1.40, country code: 43, area code: 05672)

Reutte is a mellow Füssen with fewer crowds and easygoing locals with a contagious love of life. Come here for a good dose of Austrian ambience and lower prices. While it's not impossible by public transport, staying here makes most sense for those with a car. Reutte is popular with Austrians and Germans, who come here year after year for one- or two-week vacations. The hotels are big, elegant, and full of comfy carved furnishings and creative ways to spend lots of time in one spot. They take great pride in their restaurants, and the owners send their children away to hotel-management schools. All include a great breakfast, but few accept credit cards. Most hotels give a small discount for stays of two nights or longer.

The Reutte TI has a list of 50 private homes that rent out generally good rooms *(Zimmer)* with facilities down the hall, pleasant communal living rooms, and breakfast. Most charge €20 per person per night, and the owners speak little or no English. As these are family-run places, it is especially important to cancel in advance if your plans change. I've listed a few favorites in this section, but the TI can always find you a room when you arrive.

Reutte is surrounded by several distinct "villages" that basically feel like suburbs—many of them, such as Breitenwang, within easy walking distance of the Reutte town center. If you want to hike through the woods to Neuschwanstein Castle, stay at Gutshof zum Schluxen. To locate these accommodations, see the Reutte map. Remember, to call Reutte from Germany, dial 00-43- and then the number (minus the initial zero).

In Central Reutte

These two hotels are the most practical if you're traveling by train or bus.

$$ Hotel "Das Beck" offers 17 clean, sunny rooms (many with balconies) filling a modern building in the heart of town close to the train station. It's a great value, and guests are personally taken care of by Hans, Inge, Tamara, and Pipi. Their small café offers tasty snacks and specializes in Austrian and Italian wines. Expect good conversation overseen by Hans (Sb-€46, Db-€70, Tb suite-€95, Qb suite-€112, these prices with this book in 2012, all rooms non-smoking, Internet access and Wi-Fi free for Rick Steves readers, free parking, Untermarkt 11, tel. 05672/62522, fax 05672/625-2235, www.hotel-das-beck.at, info@hotel-das-beck.at).

$$ Hotel Goldener Hirsch, also in the center of Reutte just two blocks from the station, is a grand old hotel with 56 rooms and one lonely set of antlers (Sb-€58-62, Db-€88-98, Tb-€135, Qb-€148, less for 2 nights, elevator, free Wi-Fi, restaurant, Mühlerstrasse 1, tel. 05672/62508, fax 05672/625-087, www.goldener -hirsch.at, info@goldener-hirsch.at; Monika, Helmut, and daughters Vanessa and Nina).

In Breitenwang

Now basically a part of Reutte, the older and quieter village of Breitenwang has good *Zimmer* and a fine bakery. It's a 20-minute walk from the Reutte train station: From the post office, follow Planseestrasse past the onion-dome church to the pointy straight-dome church near the two hotels. The Hosps—as well as other B&Bs—are along Kaiser-Lothar-Strasse, the first right past this church. If your train stops at the tiny Reutte-Schulzentrum station, hop out here—you're just a five-minute walk from Breitenwang.

$$ Alpenhotel Ernberg's 26 fresh rooms are run with great care by friendly Hermann, who combines Old World elegance with modern touches. Nestle in for some serious coziness among the carved-wood eating nooks, tiled stoves, and family-friendly backyard (Sb-€55, Db-€90, less for 2 nights, free Wi-Fi, popular restaurant, swimming complex nearby, Planseestrasse 50, tel. 05672/71912, fax 05672/719-1240, www.ernberg.at, info@ernberg.at).

$$ Moserhof Hotel has 40 new-feeling rooms plus an elegant dining room (Sb-€53, Db-€92, larger Db-€100, these special rates promised in 2012 if you ask for the Rick Steves discount when you reserve, extra bed-€35, most rooms have balconies, elevator, free Wi-Fi, restaurant, sauna and whirlpool, free parking, Planseestrasse 44, tel. 05672/62020, fax 05672/620-2040, www .hotel-moserhof.at, info@hotel-moserhof.at, Hosp family).

$ Walter and Emilie Hosp rent three rooms in a comfortable, quiet, and modern house two blocks from the Breitenwang church steeple. You'll feel like you're staying at Grandma's (S-€25, D-€40, T-€60, Q-€80, cash only, Kaiser-Lothar-Strasse 29, tel. 05672/65377).

In Ehenbichl, near the Ehrenberg Ruins

The next listings are a bit farther from central Reutte, a couple of miles upriver in the village of Ehenbichl (under the Ehrenberg ruins). From central Reutte, go south on Obermarkt and turn right on Kög, which becomes Reuttenerstrasse, following signs to Ehenbichl. These listings are best for car travelers—you'll need to take a taxi if you arrive by train.

$$ Hotel Maximilian offers 30 rooms at a great value. It includes table tennis, play areas for children (indoors and out), a pool table, and the friendly service of Gabi, Monika, and the rest of the Koch family. They host many special events, and their hotel has lots of wonderful extras such as a sauna and a piano (Sb-€50-57, Db-€80-90, ask for these special Rick Steves prices when you reserve, family deals, elevator, free Internet access and Wi-Fi in common areas, pay Wi-Fi in rooms, laundry service-€12/load, good restaurant, Reuttenerstrasse 1, tel. 05672/62585, fax 05672/625-8554, www.maxihotel.com, info@hotelmaximilian.at). They rent cars to guests only (€0.72/km, book in advance) and bikes to anyone (€5/half-day, €8/day, higher if you're not a guest, those staying at the hotel have free use of older bikes).

$$ Gasthof-Pension Waldrast, separating a forest and a meadow, is run by the farming Huter family and their dog, Picasso. The place feels hauntingly quiet and has no restaurant, but it's inexpensive and offers 10 nice rooms with generous sitting areas and castle-view balconies (Sb-€39, Db-€66, Tb-€82, Qb-€99; discounts with this book in 2012: 5 percent off second night, 10 percent off third night; cash only, non-smoking, free Wi-Fi, free parking; about a mile from Reutte, just off main drag toward Innsbruck, past campground and under castle ruins on Ehrenbergstrasse; tel. & fax 05672/62443, www.waldrasttirol.com, info@waldrasttirol.com, Gerd).

$$ Pension Hohenrainer, a big, quiet, no-frills place, is a good value with 12 modern rooms and some castle-view balconies (Sb-€30-32, Db-€60-64, €1.50/per person less for 2 nights, €3/person less for 3 nights, lower prices are for April-June and Sept-Oct, cash only, family rooms, non-smoking rooms, free Internet access and Wi-Fi, restaurant and reception in Gasthof Schlosswirt across the street, follow signs up the road behind Hotel Maximilian into village of Ehenbichl, Unterried 3, tel. 05672/62544 or 05672/63262, fax 05672/62052, www.hohenrainer.at, hohenrainer @aon.at).

$$ Gintherhof is a working farm that provides its guests with fresh milk, butter, and bacon. Annelies Paulweber offers geranium-covered balconies, six nice rooms with carved-wood ceilings, and a Madonna in every corner (Db-€62, Db suite-€64, €3/person less for third night, cash only, free Wi-Fi, Unterried 7, just up the road behind Hotel Maximilian, tel. 05672/67697, www.gintherhof.com, gintherhof@aon.at).

At the Ehrenberg Ruins

$$ Landgasthof Klause café, just below the Ehrenberg ruins and next to the castle museum, rents six non-smoking rooms with balconies on its upper floor. The downside is that you may have to go out for dinner (the café officially closes at 18:00), and you'll need a car to get anywhere besides Ehrenberg (Sb-€37, Db-€74, Tb-€111, ask for Rick Steves discount when you book, discount for 2 or more nights, free Wi-Fi, apartments available, closed Nov and Jan, tel. 05672/62007, fax 05672/620-0777, www.gasthof-klause.com, gasthof-klause@gmx.at).

A Hostel Across the River

The homey **$ Gästehaus am Graben hostel** has 4-6 beds per room and includes breakfast and sheets. It's lovingly run by the Reyman family—Frau Reyman, Rudi, and Gabi keep the 50-bed place traditional, clean, and friendly. This is a super value less than two miles from Reutte, and the castle views are fantastic. If you've never hosteled and are curious (and have a car or don't mind a bus ride), try it. If traveling with kids, this is a great choice. The double rooms are hotel-grade, and they accept nonmembers of any age (dorm bed-€25, hotel-style Db-€68, cash only, non-smoking, expensive Internet access and Wi-Fi, laundry service-€9, no curfew, closed April and Nov-mid-Dec; from downtown Reutte, cross bridge and follow main road left along river, or take the bus—hourly until 19:30, ask for Graben stop; Graben 1, tel. 05672/626-440, fax 05672/626-444, www.hoefen.at, info@hoefen.at).

In Pinswang

The village of Pinswang is closer to Füssen (and Ludwig's castles), but still in Austria.

$$ Gutshof zum Schluxen gets the "Remote Old Hotel in an Idyllic Setting" award. This family-friendly farm offers rustic elegance draped in goose down and pastels. Its picturesque meadow setting will turn you into a dandelion-picker, and its proximity to Neuschwanstein will turn you into a hiker—the castle is just an hour's hike away (Sb-€49-51, Db-€88-96, extra person-€29, these prices with this book in 2012, about 5-10 percent cheaper Nov-March, 5 percent discount for stays of three or more nights, free Wi-Fi in common areas, laundry-€9, mountain-bike rental-€10/day or €5/half-day, restaurant, fun bar, between Reutte and Füssen in village of Pinswang, free pickup from Reutte or Füssen but call 24 hours ahead if you'll arrive after 18:00, tel. 05677/89030, fax 05677/890-323, www.schluxen.com, info@schluxen.at).

To reach Neuschwanstein by foot or bike, follow the dirt road up the hill behind the hotel. When the road forks at the top of the hill, go right (downhill), cross the Austria-Germany border (marked by a sign and deserted hut), and follow the narrow paved road to the castles. It's a 1- to 1.5-hour hike or a great circular bike trip (allow 30 minutes; cyclists can return to Schluxen from the castles on a different 30-minute bike route via Füssen).

Eating in Reutte

The hotels here take great pride in serving local cuisine at reasonable prices to their guests and the public. Rather than go to a cheap restaurant, eat at one of the Reutte hotels recommended earlier (**Alpenhotel Ernberg, Moserhof Hotel, Hotel Maximilian,** and **Hotel Goldener Hirsch**). Hotels typically serve €10-15 dinners from 18:00 to 21:00 and are closed one night a week.

Storfwirt is *the* place for a quick and cheap weekday lunch. You can get the usual sausages here, as well as baked potatoes and salads (€5.50-9 daily specials, salad bar, always something for vegetarians, Mon-Fri 9:00-14:30, closed Sat-Sun, Schrettergasse 15, tel. 05672/62640).

Non Solo Pasta, just off the traffic circle, is a local favorite for Italian food (€7-9 pizzas and pastas, €8-12 main courses, Mon-Fri 11:30-14:00 & 18:00-23:00, Sat 18:00-23:00, closed Sun, Lindenstrasse 1, tel. 05672/72714).

Across the street from the Hotel Goldener Hirsch on Mühlerstrasse is a **Bauernladen** (farmer's shop) with rustic sandwiches and meals prepared from local ingredients (Wed-Fri 9:00-18:00, Sat 9:00-12:00, closed Sun-Tue, mobile 0676-575-4588).

Picnic Supplies: **Billa** supermarket has everything you'll need (across from TI, Mon-Fri 7:15-19:30, Sat 7:15-18:00, closed Sun).

Reutte Connections

From Reutte by Train to: Ehrwald (at base of Zugspitze lift, every 2 hours, 30 minutes), **Garmisch** (every 2 hours, 1 hour), **Innsbruck** (every 2 hours, 2.5 hours, change in Garmisch), **Munich** (every 2 hours, 2.5 hours, change in Garmisch), **Salzburg** (every 2 hours, 4.5-5.5 hours, quickest with changes in Garmisch and Munich). Train info: tel. 0180-599-6633, www.bahn.com.

By Bus to: Füssen (Mon-Fri almost hourly, Sat-Sun every 2 hours, 45 minutes, €3.90 one-way, buses depart from train station, pay driver).

Taxis cost about €35 one-way to Füssen or the King's Castles.

SALZBURG (AUSTRIA) and BERCHTESGADEN

Salzburg, just over the Austrian border, makes a fun day trip from Munich (1.5-2 hours by direct train). Thanks to its charmingly preserved old town, splendid gardens, Baroque churches, and Europe's largest intact medieval fortress, Salzburg feels made for tourism. As a musical mecca, the city puts on a huge annual festival, as well as constant concerts, and its residents—or at least its tourism industry—are forever smiling to the tunes of Mozart and *The Sound of Music*. It's a city with class. Vagabonds wish they had nicer clothes.

In the mountains just outside Salzburg is Berchtesgaden, a German alpine town that was once a favorite of Adolf Hitler's, but thrills a better class of nature-lovers today.

Planning Your Time

While Salzburg's sights are, frankly, mediocre, the town itself is a Baroque museum of cobbled streets and elegant buildings—simply a touristy stroller's delight. Even if your time is short, consider allowing half a day for the *Sound of Music* tour. The *S.O.M.* tour kills a nest of sightseeing birds with one ticket (city overview, *S.O.M.* sights, and a fine drive by the lakes).

You'd probably enjoy at least two nights in Salzburg—nights are important for swilling beer in atmospheric local gardens and attending concerts in Baroque halls and chapels. Seriously consider one of Salzburg's many evening musical events (a few are free, some are as cheap as €12, and most average €30-40).

To get away from it all, bike down the river or hike across the Mönchsberg cliffs that rise directly from the middle of town.

Or consider swinging by Berchtesgaden, just 15 miles away in Germany. A direct bus gets you there from Salzburg in 45 minutes.

Salzburg

Even without Mozart and the von Trapps, Salzburg is steeped in history. In about A.D. 700, Bavaria gave Salzburg to Bishop

Rupert in return for his promise to Christianize the area. Salzburg remained an independent city (belonging to no state) until Napoleon came in the early 1800s. Thanks in part to its formidable fortress, Salzburg managed to avoid the ravages of war for 1,200 years...until World War II. Much of the city was destroyed by WWII bombs (mostly around the train station), but the historic old town survived.

Eight million tourists crawl its cobbles each year. That's a lot of Mozart balls—and all that popularity has led to a glut of businesses hoping to catch the tourist dollar. Still, Salzburg is both a must and a joy.

Orientation to Salzburg

(country code: 43, area code: 0662)
Salzburg, a city of 150,000 (Austria's fourth-largest), is divided into old and new. The old town, sitting between the Salzach River and its mini-mountain (Mönchsberg), holds nearly all the charm and most of the tourists. The new town, across the river, has its own share of sights and museums, plus some good accommodations.

Welcome to Austria: Austria uses the same euro currency as Germany, but postage stamps and phone cards only work in the country where you buy them.

To **telephone** from Germany to Austria, dial 00-43 and then the number listed in this section (omitting the initial zero). To call from Austria to Germany, dial 00-49 and then the number (again, omitting the initial zero).

Note that **Berchtesgaden**—also covered in this chapter—is in Germany, not Austria.

Tourist Information

Salzburg has three helpful TIs (main tel. 0662/889-870, www
.salzburg.info): at the **train station** (daily June-Aug 8:15-19:30,
Sept-May 8:45-18:00, tel. 0662/
8898-7340); on **Mozartplatz** in
the old center (daily 9:00-18:00,
July-mid-Sept until 19:00, closed
Sun mid-Jan-Easter and Oct-
mid-Nov, tel. 0662/889-870);
and at the **Salzburg Süd park-
and-ride** (generally open daily
July-Aug 10:00-16:30 but some-

times longer hours, May-June Thu-Sat 10:00-16:30, Sept Mon-Sat
10:00-16:30, closed in winter, tel. 0662/8898-7360).

At any TI, you can pick up a free city-center map (the €0.70
map has a broader coverage and more information on sights, but
probably isn't necessary), the Salzburg Card brochure (listing sights
with current hours and prices), and a bimonthly events guide. Book
a concert upon arrival. The TIs also book rooms (€2.20 fee and 10
percent deposit).

Salzburg Card: The TIs sell the Salzburg Card, which covers
all your public transportation (including the Mönchsberg elevator
and funicular to the fortress) and admission to all the city sights
(including Hellbrunn Castle and a river cruise). The card is pricey,
but if you'd like to pop into all the sights, it can save money and
enhance your experience (€25/24 hours, €34/48 hours, €40/72
hours, cheaper Nov-April). To analyze your potential savings,
here are the major sights and what you'd pay without the card:
Hohensalzburg Fortress and funicular-€10.50; Mozart's Birthplace
and Residence-€12; Hellbrunn Castle-€9.50; Salzburg Panorama
1829-€2; Salzach River cruise-€13; 24-hour transit pass-€4.20.
Busy sightseers can save plenty. Get this card, feel the financial
pain once, and the city will be all yours.

Arrival in Salzburg

By Train: The Salzburg station is undergoing a huge renovation,
so for the next several years its services will be operating out of

temporary structures in the
parking lot. Still, you'll find
it all here: train information,
tourist information, luggage
lockers, and so on.

Getting downtown
couldn't be easier, as immediately in front of the station
a bus stop labeled *Zentrum-*

Altstadt has **buses** lined up and leaving every two minutes. Buses #1, #3, #5, #6, and #25 all do the same route into the city center before diverging at the far end of town. For most sights and city-center hotels, get off just after the bridge. For my recommended hotels in the new town, get off at Makartplatz, just before the bridge. (Buses to and from the airport use the *Flughafen* stop in front of the train station.) **Taxis** charge about €8 (plus €1/bag) to take you to your hotel.

To **walk** downtown (15 minutes), turn left as you leave the station, and walk straight down Rainerstrasse, which leads under the tracks past Mirabellplatz, turning into Dreifaltigkeitsgasse. From here, you can turn left onto Linzergasse for many of my recommended hotels, or cross the Staatsbrücke bridge for the old town (and more hotels). For a slightly longer but more dramatic approach, leave the station the same way but follow the tracks to the river, turn left, and walk the riverside path toward the fortress.

By Car: Coming on A-8 from Munich, cross the border into Austria. Take A-10 toward Hallein, and then take the next exit (Salzburg Süd) in the direction of Anif. First, you'll pass Hellbrunn Castle (and zoo), then the Salzburg Süd TI and a park-and-ride lot—a smart place to park while visiting Salzburg. Park your car (€5/24 hours), get sightseeing information and transit tickets from the TI, and catch the shuttle bus into town (€1.90 single-ride ticket, covered by €4.20 *Tageskarte* day pass, both sold at the TI, more expensive if you buy tickets on board, every 5 minutes; bus #3, #8, or #28). If traveling with more than one other person, take advantage of a park-and-ride combo-ticket: For €13 (€10 July-Aug), you get 24 hours of parking and a round-trip on the shuttle bus for up to five people.

Mozart never drove in the old town, and neither should you. But if you don't believe in park-and-rides, the easiest, cheapest, most central parking lot is the 1,500-car Altstadt lot in the tunnel under the Mönchsberg (€14/day, note your slot number and which of the twin lots you're in, tel. 0662/846-434). Your hotel may provide discounted parking passes.

Helpful Hints

Recommendations Skewed by Kickbacks: Salzburg is addicted to the tourist dollar, and it can never get enough. Virtually all hotels are on the take when it comes to concert and tour recommendations, influenced more by their potential kickback than by what's best for you. Take any advice with a grain of salt.

Music Festival: The Salzburg Festival (Salzburger Festspiele) runs each year from late July to the end of August.

Internet Access: Two Internet cafés at the bottom of the cliff,

SALZBURG

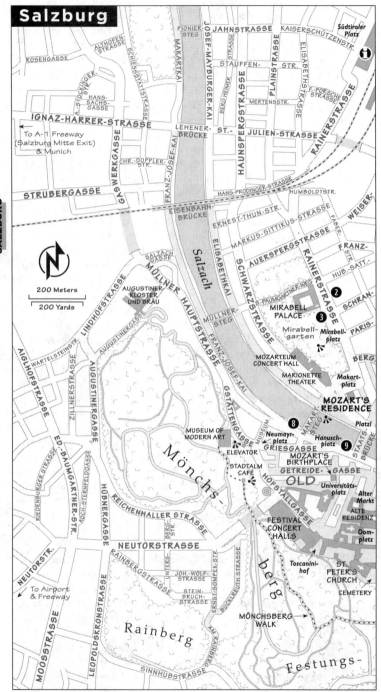

Salzburg

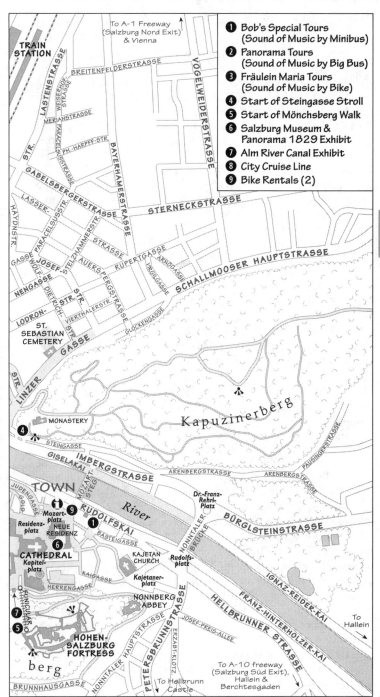

1. Bob's Special Tours
   (Sound of Music by Minibus)
2. Panorama Tours
   (Sound of Music by Big Bus)
3. Fräulein Maria Tours
   (Sound of Music by Bike)
4. Start of Steingasse Stroll
5. Start of Mönchsberg Walk
6. Salzburg Museum &
   Panorama 1829 Exhibit
7. Alm River Canal Exhibit
8. City Cruise Line
9. Bike Rentals (2)

SALZBURG

between Getreidegasse and the Mönchsberg lift, have good prices and long hours (€2/hour, daily 10:00-22:00). Across the river, there's a big, handy Internet café on Theatergasse (near Mozart's Residence, €2/hour, daily 9:00-23:00). Travelers with this book can get online free for a few minutes (long enough to check email) at the Panorama Tours terminal on Mirabellplatz (daily 8:00-18:00).

Post Office: A full-service post office is located in the heart of town, in the New Residenz (Mon-Fri 8:00-18:00, Sat 9:00-12:00, closed Sun).

Laundry: A handy launderette is at the corner of Paris-Lodron-Strasse and Wolf-Dietrich-Strasse, near my recommended Linzergasse hotels (€10 self-service, €15 same-day full-service, Mon-Fri 7:30-18:00, Sat 8:00-12:00, closed Sun, tel. 0662/876-381).

Cinema: Das Kino is an art-house movie theater that plays films in their original language (a block off the river and Linzergasse on Steingasse, tel. 0662/873-100).

Getting Around Salzburg

By Bus: Single-ride tickets for central Salzburg *(Einzelkarte-Kernzone)* are sold on the bus for €2.10. At machines and *Tabak/Trafik* shops, you can buy €1.90 single-ride tickets or a €4.20 day pass *(Tageskarte,* good for 24 hours; €5 if you buy it on the bus). To get from the old town to the station, catch bus #1 from Hanuschplatz; or, from the other side of the river, catch #1, #3, #5, or #6 at Theatergasse, near Mirabell Gardens. Bus info: tel. 800-660-660.

By Bike: Salzburg is great fun for cyclists. The following two bike-rental shops offer 20 percent off to anyone with this book—ask for it. **Top Bike** rents bikes on the river next to the Staatsbrücke (€6/2 hours, €10/4 hours, €15/24 hours, usually daily April-June and Sept-Oct 10:00-17:00, July-Aug 9:00-19:00, closed Nov-March, free helmets with this book, tel. 06272/4656, mobile 0676-476-7259, www.topbike.at, Sabine). **A'Velo Radladen** rents bikes in the old town, just outside the TI on Mozartplatz (€4.50/1 hour, €10/2 hours, €16/24 hours; electric or mountain bike-€6/hour, €22/24 hours; daily 9:00-18:00, until 19:00 July-Aug, but hours unreliable, shorter hours off-season and in bad weather, passport number for security deposit, mobile 0676-435-5950). Some of my recommended hotels and pensions also rent bikes, and several of the B&Bs on Moosstrasse have free loaner bikes for guests.

By Funicular and Elevator: The old town is connected to the top of the Mönchsberg mountain (and great views) via funicular and elevator. The **funicular** *(Festungsbahn)* whisks you up to the imposing Hohensalzburg Fortress (included in castle admission, goes every few minutes). The **elevator** *(MönchsbergAufzug)* on the east side of the old town propels you to the recommended Gasthaus Stadtalm café and hostel, the Museum of Modern Art, wooded paths, and more great views (€2 one-way, €3.20 round-trip, daily 8:30-19:00, Wed until 21:00, July-Aug daily until 1:00 in the morning, May-Sept starts running at 8:00).

By Taxi: Meters start at about €3 (from train station to your hotel, allow about €8). Small groups can taxi for about the same price as riding the bus.

By Buggy: The horse buggies *(Fiaker)* that congregate at Residenzplatz charge €36 for a 25-minute trot around the old town (www.fiaker-salzburg.at).

SALZBURG

Tours in Salzburg

Walking Tours—On any day of the week, you can take a two-language, one-hour guided walk of the old town without a reservation—just show up at the TI on Mozartplatz and pay the guide. The tours are informative, but you'll likely be listening to everything in both German and English (€9, daily at 12:15 and 14:00, tours split into two single-language groups when turnout is sufficiently high, tel. 0662/8898-7330). To save money (and avoid all that German), you can easily do it on your own using this chapter's self-guided walk.

Local Guides—Salzburg is home to over a hundred licensed guides. I recommend two hardworking young guides in particular. **Christiana Schneeweiss** ("Snow White") has been instrumental in both my guidebook research and my TV production in Salzburg (€135/2 hours, €150/3 hours, tel. 0664/340-1757, www.kultur-tourismus.com, info@kultur-tourismus.com); check her website for bike tours, private minibus tours, and more. **Sabine Rath** also knows her city well, and is a joy to learn from (€140/2 hours, €180/4 hours, €270/8 hours, tel. 0664/201-6492, www.tourguide-salzburg.com, info@tourguide-salzburg.com). Salzburg has many other good guides (to book, call 0662/840-406).

Boat Tours—**City Cruise Line** (a.k.a. Stadt Schiff-Fahrt) runs a basic 40-minute round-trip river cruise with recorded commentary (€13, 9/day July-Aug, 7/day May-June, fewer Sept-Oct and April, no boats Nov-March). For a longer cruise, ride to Hellbrunn and return by bus (€16, 1-2/day April-Oct). Boats leave from the old-town side of the river just downstream of the Makartsteg bridge (tel. 0662/825-858, www.salzburgschifffahrt .at). While views can be cramped, passengers are treated to a fun finale just before docking, when the captain twirls a fun "waltz."

Salzburg at a Glance

▲▲▲**Salzburg's Old Town Walk** Old Town's best sights in handy orientation walk. **Hours:** Always open. See page 147.

▲▲**Salzburg Cathedral** Glorious, harmonious Baroque main church of Salzburg. **Hours:** Easter-Oct Mon-Sat 9:00-18:00, Sun 13:00-18:00; Nov-Easter Mon-Sat 10:00-17:00, Sun 13:00-17:00. See page 150.

▲▲**Getreidegasse** Picturesque old shopping lane with characteristic wrought-iron signs. **Hours:** Always open. See page 155.

▲▲**Hohensalzburg Fortress** Imposing castle capping the mountain overlooking town, with tourable grounds, several mini-museums, commanding views, and good evening concerts. **Hours:** Daily May-Sept 9:00-19:00, Oct-April 9:30-17:00. Concerts nearly nightly. See page 160.

▲▲**Mozart's Residence** Restored house where the composer lived, with the best Mozart exhibit in town. **Hours:** Daily 9:00-17:30, July-Aug until 20:00. See page 165.

▲▲**Salzburg Museum** Best place to learn more about the city's history. **Hours:** Tue-Sun 9:00-17:00, Thu until 20:00, closed Mon. See page 157.

▲▲*The Sound of Music* **Tour** Cheesy but fun tour through the S.O.M. sights of Salzburg and the surrounding Salzkammergut Lake District, by minibus, big bus, or bike. **Hours:** Various options daily at 9:00, 9:30, 14:00, and 16:30. See below.

▲**Old Residenz** Prince archbishop Wolf Dietrich's palace, with ornate rooms and good included audioguide. **Hours:** Daily 10:00-17:00. See page 150.

▲**Salzburg Panorama 1829** A vivid peek at the city in 1829. **Hours:** Daily 9:00-17:00, Thu until 20:00. See page 157.

▲▲*The Sound of Music* **Tour**—I took this tour skeptically (as part of my research)—and liked it. It includes a quick but good general city tour, hits the *S.O.M.* spots (including the stately home used in the movie, flirtatious gazebo, and grand wedding church), and shows you a lovely stretch of the Salzkammergut Lake District. This is worthwhile for *S.O.M.* fans and those who won't otherwise be going into the Salzkammergut. Warning: Many think rolling through the Austrian countryside with 30 Americans singing "Doe, a deer..." is pretty schmaltzy. Local

▲**Mozart's Birthplace** House where Mozart was born in 1756, featuring his instruments and other exhibits. **Hours:** Daily 9:00-17:30, July-Aug until 20:00. See page 158.

▲**Mönchsberg Walk** "The hills are alive" stroll you can enjoy right in downtown Salzburg. **Hours:** Doable anytime during daylight hours. See page 162.

▲**Mirabell Gardens and Palace** Beautiful palace complex with fine views, Salzburg's best concert venue, and *Sound of Music* memories. **Hours:** Gardens—always open; concerts—free in the park May-Aug Sun at 10:30 and Wed at 20:30, in the palace nearly nightly. See page 164.

▲**Steingasse** Historic cobbled lane with trendy pubs—a tranquil, tourist-free section of old Salzburg. **Hours:** Always open. See page 165.

▲**St. Sebastian Cemetery** Baroque cemetery with graves of Mozart's wife and father, and other Salzburg VIPs. **Hours:** Daily April-Oct 9:00-18:30, Nov-March 9:00-16:00. See page 167.

▲**Hellbrunn Castle** Palace on the outskirts of town featuring gardens with trick fountains. **Hours:** Daily May-Sept 9:00-17:30, July-Aug until 21:00, mid-March-April and Oct 9:00-16:30, closed Nov-mid-March. See page 167.

St. Peter's Cemetery Atmospheric old cemetery with mini-gardens overlooked by cliff face with monks' caves. **Hours:** Cemetery—daily April-Sept 6:30-19:00, Oct-March 6:30-18:00; caves—May-Sept Tue-Sun 10:30-17:00, closed Mon, shorter hours Oct-April. See page 153.

St. Peter's Church Romanesque church with Rococo decor. **Hours:** Open long hours daily. See page 153.

Austrians don't understand all the commotion, and the audience is mostly native English speakers.

Of the many companies doing the tour, consider Bob's Special Tours (usually uses a minibus) and Panorama Tours (more typical and professional, big 50-seat bus). Each one provides essentially the same tour (in English with a live guide, 4 hours) for essentially the same price: €37 for Panorama, €45 for Bob's. You'll get a €5 discount from either if you book direct, mention Rick Steves, pay cash, and bring this book along (you'll need to show them this book to get the deal). Getting a spot is simple—just call and make a reservation (calling Bob's a week or two in advance is smart). Note: Your hotel will be eager to call to reserve for you—to get their commission—but if you let them do it, you won't get the discount I've negotiated.

Minibus Option: Most of **Bob's Special Tours** use an eight-seat minibus (and occasionally a 20-seat bus) and therefore have good access to old-town sights, promote a more casual feel, and spend less time waiting to load and unload. Calling well in advance increases your chances of getting a seat (€45 for adults, €5 discount with this book if you pay cash and book direct, €40 for kids and students with ID, €35 for kids in car seats, daily at 9:00 and 14:00 year-round, they'll pick you up at your hotel for the morning tour, afternoon tours leave from Bob's office along the river just east of Mozartplatz at Rudolfskai 38, tel. 0662/849-511, mobile 0664-541-7492, www.bobstours.com). Nearly all of Bob's tours stop for a fun luge ride when the weather is dry (mountain bobsled-€4.30 extra, generally April-Oct, confirm beforehand). Some travelers looking for Bob's tours at Mozartplatz have been hijacked by other companies...have Bob's pick you up at your hotel (morning only), or meet the bus at their office. If you're unable to book with Bob's, and still want a minibus tour, try **Kultur Tourismus** (€45, tel. 0664/340-1757, www.kultur-tourismus.com, info@kultur-tourismus.com).

Big-Bus Option: Panorama Tours depart from their smart kiosk at Mirabellplatz daily at 9:30 and 14:00 year-round (€37, €5 discount with this book if you book direct and pay cash, book by calling 0662/874-029 or 0662/883-2110, or online at www.panoramatours.com). Many travelers appreciate their more businesslike feel, roomier buses, and slightly higher vantage point.

Bike Option: For some exercise with your tour, you can meet **Fräulein Maria** at the Mirabell Gardens (at Mirabellplatz 4, 50 yards to the left of palace entry) for a *S.O.M.* bike tour. The main attractions that you'll pass during the seven-mile pedal include the Mirabell Gardens, the horse pond, St. Peter's Cemetery, Nonnberg Abbey, Leopoldskron Palace, and, of course, the gazebo (€24 includes bike, €2 discount with this book, €15 for kids 6-15, €10 for kids under 6, daily May-Sept at 9:30, June-Aug also at 16:30, allow 3.5 hours, family-friendly, reservations required only for afternoon tours, tel. 0650/342-6297, www.mariasbicycletours.com). For €8 extra, you're welcome to keep the bike all day.

Beyond Salzburg

Both Bob's and Panorama Tours also offer an extensive array of other day trips from Salzburg (e.g., Berchtesgaden/Eagle's Nest, salt mines, and Salzkammergut lakes and mountains).

Bob's Special Tours offers two particularly well-designed day tours (both depart daily at 9:00; either one costs €90 with a €10 discount if you show this book and book direct, does not include entrance fees). Their *Sound of Music/Hallstatt Tour* first covers everything in the standard four-hour *Sound of Music* tour, then continues for a four-hour look at the scenic, lake-speckled Salzkammergut (with free time to explore charming Hallstatt). Bob's **Bavarian Mountain Tour** covers the main things you'd want to do in and around Berchtesgaden (Königssee cruise, Hitler's mountaintop Eagle's Nest, salt mine tour). Although you can do all the top Berchtesgaden sights on your own with the information I've provided later in this chapter, Bob's tour makes it easy for those without a car to see these sights in one busy day.

Self-Guided Walk

▲▲▲Salzburg's Old Town

I've linked the best sights in the old town into this handy self-guided orientation walk.

• *Begin in the heart of town, just up from the river, near the TI on...*

❶ Mozartplatz

All the happy tourists around you probably wouldn't be here if not for the man honored by this statue—Wolfgang Amadeus Mozart (erected in 1842; locals consider the statue a terrible likeness). Mozart spent much of his first 25 years (1756-1777) in Salzburg, the greatest Baroque city north of the Alps. But the city itself is much older: The Mozart statue sits on bits of Roman Salzburg, and the pink Church of St. Michael that overlooks the square dates from A.D. 800. The first Salzburgers settled right around here. Near you is the TI (with a concert box office), and just around the downhill corner is a pedestrian bridge leading over the Salzach River to the quiet and most medieval street in town, Steingasse.

• *Walk toward the cathedral and into the big square with the huge fountain.*

❷ Residenzplatz

Important buildings have long ringed this square. Salzburg's energetic prince archbishop Wolf Dietrich von Raitenau (who ruled 1587-1612) was raised in Rome, was a cousin of the influential Florentine Medici family, and had grandiose Italian ambitions for

SALZBURG

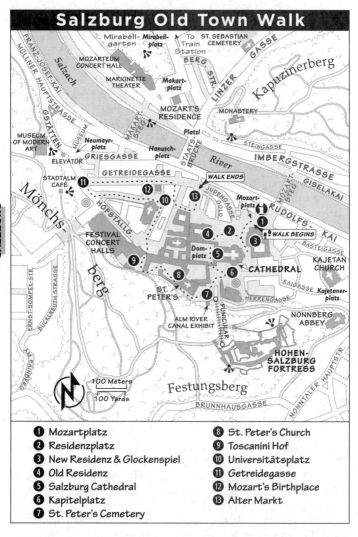

Salzburg Old Town Walk

❶ Mozartplatz
❷ Residenzplatz
❸ New Residenz & Glockenspiel
❹ Old Residenz
❺ Salzburg Cathedral
❻ Kapitelplatz
❼ St. Peter's Cemetery
❽ St. Peter's Church
❾ Toscanini Hof
❿ Universitätsplatz
⓫ Getreidegasse
⓬ Mozart's Birthplace
⓭ Alter Markt

Salzburg. After a convenient fire destroyed the town's cathedral, Wolf Dietrich set about building the "Rome of the North." This square, with his new cathedral and palace, was the centerpiece of his Baroque dream city. A series of interconnecting squares—like you'll see nowhere else—make a grand processional way, leading from here through the old town. As we enjoy this heart and soul of historic Salzburg, notice how easily we slip from noisy commercial streets to peaceful, reflective courtyards. Also notice the two dominant kinds of stone around town: a creamy red marble and a chunky conglomerate, both quarried nearby.

For centuries, Salzburg's leaders were both important church officials *and* princes of the Holy Roman Empire, hence the title "prince archbishop"—mixing sacred and secular authority. But Wolf Dietrich misplayed his hand, losing power and spending his last five years imprisoned in the Hohensalzburg Fortress. (It's a complicated story—basically, the pope counted on Salzburg to hold the line against the Protestants for several generations following the Reformation. Wolf Dietrich was a good Catholic, as were most Salzburgers. But the town's important businessmen and the region's salt miners were Protestant, and for Salzburg's financial good, Wolf Dietrich dealt with them in a tolerant and pragmatic way. So the pope—who couldn't allow any tolerance for Protestants in those heady Counter-Reformation days—had Wolf Dietrich locked up and replaced.)

The fountain is as Italian as can be, with a Triton matching Bernini's famous Triton Fountain in Rome. Situated on a busy trade route to the south, Salzburg was well aware of the exciting things going on in Italy. Things Italian were respected (as in colonial America, when a bumpkin would "stick a feather in his cap and call it macaroni"). Local artists even Italianized their names in order to raise their rates.

• *Along the left side of Residenzplatz (as you face the cathedral) is the...*

❸ New (Neue) Residenz & Glockenspiel

This former palace, long a government administration building, now houses the central post office, the **Heimatwerk** (a fine shop showing off all the best local handicrafts, Mon-Fri 9:00-18:00, Sat 9:00-17:00, closed Sun), and two worthwhile sights: the fascinating **Salzburg Panorama 1829** exhibit (definitely worth the entry fee); and the **Salzburg Museum,** which offers the best peek at the history of this one-of-a-kind city.

The famous **glockenspiel** rings atop the New Residenz. This bell tower has a carillon of 35 17th-century bells (cast in Antwerp) that chimes throughout the day and plays tunes (appropriate to the month) at 7:00, 11:00, and 18:00. A big barrel with adjustable tabs turns like a giant music-box mechanism, pulling the right bells in the appropriate rhythm. Notice the ornamental top: an upside-down heart in flames surrounding the solar system (symbolizing that God loves all of creation). Seasonal twice-weekly tours let you get up close to watch the glockenspiel action (€3, April-Oct Thu at 17:30 and Fri at 10:30, no tours Nov-March, meet in Salzburg Panorama 1829, just show up).

Look back, past Mozart's statue, to the 4,220-foot-high **Gaisberg**—the forested hill with the television tower. A road leads to the top for a commanding view. Its summit is a favorite destination for local nature-lovers and strong bikers.

• Head to the opposite end of the square. This building is the...

❹ Old (Alte) Residenz

Across from the New Residenz is Wolf Dietrich's palace, the Old Residenz, which is connected to the cathedral by a skyway. Its series of ornately decorated rooms is well-described in an included audioguide, which gives you a good feel for the wealth and power of the prince archbishop. Walking through 15 fancy state rooms (all on one floor), you'll see Renaissance, Baroque, and Classicist styles—200 years of let-them-eat-cake splendor.

Cost and Hours: €8.50, daily 10:00-17:00, tel. 0662/8042-2690.

• Walk under the prince archbishop's skyway and step into Domplatz (Cathedral Square), where you'll find...

❺ Salzburg Cathedral (Salzburger Dom)

This cathedral, rated ▲▲, was one of the first Baroque buildings north of the Alps. It was consecrated in 1628, during the Thirty Years' War. (Pitting Roman Catholics against Protestants, this

war devastated much of Europe and brought most grand construction projects to a halt.) Experts differ on what motivated the builders: to emphasize Salzburg's commitment to the Roman Catholic cause and the power of the Church here, or to show that there could be a peaceful alternative to the religious strife that was racking Europe at the time. Salzburg's archbishop was technically the top papal official north of the Alps, but the city managed to steer clear of the war. With its rich salt production, it had enough money to stay out of the conflict and carefully maintain its independence from the warring sides, earning it the nickname "Fortified Island of Peace."

Domplatz is surrounded by the prince archbishop's secular administration buildings. The **statue of Mary** (1771) is looking away from the church, welcoming visitors. If you stand in the rear of the square, immediately under the middle arch, you'll see that she's positioned to be crowned by the two angels on the church facade.

The dates on the iron gates refer to milestones in the church's history: In 774, the previous church (long since destroyed) was founded by St. Virgil, to be replaced in 1628 by the church you see today. In 1959, a partial reconstruction was completed, made necessary by a WWII bomb that had blown through the dome.

Cost and Hours: Free, but donation requested; Easter-Oct Mon-Sat 9:00-18:00, Sun 13:00-18:00; Nov-Easter Mon-Sat 10:00-17:00, Sun 13:00-17:00.

Touring the Cathedral: Enter the cathedral as if part of a festival procession—drawn toward the resurrected Christ by the

brightly lit area under the dome, and cheered on by ceiling paintings of the Passion.

Built in just 14 years (1614-1628), the church boasts harmonious architecture. When Pope John Paul II visited in 1998, some 5,000 people filled the cathedral (330 feet long and 230 feet tall). The baptismal font (dark bronze, left of the entry) is from the previous cathedral (basin from about 1320, although the lid is modern). Mozart was baptized here (Amadeus means "beloved by God"). Concert and Mass schedules are posted at the entrance; the Sunday Mass at 10:00 is famous for its music.

The **paintings** lining the nave, showing events leading up to Christ's death, are relatively dark. But the Old Testament themes that foreshadow Jesus' resurrection, and the Resurrection scene painted at the altar, are well-lit. The church has never had stained glass—just clear windows to let light power the message.

The stucco, by a Milanese artist, is exceptional. Sit under the **dome**—surrounded by the tombs of 10 archbishops from the 17th century—and imagine all four organs playing, each balcony filled with musicians...glorious surround-sound. Mozart, who was the organist here for two years, would advise you that the acoustics are best in pews immediately under the dome. Study the symbolism of the decor all around you—intellectual, complex, and cohesive. Think of the altar in Baroque terms, as the center of a stage, with sunrays as spotlights in this dramatic and sacred theater.

In the left transept, stairs lead down into the **crypt** *(Krypta),* where you can see foundations of the earlier church, more tombs, and a tourist-free chapel (reserved for prayer) directly under the dome.

Other Cathedral Sights: The **Cathedral Excavations Museum** (outside the church on Residenzplatz and down the stairs) offers a chance to see the foundations of the medieval church, some Roman engineering, and a few Roman mosaics from Roman street level. It has the charm of an old basement garage; unless you've never seen anything Roman, I'd skip it (€2.50, July-Aug daily 9:00-17:00, closed Sept-June).

The **Cathedral Museum** (Dom Museum) has a rich collection of church art (entry at portico, €6, mid-May-Oct Mon-Sat 10:00-17:00, Sun 11:00-18:00, closed Nov-mid-May except during Advent, tel. 0662/8047-1870).
• *From the cathedral, exit left and walk toward the fortress into the next square.*

❻ Kapitelplatz
Head past the underground public WCs (€0.50) to the giant **chessboard.** It's just under the golden orb topped by a man gazing up at the castle, trying to decide whether to walk up or shell out €10.50 for the funicular. Every year since 2002, a foundation has commissioned a different artist to create a new work of public art somewhere in the city; this is the piece from 2007. A small road leads uphill to the fortress (and fortress funicular; see arrow pointing to the *Stieglkeller*).

Keep going across the square to the pond. This was a **horse bath,** the 18th-century equivalent of a car wash. Notice the puzzle above it—the artist wove the date of the structure into a phrase. It says, "Leopold the Prince Built Me," using the letters LLDVICMXVXI, which total 1732 (add it up...it works)—the year it was built. With your back to the cathedral, leave the square through a gate in the right corner that reads *zum Peterskeller.* It leads to a waterfall and St. Peter's Cemetery (described later).

The **waterwheel** is part of a clever canal system that has brought water into Salzburg from Berchtesgaden, 15 miles away, since the 13th century. Climb uphill a few steps to feel the medieval water power. The stream was divided into smaller canals and channeled through town to provide fire protection, to flush out the streets (Thursday morning was flood-the-streets day), and to power factories (there were more than 100 watermill-powered firms as late as the 19th century). Because of its water-powered hygiene (relatively good for the standards of the time), Salzburg never suffered from a plague—it's probably the only Austrian town you'll see with no plague monument. For more on the canal system, check out the **Alm River Canal exhibit** (at the exit of the funicular).

Before leaving, drop into the fragrant and traditional **bakery** at the waterfall, which sells various fresh rolls—both sweet and not, explained on the wall, for less than €1 (Thu-Tue 7:00-17:30, Sat until 13:00, closed Wed). There's a good view of the funicular climbing up to the castle from here.

• *Now find the* Katakomben *sign and step into...*

❼ St. Peter's Cemetery

This collection of lovingly tended mini-gardens abuts the Mönchberg's rock wall. Walk in about 50 yards to the intersection of lanes at the base of the cliff marked by a stone ball. You're surrounded by three churches, each founded in the early Middle Ages atop a pagan Celtic holy site. St. Peter's Church is closest to the stone ball. Notice the fine Romanesque stonework on the apse of the chapel nearest you, and the rich guys' fancy Renaissance-style tombs decorating its walls.

Wealthy as those guys were, they ran out of caring relatives. The graves surrounding you are tended by descendants of the deceased. In Austria, gravesites are rented, not owned. Rent bills are sent out every 10 years. If no one cares enough to make the payment, your tombstone is removed.

While the cemetery where the von Trapp family hid out in *The Sound of Music* was a Hollywood set, it was inspired by this one.

Look up the cliff. Legendary medieval hermit monks are said to have lived in the hillside—but "catacombs" they're not. You can climb lots of steps to see a few old caves, a chapel, and some fine views.

Cost and Hours: Cemetery—free, silence is requested, daily April-Sept 6:30-19:00, Oct-March 6:30-18:00; caves—€1, May-Sept Tue-Sun 10:30-17:00, closed Mon, shorter hours Oct-April.

Nearby: To enjoy a peaceful side-trip, stroll past the stark Gothic funeral chapel (c. 1491) to the uphill corner of the cemetery, and return along the high lane to see the finer tombs in the arcade. Tomb #XXXI belongs to the cathedral's architect—forever facing his creation. Tomb #LIV, at the catacomb entry, is a chapel carved into the hillside, holding the tombs of Mozart's sister and Joseph Haydn's younger brother Michael, also a composer of great note.

• *Continue downhill through the cemetery and out the opposite end. Just outside, hook right and drop into...*

❽ St. Peter's Church

Just inside, enjoy a carved Romanesque welcome. Over the inner doorway, a fine tympanum shows Jesus on a rainbow flanked by Peter and Paul over a stylized Tree of Life and under a Latin inscription reading, "I am the door to life, and only through me can you find eternal life." Enter the nave and notice how the once purely Romanesque vaulting has since been iced with a sugary Rococo finish. Salzburg's only Rococo interior feels Bavarian (because it is—the fancy stucco work was done by Bavarian artists). Up the right side aisle is the tomb of St. Rupert, with a painting showing Salzburg in 1750 (one bridge, salt ships sailing the river, and angels hoisting barrels of salt to heaven as St. Rupert prays for his city). If you're here during the town's Ruperti-Kirtag festival in late September, you'll see candles and fresh flowers, honoring the city's not-forgotten saint. On pillars farther up the aisle are faded bits of 13th-century Romanesque frescoes. Similar frescoes hide under Rococo whitewash throughout the church.

Cost and Hours: Free, long hours daily.

• *Leaving the church, notice on the left the recommended* **Stiftskeller St. Peter** *restaurant—known for its Mozart Dinner Concert. Charlemagne ate here in A.D. 803, allowing locals to claim that it's the oldest restaurant in Europe. Opposite where you entered the square (look through the arch), you'll see St. Rupert waving you into the next square. Once there, you're surrounded by early 20th-century Bauhaus-style dorms for student monks. Notice the modern crucifix (1926) painted on the far wall. Here's a good place to see the two locally quarried stones (marble and conglomerate) so prevalent in all the town's buildings.*

Walk through the archway under the crucifix into...

❾ Toscanini Hof

This square faces the 1925 **Festival Hall.** The hall's three theaters seat 5,000. This is where Captain von Trapp nervously waited before walking onstage (in the movie, he sang "Edelweiss"), just before he escaped with his family. On the left is the city's 1,500-space, inside-the-mountain parking lot; ahead, behind the *Felsenkeller* sign, is a tunnel (generally closed) leading to the actual concert hall; and to the right is the backstage of a smaller hall where carpenters are often building stage sets (door open on hot days). The stairway leads a few flights up to a picnic perch with a fine view, and then up to the top of the cliff and the recommended Stadtalm Café and hostel.

Walk downhill to **Max-Reinhardt-Platz.** Pause here to survey the line of Salzburg Festival concert halls. As the festival was started in the austere 1920s, the city remodeled existing buildings (e.g., the prince archbishop's stables and riding school) for venues.

• *Continue straight—passing the big church on your left, along with lots of popular wurst stands and a public WC—into...*

❿ Universitätsplatz

This square hosts an **open-air produce market**—Salzburg's liveliest (mornings Mon-Sat, best on Sat). Salzburgers are happy to pay more here for the reliably fresh and top-quality produce. (These days, half of Austria's produce is grown organically.) The market really bustles on Saturday mornings, when the farmers are in

town. Public marketplaces have fountains for washing fruit and vegetables. The fountain here—a part of the medieval water system—plummets down a hole and to the river. The sundial (over the water hole) is accurate (except for the daylight savings hour) and two-dimensional, showing both the time (obvious) and the date (less obvious). The fanciest facade overlooking the square (the yellow one) is the backside of Mozart's Birthplace (we'll see the front soon).

• *Continue past the fountain to the end of the square, passing several characteristic and nicely arcaded medieval tunnels (on right) that connect the square to Getreidegasse (described next). Just for fun, weave between this street and Getreidegasse several times, following these "through houses" as you work your way toward the cliff face. For a look at the giant horse troughs, adjacent to the prince's stables, cross the big road (looking left at the string of Salzburg Festival halls again). Paintings show the various breeds and temperaments of horses in his stable. Like Vienna, Salzburg had a passion for the equestrian arts.*

Turn right (passing a courtyard on your left that once housed a hospital for the poor, and now houses a toy museum and a museum of historic musical instruments), and then right again, which brings you to the start of a long and colorful pedestrian street.

⓫ Getreidegasse

This street, rated ▲▲, was old Salzburg's busy, colorful main drag. It's been a center of trade since Roman times (third century). It's lined with *Schmuck* (jewelry) shops and other businesses. This is the burgher's (businessman's) Salzburg. The buildings, most of which date from the 15th century, are tall for that age, and narrow, and densely packed. Space was tight here because such little land was available between the natural fortifications provided by the mountain and the river, and much of what was available was used up by the Church. Famous for its old wrought-iron signs (best viewed from this end), the architecture on the street still looks much as

it did in Mozart's day—though its former elegance is now mostly gone, replaced by chain outlets.

As you walk away from the cliffs, look up and enjoy the traditional signs indicating what each shop made or sold: Watch for spirits, bookmakers, a horn (indicating a place for the postal coach), brewery (the star for the name of the beer, Sternbräu—"Star Brew"), glazier (window-maker), locksmith, hamburgers, pastries, tailor, baker (the pretzel), pharmacy, and a hatter.

On the right at #39, **Sporer** serves up homemade spirits (€1.50/shot, open 8:30-17:00). This has been a family-run show for a century—fun-loving, proud, and English-speaking. *Nuss* is nut, *Marille* is apricot (typical of this region), the *Kletzen* cocktail is like a super-thick Baileys with pear, and *Edle Brande* are the stronger schnapps. The many homemade firewaters are in jugs at the end of the bar.

Continue down Getreidegasse, noticing the old doorbells—one per floor. At #40, **Eisgrotte** serves good ice cream. Across from Eisgrotte, a tunnel leads to the recommended **Balkan Grill** (signed as *Bosna Grill*), the local choice for the very best wurst in town. At #28, Herr Wieber, the iron- and locksmith, welcomes the curious. Farther along, you'll pass McDonald's (required to keep its arches Baroque and low-key).

The knot of excited tourists and salesmen hawking goofy gimmicks marks the home of Salzburg's most famous resident. **Mozart's Birthplace** (*Geburtshaus,* ⑫ on map)—the house where Mozart was born, and where he composed many of his early works—is worth a visit for his true fans. But for most, his **Residence,** across the river, is more interesting.

At #3, dip into the passage and walk under a whalebone, likely once used to advertise the wares of an exotic import shop. Look up at the arcaded interior. On the right, at the venerable **Schatz Konditorei,** you can enjoy coffee under the vaults with your choice of top-end cakes and pastries (Mon-Fri 8:30-18:30, Sat 8:00-17:00, closed Sun).

Leaving the pastry shop, go straight ahead through the passage to Sigmund-Haffner-Gasse. Before heading right, look left to see the tower of the old City Hall at the end. The blue-and-white ball halfway up is an 18th-century moon clock. It still tells the phase of the moon.

• *Go right, then take your first left to....*

⓭ Alter Markt

Here in Salzburg's old marketplace, you'll find a sausage stand, the recommended **Café Tomaselli,** a fun **candy shop** at #7, and, next door, the beautifully old-fashioned **Alte F.E. Hofapotheke** pharmacy—duck in discreetly to peek at the Baroque shelves and containers (be polite—the people in line are here for medicine, no photography).

• *Our walk is finished. From here, you can circle back to some of the old town sights (such as those in the New Residenz, described next); head up to the Hohensalzburg Fortress on the cliffs over the old town (see next page); or continue to some of the sights across the river. To reach those sights, head for the river, jog left (past the fast-food fish restaurant and free WCs), and climb to the top of the Makartsteg pedestrian bridge.*

Sights in Salzburg

In the Old Town

In the New (Neue) Residenz

▲▲Salzburg Museum—This two-floor exhibit is the best in town for history. The included audioguide wonderfully describes the great artifacts in the lavish prince archbishop's residence.

The Salzburg Personalities exhibit fills the first floor with a charming look at Salzburg's greatest historic characters—mostly artists, scientists, musicians, and writers who would otherwise be forgotten. And upstairs is the real reason to come: lavish ceremonial rooms filled with an exhibit called The Salzburg Myth, which traces the city's proud history, art, and culture since early modern times. The focus is on its quirky absolutist prince archbishop and its long-standing reputation as a fairy-tale "Alpine Arcadia." The *Kunsthalle* in the basement shows off special exhibits.

From the Salzburg Museum, the Panorama Passage (clearly marked from the entry) leads underground to the Salzburg Panorama (described next). This passage is lined with archaeological finds (Roman and early medieval), helping you trace the development of Salzburg from its Roman roots until today.

Cost and Hours: €7, €8 combo-ticket with Salzburg Panorama, includes audioguide, Tue-Sun 9:00-17:00, Thu until 20:00, closed Mon, tel. 0662/620-8080, www.smca.at.

▲Salzburg Panorama 1829—In the early 19th century, before the advent of photography, 360-degree "panorama" paintings of great cities or events were popular. These creations were even taken on extended road trips. When this one was created, the 1815 Treaty of Vienna had just divvied up post-Napoleonic Europe, and Salzburg had become part of the Habsburg realm. This photorealistic painting served as a town portrait done at the emperor's request. The circular view, painted by Johann Michael Sattler, shows the city as seen from the top of its castle. When complete, it spent 10 years touring the great cities of Europe, showing off Salzburg's breathtaking setting.

Today, the exquisitely restored painting offers a fascinating look at the city in 1829. The river was slower and had beaches. The old town looks essentially as it does today, and Moosstrasse still leads into idyllic farm country. Paintings from that era of other great cities around the world are hung around the outside wall with numbers but without labels, as a kind of quiz game. A flier gives the cities' names on one side, and keys them to the numbers. See how many 19th-century cities you can identify.

Cost and Hours: €2, €8 combo-ticket with Salzburg Museum, open daily 9:00-17:00, Thu until 20:00, Residenzplatz 9.

▲Mozart's Birthplace (Geburtshaus)

Mozart was born here in 1756. It was in this building that he composed most of his boy-genius works. Today it's the most popular Mozart sight in town—for fans, it's almost a pilgrimage. American artist Robert Wilson was hired to spiff up the exhibit, to make it feel more conceptual and less like a museum. Even so, I was unimpressed. If you're tackling just one Mozart sight, skip this one. Instead, walk 10 minutes from here to Mozart's Residence  (described later), which provides a more informative visit. But if you want to max out on Mozart, a visit here is worthwhile.

Shuffling through with all the crowds, you'll peruse three floors of rooms with old-school exhibits displaying paintings, letters, personal items, and lots of facsimiles, all attempting to bring life to the Mozart story (and all explained in English). A period living room shows what Wolfgang's world likely looked like, and portraits introduce you to the family. A particular highlight is an old clavichord he supposedly composed on. (A predecessor of the more complicated piano, the clavichord's keys hit the strings with a simple teeter-totter motion that allowed you to play very softly—ideal for composers living in tight apartment quarters.) At the end, there's a room of dioramas dedicated to Mozart's operas.

Cost and Hours: €7, €12 for combo-ticket includes Mozart's Residence, daily 9:00-17:30, July-Aug until 20:00, last entry 30 minutes before closing, only the shop has air-con, Getreidegasse 9, tel. 0662/844-313.

Atop the Cliffs Above the Old Town

The main "sight" above town is the Hohensalzburg Fortress. But if you just want to enjoy the sweeping views over Salzburg, you have a couple of cheap options: Head up to the castle grounds on foot, take the elevator up the cliffs of Mönchsberg, or visit the castle in the evening on a night when they're hosting a concert

Battlefield Salzburg:
Popes vs. Emperors

Salzburg is so architecturally impressive today to a great degree because of the Roman Catholic Church. This town was on the frontline of a centuries-long power struggle between Church and emperor. The town's mighty Hohensalzburg Fortress—a symbol of the Church's determination to assert its power here—was built around 1100, just as the conflict was heating up.

The medieval church-state argument, called the "Lay Investiture Controversy," was a classic tug-of-war between a series of popes and Holy Roman Emperors. The prize: the right to appoint (or "invest") church officials in the Holy Roman Emperor's domain. (Although called "Holy," the empire was headed not by priests, but by secular—or "lay"—rulers.)

The Church impinged on the power of secular leaders in several ways: Their subjects' generous tithes went to Rome, leaving less for the emperor to tax. In many areas, the Church was the biggest landowner (people willed their land to the Church in return for prayers for their salvation). And the pope's appointees weren't subject to secular local laws. Holy Roman Emperors were plenty powerful, but not as powerful as the Church.

In 1075, Emperor Henry IV bucked the system, appointing his own set of church officials and boldly renouncing Gregory VII as pope. In retaliation, Gregory excommunicated both Henry and the bishops he'd appointed. One of Henry's chief detractors was Salzburg's pope-appointed archbishop, Gebhard, who started construction of Hohensalzburg Fortress in a face-off with the defiant emperor.

The German nobility seized on the conflict as an opportunity to rebel, seizing royal property and threatening to elect a new emperor. To placate the nobles, Henry sought to regain the Church's favor. In January of 1077, Henry traveled south to Italy—supposedly crossing the Alps barefoot and in a monk's hair-shirt—to Canossa, where the pope was holed up. The emperor knelt in the snow outside the castle gate for three days, begging the pope's forgiveness. (To this day, the phrase "go to Canossa" is used to refer to any act of humility.)

But the German princes continued their revolt, electing their own king (Henry's brother-in-law, Rudolf of Rheinfelden). Henry's reconciliation with the Church was brief: In short order he named an antipope (Clement III), killed Rudolf in battle, and invaded Rome. Archbishop Gebhard was forced out of Salzburg and spent a decade in exile, raising forces against Henry in an attempt to reclaim the Salzburg archdiocese.

The back-and-forth continued until 1122, when a power-sharing accord was finally reached between Henry's son, Emperor Henry V, and Pope Calistus II.

SALZBURG

(about 300 nights a year). This is the only time you can buy a funicular ticket without paying for the castle entrance—since the castle museums are closed, but the funicular still runs to bring up concert-goers.

▲▲Hohensalzburg Fortress (Festung)

Construction of Hohensalzburg Fortress was begun by Archbishop Gebhard of Salzburg as a show of the Catholic Church's power (see sidebar). Built on a rock (called Festungsberg) 400 feet above the Salzach River, this fortress was never really used. That's the idea. It was a good investment—so foreboding, nobody attacked the town for 1,000 years. The city was never taken by force, but when

Napoleon stopped by, Salzburg wisely surrendered. After a stint as a military barracks, the fortress was opened to the public in the 1860s by Habsburg Emperor Franz Josef. Today, it remains one of Europe's mightiest castles, dominating Salzburg's skyline and offering incredible views.

Cost: Your daytime funicular ticket includes admission to the fortress grounds and all the museums inside—whether you want to see them or not (€10.50, €24.30 family ticket). Save a few euros by walking up—the climb is much easier than it looks, and the views are fantastic. At the top, you'll pay €7.40 to enter (includes grounds and museums). If you'd rather take the funicular but want to skip the museums, head up the hill in the evening: Within one hour of the museums' closing time, the funicular and entry to the castle grounds cost €6.20 one-way/€7.60 round-trip; on concert nights and in summer, after the museums have closed, the funicular is just €3.80 round-trip.

Hours: The complex is open daily year-round (May-Sept 9:00-19:00, Oct-April 9:30-17:00, last entry 30 minutes before closing, tel. 0662/8424-3011). On nights when there's a concert, and nightly in July and August, the castle grounds are free and open from after the museums close until 22:00.

Concerts: The fortress also serves as a venue for evening concerts (Festungskonzerte).

Café: The café between the funicular station and the castle entry is a great place to nibble on apple strudel while taking in the jaw-dropping view.

Orientation: The fortress visit has three parts: a relatively dull courtyard with some fine views from its various ramparts; the fortress itself (with a required and escorted 45-minute audio tour); and the palace museum (by far the best exhibit of the lot). At the bottom of the funicular, you'll pass through an interesting little exhibit on the town's canal system (free).

➋ **Self-Guided Tour:** From the top of the funicular, head to your right and down the stairs to bask in the **view,** either from the café or the view terrace a little farther along.

Once you're done snapping photos, walk through to the castle grounds and go left, following the path up and around to reach the inner courtyard (labeled *Inneres Schloß*). Immediately inside, circling to the right (clockwise), you'll encounter cannons (still poised to defend Salzburg against an Ottoman invasion), a marionette exhibit, the palace museum, the Kuenburg Bastion, scant ruins of a Romanesque church, the courtyard (with path down for those walking), toilets, shops, a restaurant, and the fortress tour.

• *Begin at the...*

Marionette Exhibit: Several fun rooms show off this local tradition, with three videos playing continuously: two with peeks at Salzburg's ever-enchanting Marionette Theater performances of Mozart classics (described under "Music in Salzburg," later) and one with a behind-the-scenes look at the action. Give the hands-on marionette a whirl.

• *Hiking through the former palace, you'll find the best exhibits at the...*

Palace Museum (Festungsmuseum Carolino Augusteum): The second floor has exhibits on castle life, from music to torture. The top floor shows off fancy royal apartments, a sneak preview of the room used for the nightly fortress concerts, and the Rainier military museum, dedicated to the Salzburg regiments that fought in both world wars.

Castle Courtyard: The courtyard was the main square for the castle's 1,000-some medieval residents, who could be self-sufficient when necessary. The square was ringed by the shops of craftsmen, blacksmiths, bakers, and so on. The well dipped into a rain-fed cistern. The church is dedicated to St. George, the protector of horses (logical for an army church) and decorated by fine red marble reliefs (c. 1502). Behind the church is the top of the old lift that helped supply the fortress. (From near here, steps lead back into the city, or to the mountaintop "Mönchsberg Walk," described later.) You'll also see the remains of a Romanesque chapel, which are well-described.

• *Near the chapel, turn left into the Kuenburg Bastion (once a garden) for fine city and castle views.*

Kuenburg Bastion: Notice how the castle has three parts: the

original castle inside the courtyard, the vast whitewashed walls (built when the castle was a residence), and the lower, beefed-up fortifications (added for extra defense against the expected Ottoman invasion). Survey Salzburg from here and think about fortifying an important city by using nature. Mönchsberg (the cliffs to the left) and Festungsberg (the little mountain you're on) naturally cradle the old town, with just a small gate between the ridge and the river needed to bottle up the place. The new town across the river needed a bit of a wall arcing from the river to its hill. Back then, only one bridge crossed the Salzach into town, and it had a fortified gate.

• *Back inside the castle courtyard, continue your circle. The Round Tower (1497) helps you visualize the inner original castle.*

Fortress Interior: Tourists are allowed in this part of the fortified palace only with an escort. (They say that's for security, though while touring it, you wonder what they're protecting.) A crowd assembles at the turnstile, and every quarter-hour 40 people are issued their audioguides and let in for the escorted walk. You'll go one room at a time, listening to a 45-minute commentary. While the interior furnishings are mostly gone—taken by Napoleon—the rooms survived as well as they did because no one wanted to live here after 1500, so the building was never modernized. Your tour includes a room dedicated to the art of "excruciating questioning" ("softening up" prisoners, in American military jargon)—filled with tools of that gruesome trade. The highlight is the commanding city view from the top of a tower.

• *After seeing the fortress, consider hiking down to the old town, or along the top of Mönchsberg (see "Mönchsberg Walk," below). If you take the funicular down, don't miss (at the bottom of the lift) the...*

Alm River Canal Exhibit: At the base of the funicular, below the castle, is this fine little exhibit on how the river was broken into five smaller streams—powering the city until steam took up the energy-supply baton. Pretend it's the year 1200 and follow (by video) the flow of the water from the river through the canals, into the mills, and as it's finally dumped into the Salzach River. (The exhibit technically requires a funicular ticket—but you can see it by slipping through the exit at the back of the amber shop, just uphill from the funicular terminal.)

Mönchsberg Sights

▲**Mönchsberg Walk**—For a great 30-minute hike, exit the fortress by taking the steep lane down from the castle courtyard. At the first intersection, right leads into the old town, and left leads across the Mönchsberg. The lane leads 20 minutes through the woods high above the city (stick to the high lanes, or you'll end up back in town), taking you to the recommended Gasthaus Stadtalm café (light meals, cheap beds). From the Stadtalm, pass under the medieval wall and walk left along the wall to a tableau showing how it once looked. Take the switchback to the right and follow the lane downhill to the Museum of Modern Art (described next), where the *MönchsbergAufzug* elevator zips you back into town (€2 one-way, €3.20 round-trip, daily 8:00-19:00, Wed and July-Aug until 21:00). If you stay on the lane past the elevator, you eventually pass the Augustine church that marks the rollicking Augustiner Bräustübl beer garden.

In 1669, a huge Mönchsberg landslide killed more than 200 townspeople. Since then the cliffs have been carefully checked each spring and fall. Even today, you might see crews on the cliff, monitoring its stability.

Museum of Modern Art on Mönchsberg—The modern-art museum on top of Mönchsberg was built in 2004. While the collection is not worth climbing a mountain for, the M32 restaurant has some of the best views in town.

Cost and Hours: €8, €9.70 including elevator ticket, Tue-Sun 10:00-18:00, Wed until 20:00, closed Mon except during festival; restaurant open Tue-Sat 9:00-24:00, closed Mon except during festival; at top of Mönchsberg elevator, tel. 0662/842-220-403, www.museumdermoderne.at.

In the New Town, North of the River

The following sights are across the river from the old town. I've connected them with walking instructions.

• *Begin at the Makartsteg pedestrian bridge, where you can survey the...*

Salzach River

Salzburg's river is called "salt river" not because it's salty, but because of the precious cargo it once carried—the salt mines of Hallein are just nine miles upstream. Salt could be transported from here all the way to the Danube, and on to the Mediterranean via the Black Sea. The riverbanks and roads were built when the river was regulated in the 1850s. Before that, the Salzach was much wider and slower moving. Houses opposite the old town fronted the river with docks and "garages" for boats. The grand buildings just past the bridge (with their elegant promenades and cafés) were built on reclaimed land in the late 19th century.

Scan the cityscape. Notice all the churches. Salzburg, nicknamed the "Rome of the North," has 38 Catholic churches (plus two Protestant churches and a synagogue). Find the five streams gushing into the river. These date from the 13th century, when the river was split into five canals running through the town to power its mills. The Stein Hotel (upstream, just left of next bridge) has a popular roof-terrace café. Downstream, notice the Museum of Modern Art atop Mönchsberg, with a view restaurant and a faux castle (actually a water reservoir). The Romanesque bell tower with the green copper dome in the distance is the Augustine church, site of the best beer hall in town (the recommended Augustiner Bräustübl).

• *Cross the bridge, pass the recommended Café Bazar (a fine place for a drink), walk two blocks inland, and take a left past the heroic statues into...*

▲Mirabell Gardens and Palace (Schloss)

The bubbly gardens laid out in 1730 for the prince archbishop have been open to the public since 1850 (thanks to Emperor Franz Josef, who was rattled by the popular revolutions of 1848). The gardens are free and open until dusk. The palace is open only as a concert venue (explained later). The statues and the arbor (far left) were featured in *The Sound of Music*. Walk through the gardens to the palace. Look back, enjoy the garden/cathe-

dral/castle view, and imagine how the prince archbishop must have reveled in a vista that reminded him of all his secular and religious power. Then go around to the river side of the palace and find the horse.

The rearing **Pegasus statue** (rare and very well-balanced) is the site of a famous *Sound of Music* scene where the kids all danced before lining up on the stairs (with Maria 30 yards farther along). The steps lead to a small mound in the park (made of rubble from a former theater, and today a rendezvous point for Salzburg's gay community).

Nearest the horse, stairs lead between two lions to a pair of tough dwarfs (early volleyball players with spiked mittens) welcoming you to Salzburg's **Dwarf Park.** Cross the elevated walk (noticing the city's fortified walls) to meet statues of a dozen dwarfs who served the prince archbishop—modeled after real people with real fashions in about 1600. This was Mannerist art, from the hyper-realistic age that followed the Renaissance.

There's plenty of **music** here, both in the park and in the palace. A brass band plays free park concerts (May-Aug Sun at 10:30

and Wed with lighted fountains at 20:30, unless it's raining). To properly enjoy the lavish Mirabell Palace—once the prince archbishop's summer palace and now the seat of the mayor—get a ticket to a Schlosskonzerte (my favorite venue for a classical concert).

• *To visit Salzburg's best Mozart sight, go a long block southeast to Makartplatz, where, opposite the big and bright Hotel Bristol, you'll find...*

▲▲Mozart's Residence (Wohnhaus)

This reconstruction of Mozart's second home (his family moved here when he was 17) is the most informative Mozart sight in town. The English-language audioguide provides fascinating insight into Mozart's life and music, with the usual scores, old pianos, and an interesting 30-minute film (#17 on your audioguide for soundtrack) that runs continuously.

In the main hall—used by the Mozarts to entertain Salzburg's high society—you can hear original instruments from Mozart's time. Mozart was proud to be the first in his family to compose a duet. Notice the family portrait (c. 1780) on the wall, showing Mozart with his sister Nannerl, their father, and their mother—who'd died two years earlier in Paris. Mozart also had silly crude bull's-eyes made for the pop-gun game popular at the time (licking an "arse," Wolfgang showed his disdain for the rigors of high society). Later rooms feature real artifacts that explore his loves, his intellectual pursuits, his travels, and more.

Cost and Hours: €7, includes 1.5-hour audioguide, €12 combo-ticket includes Mozart's Birthplace in the old town, daily 9:00-17:30, July-Aug until 20:00, last entry 30 minutes before closing, allow at least one hour for visit, Makartplatz 8, tel. 0662/8742-2740.

• *From here, you can walk a few blocks back to the main bridge (Staatsbrücke), where you'll find the Platzl, a square once used as a hay market. Pause to enjoy the kid-pleasing little fountain. Near the fountain (with your back to the river), Steingasse leads darkly to the right.*

▲Steingasse Stroll

This street, a block in from the river, was part of the only road in the Middle Ages going south over the Alps to Venice (this was the first stop north of the Alps). Today, it's wonderfully tranquil and free of Salzburg's touristy crush. Inviting cocktail bars along here come alive at night.

At #9, a plaque (of questionable veracity) shows where Joseph Mohr, who wrote the words to "Silent Night," was born—poor and illegitimate—in 1792. There is no doubt, however, that the popular Christmas carol was composed and first sung in the village of Oberndorf, just outside of Salzburg, in 1818. Stairs lead from near here up to a 17th-century Capuchin monastery.

On the next corner, the wall is gouged out. This scar was left even after the building was restored, to serve as a reminder of the American GI who tried to get a tank down this road during a visit to the town brothel—two blocks farther up Steingasse.

At #19, find the carvings on the old door. Some say these are notices from beggars to the begging community (more numerous after post-Reformation religious wars, which forced many people out of their homes and towns)—a kind of "hobo code" indicating whether the residents would give or not. Trace the wires of the old-fashioned doorbells to the highest floors.

Farther on, you'll find a commanding Salzburg view across the river. Notice the red dome marking the oldest nunnery in the German-speaking world (established in 712) under the fortress and to the left. The real Maria, who inspired *The Sound of Music,* taught in this nunnery's school. In 1927, she and Captain von Trapp were married in the church you see here (not the church filmed in the movie). He was 47. She was 22. Hmmmm.

From here look back, above the arch you just passed through, at part of the town's medieval fortification. The coat of arms on the arch is of the prince archbishop who paid Bavaria a huge ransom to stay out of the Thirty Years' War (smart move). He then built this fortification (in 1634) in anticipation of rampaging armies from both sides.

Today, this street is for making love, not war. The Maison de Plaisir (a few doors down, at #24) has for centuries been a Salzburg brothel. But the climax of this walk is more touristic.

• *For a grand view, head back to the Platzl and the bridge, enter the Stein Hotel (left corner, overlooking the river), and ride the elevator to...*

Stein Terrasse

This café offers perhaps the best views in town (aside from the castle). Hidden from the tourist crush, it's a trendy, professional, local scene. You can discreetly peek at the view, or enjoy a drink or light meal (small snacks, indoor/outdoor seating, Sun-Thu 9:00-24:00, Fri-Sat 9:00-1:00 in the morning).

• *Back at the Platzl and the bridge, you can head straight up Linzergasse (away from the river) into a neighborhood packed with recommended accommodations, as well as our final new-town sight, the...*

▲St. Sebastian Cemetery

Wander through this quiet oasis. Mozart is buried in Vienna, his mom's in Paris, and his sister is in Salzburg's old town (St. Peter's)—but Wolfgang's wife Constanze ("Constantia") and his father Leopold are buried here (from the black iron gate entrance on Linzergasse, walk 17 paces and look left). When prince archbishop Wolf Dietrich had the cemetery moved from around the cathedral and put here, across the river, people didn't like it. To help popularize it, he had his own mausoleum built as its centerpiece. Continue straight past the Mozart tomb to this circular building (English description at door). In the corner to the left of the entrance is the tomb of

the Renaissance scientist and physician Paracelsus, best known for developing laudanum as a pain-killer.

Cost and Hours: Free, daily April-Oct 9:00-18:30, Nov-March 9:00-16:00, entry at Linzergasse 43 in summer; in winter go around the corner to the right, through the arch at #37, and around the building to the doorway under the blue seal.

Near Salzburg

▲Hellbrunn Castle—About the year 1610, prince archbishop Sittikus (after meditating on stewardship and Christ-like val-

ues) decided he needed a lavish palace with a vast and ornate garden purely for pleasure. He built this and just loved inviting his VIP guests out for fun with his trick fountains. Today, the visit is worthwhile for the Baroque garden, one of the oldest in Europe. More notably, it's full of clever fountains...and tour guides getting sadistic joy from soaking tourists. (Hint: When you see a wet place, cover your camera.) After buying your ticket, you must wait for the English tour and laugh and scramble through the entertaining 40-minute trick-water-toy tour, and are then free to tour the forgettable palace with an included audioguide.

While it can be fun—especially on a hot day or with kids—for many, it's a lot of trouble for a few water tricks. *Sound of Music* fans not taking an *S.O.M.* tour, however, may want to visit just to see the "Sixteen Going on Seventeen" gazebo, now located in the gardens.

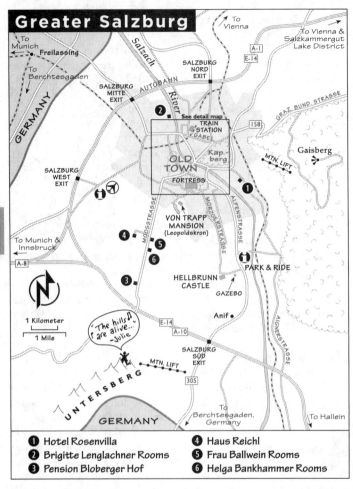

Greater Salzburg

1 Hotel Rosenvilla
2 Brigitte Lenglachner Rooms
3 Pension Bloberger Hof
4 Haus Reichl
5 Frau Ballwein Rooms
6 Helga Bankhammer Rooms

Cost and Hours: €9.50, daily May-Sept 9:00-17:30, July-Aug until 21:00—but tours from 18:00 on don't include the castle, mid-March-April and Oct 9:00-16:30, these are last tour times, closed Nov-mid-March, tel. 0662/820-3720, www.hellbrunn.at.

Getting There: Hellbrunn is nearly four miles south of Salzburg (bus #25 from station or from Staatsbrücke bridge, 2-3/hour, 20 minutes). In good weather, it makes a pleasant 30-minute bike excursion along the riverbank from Salzburg (described next).

▲▲**Riverside or Meadow Bike Ride**—The Salzach River has smooth, flat, and scenic bike lanes along each side (thanks to medieval tow paths—cargo boats would float downstream and be dragged back up by horses). On a sunny day, I can think of no more shout-worthy escape from the city. The nearly four-mile path upstream to Hellbrunn Castle is easy, with a worthy destination (leave Salzburg on castle side). For a nine-mile ride, continue on to Hallein (where you can tour a salt mine—see next listing; the north, or new-town, side of river is most scenic). Perhaps the most pristine, meadow-filled farm-country route is the four-mile Hellbrunner Allee from Akademiestrasse. Even a quickie ride across town is a great Salzburg experience. In the evening, the riverbanks are a world of floodlit spires.

▲**Hallein Bad Dürrnberg Salt Mine (Salzbergwerke)**—You'll be pitched plenty of different salt-mine excursions from Salzburg,

all of which cost substantial time and money. One's plenty. This salt-mine tour (above the town of Hallein, 9 miles from Salzburg) is a good choice. Wearing white overalls and sliding down the sleek wooden chutes, you'll cross underground from Austria into Germany while learning about the old-time salt-mining process. The tour entails lots of time on your feet as you walk from cavern to cavern, learning the history of the mine by watching a series of video skits with an actor channeling prince archbishop Wolf Dietrich. The visit also includes a "Celtic Village" open-air museum.

Cost and Hours: €18, allow 2.5 hours for the visit, daily April-Oct 9:00-17:00, Nov-March 10:00-15:00—these are last tour times, English-speaking guides—but let your linguistic needs be known loud and clear, tel. 06132/200-8511, www.salzwelten.at.

Getting There: The convenient *Salz Erlebnis* ticket from Salzburg's train station covers admission, train, and shuttle bus tickets, all in one money-saving round-trip ticket (€42, buy ticket at train station, no discount with railpass; 40-minute trip with hourly departures in each direction at about :15 after the hour, with synchronized train-bus connection in Hallein—schedule posted in flier).

▲▲**Hallstatt and Berchtesgaden**—Rustic Hallstatt, crammed like a swallow's nest into the narrow shore between a lake and a steep mountainside, is a 2.5-hour train ride from Salzburg, and my favorite town in the scenic Salzkammergut Lake District. Berchtesgaden (covered later in this chapter) is equally scenic, and home to Hitler's Eagle's Nest and other interesting sights. Both of these towns make for busy but worthwhile side-trips from Salzburg, and both are easy enough to do on your own. But if you're on a quick schedule, taking an all-day bus tour to these places can be a good use of your time and money.

Music in Salzburg

▲▲Salzburg Festival (Salzburger Festspiele)

Each summer, from late July to the end of August, Salzburg hosts its famous Salzburg Festival, founded in 1920 to employ Vienna's musicians in the summer. This fun and festive time is crowded, but there are usually plenty of beds (except for a few August weekends). Events take place primarily in three big halls: the Opera and Orchestra venues in the Festival House, and the Landes Theater, where German-language plays are performed. Tickets for the big festival events are generally expensive (€50-600) and sell out well in advance (bookable from January). Most tourists think they're "going to the Salzburg Festival" by seeing smaller non-festival events that go on during the festival weeks. For these lesser events, same-day tickets are normally available (the ticket office on Mozartplatz, in the TI, prints a daily list of concerts and charges a 30 percent fee to book them). For specifics on this year's festival schedule and tickets, visit www.salzburg festival.at, or contact the Austrian National Tourist Office in the United States (tel. 212/944-6880, fax 212/730-4568, www.austria .info, travel@austria.info).

▲▲Musical Events Year-Round

Salzburg is busy throughout the year, with 2,000 classical performances in its palaces and churches annually. Pick up the events calendar at the TI (free, bimonthly). I've never planned in advance, and I've enjoyed great concerts with every visit. Whenever you visit, you'll have a number of concerts (generally small chamber groups) to choose from. Here are some of the more accessible events:

Concerts at Hohensalzburg Fortress (Festungskonzerte)— Nearly nightly concerts—Mozart's greatest hits for beginners—are held atop Festungsberg, in the "prince's chamber" of the fortress, featuring small chamber groups (open seating after the first six more expensive rows, €31 or €38 plus €3.80 for the funicular; at 19:30, 20:00, or 20:30; doors open 30 minutes early, tel. 0662/825-858 to reserve, pick up tickets at the door). The medieval-feeling chamber has windows overlooking the city, and the concert gives you a chance to enjoy the grand city view and a stroll through the castle courtyard. (The funicular ticket costs €3.80 within an hour of the show—ideal for people who just want to ascend for the view.) For €51, you can combine the concert with a four-course dinner (starts 2 hours before concert).

Concerts at the Mirabell Palace (Schlosskonzerte)—The nearly nightly chamber music concerts at the Mirabell Palace are performed in a lavish Baroque setting. They come with more sophisticated programs and better musicians than the fortress concerts. Baroque music flying around a Baroque hall is a happy bird in the right cage (open seating after the first five pricier rows, €29-35, usually at 20:00—but check flier for times, doors open one hour ahead, tel. 0662/848-586, www.salzburger-schlosskonzerte.at).

"Five O'Clock Concerts" (5-Uhr-Konzerte)—These concerts—next to St. Peter's in the old town—are cheaper, since they feature young artists. While the series is formally named after the brother of Joseph Haydn, it offers music from various masters (€12-15, July-Sept Tue and Thu at 17:00, no concerts Oct-June, 45-60 minutes, tel. 0662/8445-7619, www.5-uhr-konzerte.com).

Mozart Piano Sonatas—St. Peter's Abbey hosts these concerts each weekend. This short (45-minute) and inexpensive concert is ideal for families (€18, €9 for children, €45 for a family of four, Fri and Sat at 19:00 year-round, in the abbey's Romanesque Hall—a.k.a. Romanischer Saal, tel. 0664/423-5645).

Marionette Theater—Salzburg's much-loved marionette theater offers operas with spellbinding marionettes and recorded music. Adults and kids alike are mesmerized by the little people on stage (€18-35, June-Sept nearly nightly at 17:00 or 19:30, none on Sun, also 3-4/week in May, some 14:00 matinees, box office open Mon-Sat 9:00-13:00 and 2 hours before shows, near the Mirabell Gardens and Mozart's Residence at Schwarzstrasse 24, tel. 0662/872-406, www.marionetten.at). For a sneak preview, check out the videos playing at the marionette exhibit up in the fortress.

Mozart Dinner Concert—For those who'd like some classical music but would rather not sit through a concert, the recommended Stiftskeller St. Peter restaurant offers a traditional candlelit meal with Mozart's greatest hits performed by a string quartet and singers in historic costumes gavotting among the tables. In this elegant Baroque setting, tourists clap between movements and get three courses of food (from Mozart-era recipes) mixed with three 20-minute courses of crowd-pleasing music (€51, Mozart-lovers with this guidebook pay €42 when booking direct, almost nightly at 20:00, dress is "smart casual," call to reserve at 0662/828-695, www.mozartdinnerconcert.com).

Sound of Salzburg Dinner Show—The show at the recommended Sternbräu Inn is Broadway in a dirndl with tired food. But it's a fun show, and *Sound of Music* fans leave with hands red from clapping. A piano player and a hardworking quartet of singers wearing historical costumes perform an entertaining mix of *S.O.M.* hits and traditional folk songs (€46 for dinner, begins at 19:30). You can also come by at 20:30, pay €32, skip the dinner, and get the show and a drink. Those who book direct (not through a hotel) and pay cash get a 10 percent discount with this

The Sound of Music Debunked

Rather than visit the real-life sights from the life of Maria von Trapp and family, most tourists want to see the places where Hollywood chose to film this fanciful story. Local guides are happy not to burst any *S.O.M.* pilgrim's bubble, but keep these points in mind:

- "Edelweiss" is not a cherished Austrian folk tune or national anthem. Like all the "Austrian" music in *The S.O.M.*, it was composed for Broadway by Rodgers and Hammerstein. It was, however, the last composition that the famed team wrote together, as Hammerstein died in 1960—nine months after the musical opened.
- *The S.O.M.* implies that Maria was devoutly religious throughout her life, but Maria's foster parents raised her as a socialist and atheist. Maria discovered her religious calling while studying to be a teacher. After completing school, she joined the convent not as a nun, but as a novitiate (that is, she hadn't taken her vows yet).
- Maria's position was not as governess to all the children, as portrayed in the musical, but specifically as governess and teacher for the Captain's second-oldest daughter, also called Maria, who was bedridden with rheumatic fever.
- The Captain didn't run a tight domestic ship. In fact, his seven children were as unruly as most. But he did use a whistle to call them—each kid was trained to respond to a certain pitch.
- Though the von Trapp family did have seven children, the show changed all their names and even their genders. Rupert, the eldest child, responded to the often-asked question, "Which one are you?" with a simple, "I'm Liesl!"
- The family didn't escape by hiking to Switzerland (which is a five-hour drive away). Rather, they pretended to go on one of their frequent mountain hikes. With only the possessions in their backpacks, they "hiked" all the way to the train station

book (nightly mid-May-mid-Oct, Griesgasse 23, tel. 0662/826-617, www.soundofsalzburgshow.com).

Music at Mass—Each Sunday morning, three great churches offer a Mass, generally with glorious music. The Salzburg Cathedral is likely your best bet for fine music to worship by (10:00). The Franciscan church—the locals' choice—is enthusiastic about its musical Masses (at 9:00). St. Peter's Church also has music (10:30). See the Salzburg events guide (available at TIs) for details.

Free Brass Band Concert—A traditional brass band plays in the Mirabell Gardens (May-Aug Sun at 10:30 and Wed with lighted fountains at 20:30).

(it was at the edge of their estate) and took a train to Italy. The movie scene showing them climbing into Switzerland was actually filmed near Berchtesgaden, Germany...home to Hitler's Eagle's Nest, and certainly not a smart place to flee to.

- The actual von Trapp family house exists...but it's not the one in the film. The mansion in the movie is actually two different buildings—one used for the front, the other for the back. The interiors were all filmed on Hollywood sets.

- For the film, Boris Levin designed a reproduction of the Nonnberg Abbey courtyard so faithful to the original (down to its cobblestones and stained-glass windows) that many still believe the cloister scenes were really shot at the abbey. And no matter what you hear in Salzburg, the graveyard scene (in which the von Trapps hide from the Nazis) was also filmed on the Fox lot.

- In 1956, a German film producer offered Maria $10,000 for the rights to her book. She asked for royalties, too, and a share of the profits. The agent claimed that German law forbids film companies from paying royalties to foreigners (Maria had by then become a US citizen). She agreed to the contract and unknowingly signed away all film rights to her story. Only a few weeks later, he offered to pay immediately if she would accept $9,000 in cash. Because it was more money than the family had seen in all of their years of singing, she accepted the deal. Later, she discovered the agent had swindled them—no such law existed.

  Rodgers, Hammerstein, and other producers gave the von Trapps a percentage of the royalties, even though they weren't required to—but it was a fraction of what they otherwise would have earned. But Maria wasn't bitter. "The great good the film and the play are doing to individual lives is far beyond money," she said.

Sleeping in Salzburg

Finding a room in Salzburg, even during its music festival (mid-July-Aug), is usually easy. Rates rise significantly (20-30 percent) during the music festival, and sometimes around Easter and Christmas; these higher prices do not appear in the ranges I've listed. Many places charge 10 percent extra for a one-night stay. Remember, to call

SALZBURG

Sleep Code

(€1 = about $1.40, country code: 43, area code: 0662)
S = Single, **D** = Double/Twin, **T** = Triple, **Q** = Quad, **b** = bathroom,
s = shower only. Unless otherwise noted, credit cards are
accepted and breakfast is included. All of these places speak
English.

To help you sort easily through these listings, I've divided
the accommodations into three categories, based on the price
for a standard double room with bath:

$$$ Higher Priced—Most rooms €90 or more.
  $$ Moderately Priced—Most rooms between €60-90.
   $ Lower Priced—Most rooms €60 or less.

Prices can change without notice; verify the hotel's
current rates online or by email. For other updates, see www
.ricksteves.com/update.

Salzburg from Germany, dial 00-43 and then the number (minus
the initial zero).

In the New Town, North of the River

These listings, clustering around Linzergasse, are in a pleasant
neighborhood (with easy parking) a 15-minute walk from the
train station (for directions, see "Arrival in Salzburg," earlier) and
a 10-minute walk to the old town. If you're coming from the old
town, simply cross the main bridge (Staatsbrücke) to the mostly
traffic-free Linzergasse. If driving, exit the highway at Salzburg-
Nord, follow Vogelweiderstrasse straight to its end, and turn
right.

$$$ Altstadthotel Wolf-Dietrich, around the corner from
Linzergasse on pedestrians-only Wolf-Dietrich-Strasse, is well-
located (half its rooms overlook St. Sebastian Cemetery). With
27 tastefully plush rooms, it's a good value for a big, stylish hotel
(Sb-€80, Db-€120, price depends on size, family deals, €20-40
more during festival, complex pricing but readers of this book
get a 10 percent discount on prevailing price—insist on this dis-
count deducted from whatever price is offered that day, elevator,
free Internet access and Wi-Fi, pool with loaner swimsuits, sauna,
free DVD library, Wolf-Dietrich-Strasse 7, tel. 0662/871-275, fax
0662/871-2759, www.salzburg-hotel.at, office@salzburg-hotel.at).
Their annex across the street has 14 equally comfortable rooms
(€20 less, no elevator).

$$$ Hotel Trumer Stube, well-located three blocks from
the river just off Linzergasse, has 20 clean rooms and is warmly

run by the Hirschbichler family (official rates: Sb-€65, Db-€105, Tb-€128, Qb-€147—email and ask for the best Rick Steves cash-only rate; buffet breakfast extra, non-smoking, elevator, free Wi-Fi, easy parking, Bergstrasse 6, tel. 0662/874-776, fax 0662/874-326, www.trumer-stube.at, info@trumer-stube.at; the mom and daughter, both named Marianne, may charm you into extending your Salzburg stay).

$$$ **Hotel Goldene Krone,** about five blocks from the river, is plain and basic, with 20 big, quiet, creaky, and well-kept rooms. Stay a while in their pleasant cliffside garden (Sb-€69, Db-€119, Tb-€159, Qb-€189, claim your 15 percent discount off these prices with this book, dim lights, elevator, free Wi-Fi, parking-€12/day, Linzergasse 48, tel. 0662/872-300, fax 0662/8723-0066, www.hotel-goldenekrone.com, office@hotel-goldenekrone.com, Günther Hausknost). Günther offers tours (€10/person, 2 hours, 5 people minimum) and a "Rick Steves Two Nights in Salzburg" deal, which covers your room, a 24-hour Salzburg Card, a concert in Mirabell Palace, and a tour with Günther (Sb-€171, Db-€304, Tb-€429, Qb-€532; book on the hotel's website).

$$ **Hotel Schwarzes Rössl** is a university dorm that becomes a student-run hotel each July, August, and September. The location couldn't be handier. It looks like a normal hotel from the outside, and its 50 rooms, while a bit spartan, are as comfortable as a hotel on the inside (S-€50, Sb-€60, D-€80, Db-€100, Tb-€132, good breakfast, Internet access and Wi-Fi, no rooms rented Oct-June, just off Linzergasse at Priesterhausgasse 6, tel. 0662/874-426, www.academiahotels.at, schwarzes.roessl@academiahotels.at).

$$ **Institute St. Sebastian** is in a somewhat sterile but very clean historic building next to St. Sebastian Cemetery. From October through June, the institute houses female students from various Salzburg colleges and also rents 40 beds for travelers (men and women). From July through September, the students are gone, and they rent all 100 beds (including 20 twin rooms) to travelers. The building has spacious public areas, a roof garden, a piano that guests are welcome to play, and some of the best rooms and dorm beds in town for the money. The immaculate doubles come with modern baths and head-to-toe twin beds (S-€36, Sb-€44, D-€55, Db-€70, Tb-€84, Qb-€98, includes simple breakfast, elevator, self-service laundry-€4/load; reception open daily July-Sept 7:30-12:00 & 13:00-21:30, Oct-June 8:00-12:00 & 16:00-21:00; Linzergasse 41, enter through arch at #37, tel. 0662/871-386, fax 0662/8713-8685, www.st-sebastian-salzburg.at, office@st-sebastian-salzburg.at). Students like the €21 bunks in 4- to 10-bed dorms (€2 less if you have sheets, no lockout, free lockers, free showers). You'll find self-service kitchens on each floor (fridge space is free; request a key). If you need parking, request it well in advance.

Salzburg Hotels

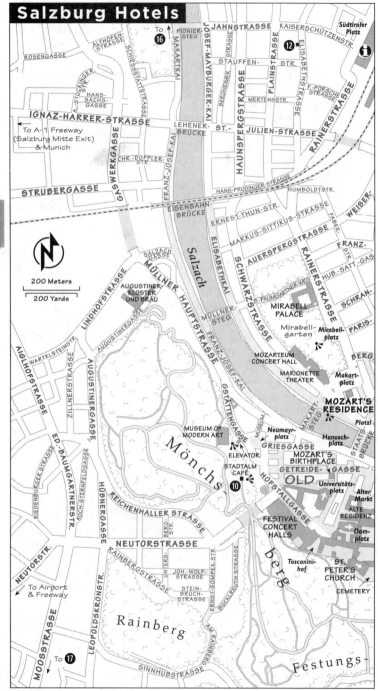

SALZBURG

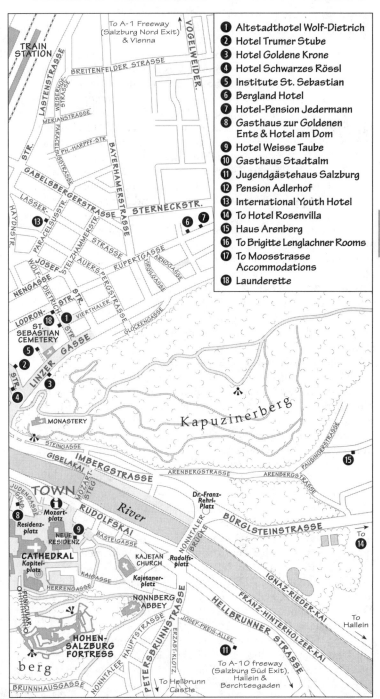

1 Altstadthotel Wolf-Dietrich
2 Hotel Trumer Stube
3 Hotel Goldene Krone
4 Hotel Schwarzes Rössl
5 Institute St. Sebastian
6 Bergland Hotel
7 Hotel-Pension Jedermann
8 Gasthaus zur Goldenen Ente & Hotel am Dom
9 Hotel Weisse Taube
10 Gasthaus Stadtalm
11 Jugendgästehaus Salzburg
12 Pension Adlerhof
13 International Youth Hotel
14 To Hotel Rosenvilla
15 Haus Arenberg
16 To Brigitte Lenglachner Rooms
17 To Moosstrasse Accommodations
18 Launderette

SALZBURG

Pensions on Rupertgasse: These two hotels are about five blocks farther from the river on Rupertgasse, a breeze for drivers but with more street noise than the places on Linzergasse. They're both modern and well-run—good values if you don't mind being a bit away from the old town. **$$$ Bergland Hotel** is charming and classy, with comfortable neo-rustic rooms. It's a modern building and therefore spacious and solid (Sb-€65, Db-€100, Tb-€125, Qb-€155, elevator, pay Internet access, free Wi-Fi, English library, bike rental-€6/day, Rupertgasse 15, tel. 0662/872-318, fax 0662/872-3188, www.berglandhotel.at, office@berglandhotel.at, Kuhn family). The similar, boutique-like **$$$ Hotel-Pension Jedermann,** a few doors down, is tastefully done and comfortable, with an artsy painted-concrete ambience and a backyard garden (Sb-€65, Db-€95, Tb-€120, Qb-€160, much more during festival, elevator, free Internet access and Wi-Fi, Rupertgasse 25, tel. 0662/873-2410, fax 0662/873-2419, www.hotel-jedermann.com, office@hotel-jedermann.com, Herr und Frau Gmachl).

In or Above the Old Town

Most of these hotels are near Residenzplatz. While this area is car-restricted, you're allowed to drive your car in to unload, pick up a map and parking instructions, and head for the €14-per-day garage in the mountain.

$$$ Gasthaus zur Goldenen Ente is in a 600-year-old building with medieval stone arches and narrow stairs. Located above a good restaurant, it's as central as you can be on a pedestrian street in old Salzburg. The 22 rooms are modern and newly renovated, and include classy amenities. While the advertised rates are too high, travelers with this book get 10 percent off (except in July-Aug), and prices may dip lower according to demand. Ulrike, Franziska, and Anita run a tight ship for the absentee owners (most of the year: Sb-€85, Db-€125; late July-Aug and Dec: Sb-€95, Db-€160; extra person-€40, firm mattresses, elevator, free Internet access, Goldgasse 10, tel. 0662/845-622, fax 0662/845-6229, www.ente.at, hotel@ente.at).

$$$ Hotel Weisse Taube has 30 comfortable rooms in a quiet dark-wood 14th-century building, well-located about a block off Mozartplatz (Sb-€69-88, Db with shower-€98-139, bigger Db with bath-€119-172, 10 percent discount with this book if you reserve direct and pay cash, elevator, pay Internet access and Wi-Fi, tel. 0662/842-404, fax 0662/841-783, Kaigasse 9, www.weissetaube.at, hotel@weissetaube.at).

$$$ Hotel am Dom is perfectly located—on Goldgasse a few steps from the cathedral—and offers 15 chic rooms, some with their original wood-beam ceilings (twin Db-€90-160, standard Db-€130-240, "superior" Db-€150-290, air-con, non-smoking, free Internet access and Wi-Fi, Goldgasse 17, tel. 0662/842-765, fax 0662/8427-6555, www.hotelamdom.at, office@hotelamdom.at).

Hostels

For another hostel (on the other side of the river), see "International Youth Hotel," on the next page.

$ **Gasthaus Stadtalm** (a.k.a. the *Naturfreundehaus*) is a local version of a mountaineer's hut and a great budget alternative. Snuggled in a forest on the remains of a 15th-century castle wall atop the little mountain overlooking Salzburg, it has magnificent town and mountain views. While the 22 beds are designed-for-backpackers basic, the price and view are the best in town—with the right attitude, it's a fine experience (€18.50/person in 4- and 6-bed dorms, same price for room with double bed; includes breakfast, sheets, and shower; lockers, 2 minutes from top of €2 Mönchsberg elevator, Mönchsberg 19C, tel. & fax 0662/841-729, www.diestadtalm.com, info@diestadtalm.com, Peter). Once you've dropped your bags here, it's a five-minute walk down the cliffside stairs into Toscanini Hof, in the middle of the old town (path always lit).

$ **Jugendgästehaus Salzburg,** just steps from the old town center, is nevertheless removed from the bustle. While its dorm rooms are the standard crammed-with-beds variety—and the hallways will bring back high-school memories—the doubles and family rooms are modern, roomy, and bright, and the public spaces are quite pleasant (bed in 8-person dorm-€23; Db, Tb, and Qb available at much higher prices; includes breakfast and sheets, pay Internet access, free Wi-Fi, *The Sound of Music* plays daily, bike rental-€10/day or €6/half-day, free parking, just around the east side of the castle hill at Josef-Preis-Allee 18; from train station, take bus #5 or #25 to the Justizgebäude stop, then head left one block along the bushy wall, cross Petersbrunnstrasse, find shady Josefs-Preis-Alle, and walk a few minutes to the end—the hostel is the big orange/green building on the right; tel. 0662/842-670, fax 0662/841-101, www.jufa.at/salzburg, salzburg@jufa.at). The hotel at the back of the hostel isn't as cheap, but does offer more standard hotel amenities, such as TVs (Db-€110 depending on season, includes breakfast).

Near the Train Station

$$ **Pension Adlerhof,** a plain and decent old pension, is two blocks in front of the train station (left off Kaiserschutzenstrasse), but a 15-minute walk from the sightseeing action. It has a quirky staff, a boring location, and 30 stodgy-but-spacious rooms (Sb-€56, Db-€80, Tb-€115, Qb-€130, price varies a bit with the season and size of room, cash only, elevator, pay Internet access and free

Wi-Fi, limited free parking, Elisabethstrasse 25, tel. 0662/875-236, fax 0662/873-663, www.gosalzburg.com, adlerhof@pension-adlerhof.at).

$ International Youth Hotel, a.k.a. the "Yo-Ho," is the most lively, handy, and American of Salzburg's hostels. This backpacker haven is a youthful and easygoing place that speaks English first; has cheap meals, 186 beds, lockers, tour discounts, and no curfew; plays *The Sound of Music* free daily at 10:30; runs a lively bar; and welcomes anyone of any age. The noisy atmosphere and lack of a curfew can make it hard to sleep (€18-19/person in 4- to 8-bed dorms, €21-22 in dorms with bathrooms, D-€55, Ds-€65, Q-€72, Qs-€81, includes sheets, cheap breakfast, pay Internet access, free Wi-Fi, laundry-€4 wash and dry, 6 blocks from station toward Linzergasse and 6 blocks from river at Paracelsusstrasse 9, tel. 0662/879-649, fax 0662/878-810, www.yoho.at, office@yoho.at).

Four-Star Hotels in Residential Neighborhoods away from the Center

If you want plush furnishings, spacious public spaces, generous balconies, gardens, and free parking, consider the following places. These two modern hotels in nondescript residential neighborhoods are a fine value if you don't mind the 15-minute walk from the old town. While not ideal for train travelers, drivers in need of no-stress comfort for a home base should consider these.

$$$ Hotel Rosenvilla, close to the river, offers 16 rooms with bright furnishings, surrounded by a leafy garden (Sb-€79-108, Db-€135-165, bigger Db-€145-199, Db suite-€168-255, at least €30 more during festival, free Wi-Fi, Höfelgasse 4, tel. 0662/621-765, fax 0662/625-2308, www.rosenvilla.com, hotel@rosenvilla.com).

$$$ Haus Arenberg, higher up opposite the old town, rents 17 big, breezy rooms—most with generous balconies—in a quiet garden setting (Sb-€85-105, Db-€129-165, Tb-€149-176, Qb-€158-185, higher prices are during festival, Blumensteinstrasse 8, tel. 0662/640-097, fax 0662/640-0973, www.arenberg-salzburg.at, info@arenberg-salzburg.at, family Leobacher).

Private Rooms (Privatzimmer)

These are generally roomy and comfortable, and come with a good breakfast, easy parking, and tourist information. Off-season, competition softens prices. While they are a bus ride from town, with a €4.20 transit day pass *(Tageskarte)* and the frequent service, this shouldn't keep you away. In fact, most homeowners will happily pick you up at the train station if you simply telephone them and ask. Most will also do laundry for a small fee for those staying at least two nights. I've listed prices for two nights or more—if staying only one night, expect a 10 percent surcharge. Most push tours and concerts to make money on the side. As they are earning a commission, if you go through them, you'll probably lose the discount I've negotiated for my readers who go direct.

Beyond the Train Station

$ **Brigitte Lenglachner** rents eight basic, well-cared-for rooms in her home in a quiet suburban-feeling neighborhood that's a 25-minute walk, 10-minute bike ride, or easy bus ride away from the center. Frau Lenglachner serves breakfast in the garden (in good weather) and happily provides plenty of local information and advice (S-€25, D-€40, Db-€49, Tb-€68, Qb-€96, 5b-€113; apartment with kitchen—Db-€56, Tb-€95, Qb-€110; apartment requires minimum 3-night stay, easy and free parking, Scheibenweg 8, tel. & fax 0662/438-044, www.bei-brigitte.at, bedandbreakfast 4u@yahoo.de). It's a 10-minute walk from the station: Head for the river, cross the pedestrian Pioneer Bridge (Pioniersteg), turn right, and walk along the river to the third street (Scheibenweg). Turn left, and it's halfway down on the right.

On Moosstrasse

The busy street called Moosstrasse, which runs southwest of Mönchsberg (behind the mountain and away from the old town center), is lined with farmhouses offering rooms. Handy bus #21 connects Moosstrasse to the center frequently (Mon-Fri 4/hour until 19:00, Sat 4/hour until 17:00, evenings and Sun 2/hour, 20 minutes). To get to these pensions from the train station, take bus #1, #5, #6, or #25 to Makartplatz, where you'll change to #21. If you're coming from the old town, catch bus #21 from Hanuschplatz, just downstream of the Staatsbrücke bridge near the *Tabak* kiosk. Buy a €1.90 *Einzelkarte-Kernzone* ticket (for one trip) or a €4.20 *Tageskarte* (day pass, good for 24 hours) from the street-side machine and punch it when you board the bus. The bus stop you use for each place is included in the following listings. If you're driving from the center, go through the tunnel, continue straight on Neutorstrasse, and take the fourth left onto Moosstrasse. Drivers exit the autobahn at *Süd* and then head in the direction of *Grodig*. Each place can recommend a favorite Moosstrasse eatery (Reiterhof, at #151, is particularly popular).

$$ **Pension Bloberger Hof,** while more a hotel than a pension, is comfortable and friendly, with a peaceful, rural location

and 20 farmer-plush, good-value rooms. It's the farthest out, but reached by the same bus #21 from the center. Inge and her daughter Sylvia offer a 10 percent discount to those who have this book, reserve direct, and pay cash (Sb-€55-70, Db-€75-80, big new Db with balcony-€95-100, Db suite-€120, extra bed-€20, 10 percent extra for one-night stays, family apartment with kitchen, non-smoking, free Internet access and Wi-Fi, restaurant for guests, free loaner bikes, free station pickup if staying 3 nights, Hammerauer Strasse 4, bus stop: Hammerauer Strasse, tel. 0662/830-227, fax 0662/827-061, www.blobergerhof.at, office@blobergerhof.at).

$$ Haus Reichl, with three good rooms at the end of a long lane, feels the most remote. Franziska offers free loaner bikes for guests (20-minute pedal to the center) and bakes fresh cakes most days (Sb-€36-45, Db-€58-64, Tb-€75-84, Qb-€92-104, cash preferred, doubles and triples have balcony and view, all have in-room tea/coffee, non-smoking, between Ballwein and Bankhammer B&Bs, 200 yards down Reiterweg to #52, bus stop: Gsengerweg, tel. & fax 0662/826-248, www.privatzimmer.at/haus-reichl, haus.reichl@telering.at).

$ Frau Ballwein offers four cozy, charming, and fresh rooms in two buildings, some with intoxicating-view balconies (Sb-€35-45, Db-€53-64, Tb-€75-85, Qb-€80-95, 2-bedroom apartment for up to 5 people-€95-110, prices depend on season, family deals, cash only, farm-fresh breakfasts amid her hanging teapot collection, non-smoking, small pool, 2 free loaner bikes, free parking, Moosstrasse 69-A, bus stop: Gsengerweg, tel. & fax 0662/824-029, www.haus-ballwein.at, haus.ballwein@gmx.net).

$ Helga Bankhammer rents four nondescript rooms in a farmhouse, with a real dairy farm out back (D-€44, Db-€55, no surcharge for one-night stays, family deals, non-smoking, laundry about €6/load, Moosstrasse 77, bus stop: Marienbad, tel. & fax 0662/830-067, www.privatzimmer.at/helga.bankhammer, bankhammer@aon.at).

Eating in Salzburg

In the Old Town

Salzburg boasts many inexpensive, fun, and atmospheric eateries. Most of these restaurants are centrally located in the old town, famous with visitors but also enjoyed by locals.

Gasthaus zum Wilden Mann is *the* place if the weather's bad and you're in the mood for *Hofbräu* atmosphere and a hearty, cheap meal at a shared table in one small, smoky, well-antlered room. Notice the 1899 flood photo on the wall. For a quick lunch, get the *Bauernschmaus,* a mountain of dumplings, kraut, and peasant's meats (€11.50). While they have a few outdoor tables, the atmosphere is all indoors, and the menu is not great for hot-weather food. Owner Robert—who runs the restaurant with Schwarzenegger-like energy—enjoys fostering a convivial ambience (you'll share tables with strangers) and serving fresh traditional cuisine at great prices. I simply love this place (€8.50 two-course lunch specials, €10-12 daily specials posted on the wall, kitchen open Mon-Sat 11:00-21:00, closed Sun, 2 minutes from Mozart's Birthplace, enter from Getreidegasse 22 or Griesgasse 17, tel. 0662/841-787).

Stiftskeller St. Peter has been in business for more than 1,000 years—it was mentioned in the biography of Charlemagne. It's classy and high-end touristy, serving uninspired traditional Austrian cuisine. Through the centuries, they've learned to charge for each piece of bread and don't serve free tap water (€10-27 meals, daily 11:30-22:30, indoor/outdoor seating, next to St. Peter's Church at foot of Mönchsberg, restaurant tel. 0662/841-268). They host the Mozart Dinner Concert.

St. Paul's Stub'n Beer Garden is tucked secretly away under the castle with a decidedly untouristy atmosphere. The food is better than a beer hall, and a young, bohemian-chic clientele fills its two troll-like rooms and its idyllic tree-shaded garden. *Kasnock'n* is a tasty mountaineers' pasta with cheese served in an iron pan with a side salad for €9—it's enough for two (€6-12 daily specials, €7-15 plates, Mon-Sat 17:00-22:30, open later for drinks only, closed Sun, Herrengasse 16, tel. 0662/843-220).

Zirkelwirt serves modern Mediterranean, Italian, and Austrian dishes, a daily fish special, and always a good vegetarian option. It's an old *Gasthaus* dining room with a medieval tiki-hut terrace a block off Mozartplatz, yet a world away from the tourism of the old town. While the waitstaff, music, and vibe feel young, it attracts Salzburgers of all ages (€9-15 plates, cheese dumplings and daily fish special, nightly 17:00-24:00, Pfeifergasse 14, tel. 0662/843-472).

Fisch Krieg Restaurant, on the river where the fishermen used to sell their catch, is a great value. They serve fast, fresh, and inexpensive fish in a casual dining room—where trees grow through the ceiling—as well as great riverside seating (€2 fish-wiches to go, self-serve €7 meals, salad bar, Mon-Fri 8:30-18:30, Sat 8:30-13:00, closed Sun, Hanuschplatz 4, tel. 0662/843-732).

Sternbräu Inn, a sloppy, touristy Austrian food circus, is a sprawling complex of popular eateries (traditional, Italian, self-serve, and vegetarian) in a cheery garden setting. Explore both courtyards before choosing a seat (Bürgerstube is classic, most restaurants open daily 9:00-24:00 with food served until 23:00, enter from Getreidegasse 34, tel. 0662/842-140). One fancy, air-conditioned room hosts the Sound of Salzburg dinner show.

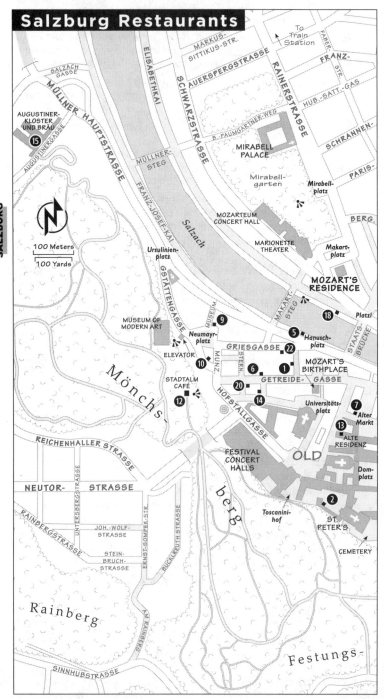

Salzburg Restaurants

SALZBURG

To Train Station

MARKUS-SITTIKUS-STR.

ELISABETHKAI

SCHWARZSTRASSE

AUERSPERGSTRASSE

RAINERSTRASSE

FRANZ-STR.

FABER-STR.

HUB.-SATT.-GAS.

SCHRANNEN-

PARIS-

SALZACH GASSE

MÜLLNER HAUPTSTRASSE

AUGUSTINER-KLOSTER UND BRÄU
15

AUGUSTINERGASSE

MÜLLNER STEG

FRANZ-JOSEF-KAI

B.-PAUMGARTNER-WEG

MIRABELL PALACE

Mirabell-garten

Mirabell-platz

BERG

Salzach

MOZARTEUM CONCERT HALL

MARIONETTE THEATER

Makart-platz

100 Meters

100 Yards

Ursulinien-platz

GSTÄTTENGASSE

MUSEUM OF MODERN ART

Neumayr-platz

ELEVATOR

9

MUSEUM

MAKART-STEG

MOZART'S RESIDENCE

18

Platzl

5

Hanusch-platz

STAATS-BRÜCKE

GRIESGASSE

22

STERN

MÜNZ

6

1

MOZART'S BIRTHPLACE

GETREIDE-GASSE

10

STADTALM CAFÉ

12

20

14

Universitäts-platz

7
Alter Markt

13

ALTE RESIDENZ

Möchs-

HOFSTALLGASSE

FESTIVAL CONCERT HALLS

OLD

Dom-platz

REICHENHALLER STRASSE

NEUTOR-

STRASSE

UNTERSBERGSTRASSE

JOH.-WOLF-STRASSE

ERNST-SOMPEK-STR.

BÜCKLREUTH STRASSE

STEIN-BRUCH-STRASSE

RAINBERGSTRASSE

berg

Toscanini-hof

2

ST. PETER'S

CEMETERY

Rainberg

AM RAINBERG

SINNHUBSTRASSE

Festungs-

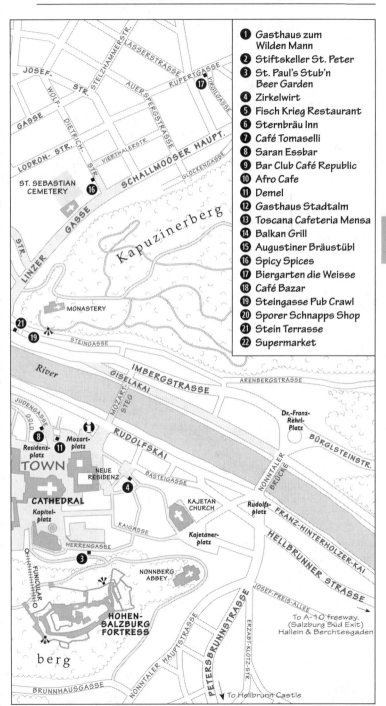

1. Gasthaus zum Wilden Mann
2. Stiftskeller St. Peter
3. St. Paul's Stub'n Beer Garden
4. Zirkelwirt
5. Fisch Krieg Restaurant
6. Sternbräu Inn
7. Café Tomaselli
8. Saran Essbar
9. Bar Club Café Republic
10. Afro Cafe
11. Demel
12. Gasthaus Stadtalm
13. Toscana Cafeteria Mensa
14. Balkan Grill
15. Augustiner Bräustübl
16. Spicy Spices
17. Biergarten die Weisse
18. Café Bazar
19. Steingasse Pub Crawl
20. Sporer Schnapps Shop
21. Stein Terrasse
22. Supermarket

Café Tomaselli (with its Kiosk annex and terrace seating across the way) has long been Salzburg's top place to see and be seen. While pricey, it is good for lingering and people-watching. Tomaselli serves light meals and lots of drinks, keeps long hours daily, and has fine seating on the square, a view terrace upstairs, and indoor tables. Despite its fancy inlaid wood paneling, 19th-century portraits, and chandeliers, it's surprisingly low-key (€3-7 light meals, daily 7:00-21:00, until 24:00 during music festival, Alter Markt 9, tel. 0662/844-488).

Saran Essbar is the product of hardworking Mr. Saran (from the Punjab), who cooks and serves with his heart. This delightful little eatery casts a rich orange glow under medieval vaults. Its fun menu is small (Mr. Saran is committed to both freshness and value), mixing Austrian (great schnitzel and strudel), Italian, and Asian vegetarian, and always offering salads (€10-15 meals, daily 11:00-22:00, often open later, a block off Mozartplatz at Judengasse 10, tel. 0662/846-628).

Bar Club Café Republic, a hip hangout for local young people near the end of Getreidegasse, feels like a theater lobby during intermission. It serves good food with smoky indoor and outdoor seating. It's ideal if you want something mod, untouristy, and un-wursty (trendy breakfasts 8:00-18:00, Asian and international menu, €9-15 plates, lots of hard drinks, daily until late, music with a DJ Fri and Sat from 23:00, salsa dance club Tue night from 21:00, no cover, Anton Neumayr Platz 2, tel. 0662/841-613).

Afro Cafe, between Getreidegasse and the Mönchsberg lift, is a hit with local students. Its agenda: to put a fun spin on African cuisine (adapted to European tastes). It serves tea, coffee, cocktails, and tasty food with a dose of '70s funk and a healthy sense of humor. The menu includes pan-African specialties—try the spicy chicken couscous—as well as standard soups and salads (€9-13 main courses, Mon-Fri 9:00-24:00, closed Sun, between Getreidegasse and cliff face at Bürgerspitalplatz 5, tel. 0662/844-888).

Demel, an outpost of Vienna's famed chocolatier, is a wonderland of desserts that are as beautiful as they are delectable. Sink into the pink couches upstairs, or have them box up a treat for later (daily 9:00-19:00, near TI and cathedral at Mozartplatz 2, tel. 0662/840-358).

On the Cliffs Above the Old Town: **Gasthaus Stadtalm,** Salzburg's mountaineers' hut, sits high above the old town on the edge of the cliff with cheap prices, good food, and great views. If hiking across Mönchsberg, make this your goal (traditional food, salads, cliffside garden seating or cozy-mountain-hut indoor seating—one indoor view table is booked for a decade of New Year's celebrations, daily 10:00-18:00, July-Aug until 23:00, 2 minutes from top of €3.20 round-trip Mönchsberg elevator, also reachable by stairs from Toscanini Hof, Mönchsberg 19C, tel. 0662/841-729, Peter).

Eating Cheaply in the Old Town

Toscana Cafeteria Mensa is the students' lunch canteen, fast and cheap—with indoor seating and a great courtyard for sitting outside with students and teachers instead of tourists. They serve a daily soup-and-main course special for €5 (Mon-Fri 8:30-18:00, hot meals served 11:00-13:30 only, closed Sat-Sun, behind the Old Residenz, in the courtyard opposite Sigmund-Haffner-Gasse 16).

Sausage stands *(Würstelstände)* serve the town's favorite "fast food." The best stands (like those on Universitätsplatz) use the same boiling water all day, which gives the weenies more flavor. The Salzburgers' favorite spicy sausage is sold at the 60-year-old **Balkan Grill,** run by chatty Frau Ebner (€3; survey the five spicy options—described in English—and choose a number; takeaway only, steady and sturdy local crowd, daily 11:00-19:00, hours vary with demand, hiding down the tunnel at Getreidegasse 33 across from Eisgrotte).

Picnickers will appreciate the bustling morning **produce market** (daily except Sun) on Universitätsplatz behind Mozart's Birthplace, as well as the well-stocked **Billa supermarket** (Mon-Fri 7:15-19:30, Sat 7:15-18:00, closed Sun), just across the street from the recommended Fisch Krieg Restaurant on Griesgasse.

Away from the Center

Augustiner Bräustübl, a huge 1,000-seat beer garden within a monk-run brewery in the Kloster Mülln, is rustic and raw. On busy nights, it's like a Munich beer hall with no music but the

volume turned up. When it's cool outside, you'll enjoy a historic setting inside beer-sloshed and smoke-stained halls. On balmy evenings, it's like a Renoir painting—but with beer breath—under chestnut trees. Local students mix with tourists eating hearty slabs of schnitzel with their fingers or cold meals from the self-serve picnic counter, while children frolic on the playground kegs. For your beer: Pick up a half-liter or full-liter mug, pay the lady (*schank* means self-serve price, *bedienung* is the price with waiter service), wash your mug, give Mr. Keg your receipt and empty mug, and you will be made happy. Waiters only bring beer; they don't bring food—instead, go up the stairs, survey the hallway of deli counters, and assemble your own meal (or, as long as you buy a drink, you can bring in a picnic). Classic pretzels from the bakery and spiraled, salty radishes make great beer even better. For dessert—after a visit to the strudel kiosk—enjoy the incomparable floodlit view of old Salzburg from the nearby Müllnersteg pedestrian bridge and a riverside stroll home (open daily 15:00-23:00, Augustinergasse 4, tel. 0662/431-246).

Getting There: It's about a 15-minute walk along the river (with the river on your right) from the Staatsbrücke bridge. After passing the pedestrian Müllnersteg bridge, just after Café am Kai, follow the stairs up to a busy street, and cross it. From here, either continue up more stairs into the trees and around the small church (for a scenic approach to the monastery), or stick to the sidewalk as it curves around to Augustinergasse. Either way, your goal is the huge yellow building. Don't be fooled by second-rate gardens serving the same beer nearby.

North of the River, near Recommended Linzergasse Hotels

Spicy Spices is a trippy vegetarian-Indian restaurant where Suresh Syal (a.k.a. "Mr. Spicy") serves tasty curry and rice, samosas, organic salads, vegan soups, and fresh juices. It's a *namaste* kind of place, where everything's proudly organic (€6.50 specials, Mon-Fri 10:30-21:30, Sat-Sun 12:00-21:30, takeout available, Wolf-Dietrich-Strasse 1, tel. 0662/870-712).

Biergarten die Weisse, close to the hotels on Rupertgasse and away from the tourists, is a longtime hit with the natives. If a beer hall can be happening, this one—modern yet with antlers—is it. Their famously good beer is made right there; favorites include their fizzy wheat beer *(Weisse)* and their seasonal beers (on request). Enjoy the beer with their good, cheap traditional food in the great garden seating, or in the wide variety of indoor rooms—sports bar, young and noisy, or older and more elegant (daily specials, Mon-Sat 10:00-24:00, closed Sun, Rupertgasse 10, east of Bayerhamerstrasse, tel. 0662/872-246).

Café Bazar, overlooking the river between Mirabell Gardens and the Staatsbrücke bridge, is as close as you'll get to a Vienna coffee house in Salzburg. It's *the* venerable spot for a classy drink with an old-town-and-castle view (light meals, Mon-Sat 7:30-23:00, Sun 9:00-18:00, Schwarzstrasse 3, tel. 0662/874-278).

Steingasse Pub Crawl

For a fun post-concert activity, crawl through medieval Steingasse's trendy pubs (all open until the wee hours). This is a local and hip scene, but accessible to older tourists: dark bars filled with well-dressed Salzburgers lazily smoking cigarettes and talking philosophy as avant-garde Euro-pop throbs on the soundtrack. Most of the pubs are in cellar-like caves...extremely atmospheric. These four pubs are all within about 100 yards of each other. Start at the Linzergasse end of Steingasse. As they are quite different, survey all before choosing your spot.

Pepe Cocktail Bar, with Mexican decor and Latin music, serves Mexican snacks *con* cocktails (nightly 19:00-3:00 in the morning, live DJs Fri-Sat from 19:00, Steingasse 3, tel. 0662/873-662).

Shrimps Bar-Restaurant, next door and less claustrophobic, is more a restaurant than a bar, serving creative international dishes (spicy shrimp sandwiches and salads, Mon-Sat 17:30-24:00, closed Sun, Steingasse 5, tel. 0662/874-484).

Saiten Sprung wins the "Best Atmosphere" award. The door is kept closed to keep out the crude and rowdy. Ring the bell and enter its hellish interior—lots of stone and red decor, with mountains of melted wax beneath age-old candlesticks and a classic soul music ambience. Stelios, who speaks English with Greek charm, serves cocktails, fine wine, and wine-friendly Italian antipasti (nightly 21:00-4:00 in the morning, Steingasse 11, tel. 0662/881-377).

Fridrich, just next door, is an intimate little place under an 11th-century vault, with lots of mirrors and a silver ceiling fan. Bernd Fridrich is famous for his martinis and passionate about Austrian wines, and has a tattered collection of vinyl that seems to keep the 1970s alive. He serves little dishes to complement the focus, which is socializing and drinking (€5-12 small dishes, Thu-Mon from 18:00 in summer, from 17:00 in winter, closed Tue-Wed, Steingasse 15, tel. 0662/876-218).

Salzburg Connections

By train, Salzburg is the first stop over the German-Austrian border. This means that if Salzburg is your only stop in Austria, and you're using a railpass that covers Germany (including the Bayern-Ticket) but not Austria, you don't have to pay extra or add Austria to your pass to get here.

From Salzburg by Train to: Berchtesgaden (hourly, 45-60 minutes; bus #840 is easier—hourly, 45 minutes, buses leave across from Salzburg train station and also stop in Mirabellplatz and near Mozartplatz), **Munich** (2/hour, 1.5-2 hours), **Füssen**

(roughly hourly, 4 hours, 1-2 changes), **Reutte,** Austria (hourly, 5 hours, change either in Munich and Kempten, or in Innsbruck and Garmisch), **Nürnberg** (hourly with change in Munich, 3 hours), **Hallstatt,** Austria (hourly, 50 minutes to Attnang Puchheim, 20-minute wait, then 1.5 hours to Hallstatt), **Innsbruck,** Austria (direct every 2 hours, 2 hours), **Vienna,** Austria (2/hour, 2.5-3 hours), **Ljubljana,** Slovenia (every 2 hours, 4.25-5 hours, some with change in Villach), **Prague,** Czech Republic (7/day, 6.5-7.5 hours, via Linz and České Budějovice, no decent overnight connection), **Interlaken,** Switzerland (7/day, 7.5-8 hours, 2-3 changes), **Florence,** Italy (4/day, 8-8.5 hours, 2 changes, 1 overnight option via Villach). Austrian train info: Austrian tel. 051-717 (to get an operator, dial 2, then 2), from Germany call 00-43-51-717, www .oebb.at. German train info: tel. 0180-599-6633, from Austria call 00-49-180-599-6633, www.bahn.com.

Berchtesgaden

This alpine ski town, just across the border from Salzburg in a finger of German territory that pokes south into Austria, is famous for its fjord-like lake and its mountaintop Nazi retreat. Long before its association with Hitler, Berchtesgaden (BERKH-tehs-gah-dehn) was one of the classic Romantic corners of Germany. In fact, Hitler's propagandists capitalized on the Führer's love of this region to establish the notion that the native Austrian was truly German at heart. Today visitors cruise up the romantic Königssee to get in touch with the soul of Bavarian Romanticism; ride a bus up to Hitler's mountain retreat (5,500 feet); see the remains of the Nazis' elaborate last-ditch bunkers; and ride an old miners' train into the mountain to learn all about salt mining in the region.

Getting There

Berchtesgaden is only 15 miles from Salzburg. The quickest way there **from Salzburg** is by bus #840 from the Salzburg train station (runs almost hourly Mon-Fri, 6/day Sat-Sun, usually at :15 past the hour, 45 minutes, buy tickets from driver, €9.60 *Tageskarte* day pass covers your round-trip plus most local buses in Berchtesgaden—except bus #849 up to the Eagle's Nest, last bus back leaves Berchtesgaden at 18:15, check schedules at www. albus.at and click "Linienverkehr"). While the Salzburg station is undergoing renovation, buses aren't necessarily leaving from the main bus platforms out front—ask around (on my last visit, bus #840 left from stall 6/Forum, beyond the bike racks and across the street). You can also catch bus #840 from the middle of Salzburg—after leaving the station, it stops a few minutes later on Mirabellplatz, and then in Salzburg's old town (on Rudolfskai, near Mozartplatz).

Coming **from Munich**, it's simplest to reach Berchtesgaden by train (almost hourly, 3 hours, change in Freilassing). You can also get to Berchtesgaden from Salzburg by train via Freilassing, but it takes twice as long as the bus and is less scenic.

Planning Your Time

The Nazi and Hitler-related sites outside Berchtesgaden are the town's main draw. Berchtesgaden also has salt mines (similar to the Hallein salt mine tour) and a romantic, pristine lake called Königssee (extremely popular with less-adventurous Germans). Plan on a full day from Salzburg, including the drive or bus ride there and back. Drivers and those taking bus tours from Salzburg can do everything in one busy day trip; otherwise I'd skip the salt mines and possibly the lake trip. If you're visiting Berchtesgaden on your way between Salzburg and points in Germany, you can leave luggage in lockers at the Berchtesgaden train station during your visit.

Remote little Berchtesgaden (pop. 7,500) can be inundated with Germans during peak season, when you may find yourself in a traffic jam of tourists desperately trying to turn their money into fun.

Orientation to Berchtesgaden

Buses from Salzburg to Berchtesgaden stop in front of the town's train station, which—though sorely dilapidated—is worth a stop for its luggage lockers (along the train platform), WC (free, also near platform), and history (specifically, its vintage 1937 Nazi architecture and the murals in the main hall). The oversized station was built to accommodate (and intimidate) the hordes of Hitler fans, who flocked here in hopes of seeing the Führer. The building next to the station, just beyond the round tower, was Hitler's own V.I.P. reception area.

Tourist Information

The TI is across from the train station, in the yellow building with green shutters (mid-June-Sept Mon-Fri 8:30-18:00, Sat 9:00-17:00, Sun 9:00-15:00; Oct-mid-June Mon-Fri 8:30-17:00, Sat 9:00-12:00, closed Sun; German tel. 08652/9670, from Austria call 00-49-8652-9670, www.berchtesgadener-land.info). Pick up a local map, and consider the 30-page local-bus schedule *(Fahrplan)* if you'll be hopping more than one bus.

Getting Around Berchtesgaden

None of the sights I list are within easy walking distance from the station, but they're all connected by convenient local buses, which use the station as a hub (all these buses—except the shuttle between the Obersalzberg Documentation Center and the Eagle's Nest chalet—are free with the €9.60 *Tageskarte* day pass from Salzburg; timetables at www.rvo-bus.de, or call 08652/94480). You'll want to note departure times and frequencies while still at the station, or pick up a schedule at the TI.

From the train station, buses #840 (the same line as the bus from Salzburg) and #837 go to the salt mines (a 20-minute walk otherwise). Bus #838 goes to the Nazi Documentation Center, and bus #841 goes to the Königssee.

Tours in Berchtesgaden

Eagle's Nest Historical Tours—For 20 years, David and Christine Harper—who rightly consider this visit more an educational opportunity than simple sightseeing—have organized thoughtful tours of the Hitler-related sites near Berchtesgaden. Their bus tours, always led by native English speakers, depart from the TI, opposite the Berchtesgaden train station. Tours start by driving through the remains of the Nazis' Obersalzberg complex, then visit the bunkers underneath the Documentation Center, and end with a guided visit to the Eagle's Nest (€50/person, €1 discount with this book, English only, daily at 13:15 mid-May-late Oct, 4 hours, 25 people maximum, reservations strongly recommended, German tel. 08652/64971, from Austria call 00-49-8652-64971, www.eagles-nest-tours.com). While the price is €50, your actual cost for the guiding is only about €23, as the tour takes care of your transport and admissions, not to mention relieving you of having to figure out the local buses up to Obersalzberg. Coming from Salzburg, you can take the 10:15 or 11:15 bus to Berchtesgaden, eat a picnic lunch, take the tour, then return on the 18:15 bus from Berchtesgaden, which gets you back to Salzburg at 19:00. If you're visiting near the beginning or end of the season, be aware that tours will be cancelled if it's snowing at the Eagle's Nest (as that makes the twisty, precipitous mountain roads too dangerous to drive). David and Christine also arrange off-season tours, though the Eagle's Nest isn't open for visitors in winter (€100/up to 4 people; see website for details).

Bus Tours from Salzburg—**Bob's Special Tours,** based in Salzburg, make it easy to see all the sights described here on one busy day trip in a cheerful minibus, and offers a €10 discount with this book. **Panorama Tours,** which usually runs larger buses, also offers excursions to Berchtesgaden (€5 discount with this book).

Sights in Berchtesgaden

▲▲▲Nazi Sites near Berchtesgaden

Early in his career as a wannabe tyrant, Adolf Hitler had a radical friend who liked to vacation in Berchtesgaden, and through him Hitler came to know and love this dramatic corner of Bavaria. Berchtesgaden's part-Bavarian, part-Austrian character held a special appeal to the Austrian-German Hitler. In the 1920s, just out

of prison, he checked into an alpine hotel in Obersalzberg, three miles uphill from Berchtesgaden, to finish work on his memoir and Nazi primer, *Mein Kampf.* Because it was here that he claimed to be inspired and laid out his vision, some call Obersalzberg the "cradle of the Third Reich."

In the 1930s, after becoming the German Chancellor, Hitler chose Obersalzberg to build his mountain retreat, a supersized alpine farmhouse called the Berghof. His handlers crafted Hitler's image here—surrounded by nature, gently receiving alpine flowers from adoring little children, lounging around with farmers in lederhosen...no modern arms industry, no big-time industrialists, no ugly extermination camps. In reality, Obersalzberg was home to much more than Hitler's alpine chalet. It was a huge compound of 80 buildings—built largely by forced labor and fenced off from the public after 1936—where the major decisions leading up to World War II were hatched. Hitler himself spent about a third of his time at the Berghof, hosted world leaders in the compound, and later had it prepared for his last stand.

Some mistakenly call the entire area "Hitler's Eagle's Nest." But that name actually belongs only to the Kehlsteinhaus, a small mountaintop chalet on a 6,000-foot peak that juts up two miles south of Obersalzberg. (A visiting diplomat humorously dubbed it the "Eagle's Nest," and the name stuck.) In 1939, it was given to the Führer for his 50th birthday. While a fortune was spent building this perch and the road up to it, Hitler, who was afraid of heights, visited only 14 times. Hitler's mistress, Eva Braun, though, liked to hike up to the Eagle's Nest to sunbathe.

In April of 1945, Britain's Royal Air Force bombed the Obersalzberg compound nearly flat, but missed the difficult-to-target Eagle's Nest entirely. Almost all of what survived the bombing at Obersalzberg was blown up in 1952 by the Allies, who wanted to leave nothing as a magnet for future neo-Nazi pilgrims before turning the site over to the German government. The most extensive surviving remains are of the Nazis' bunker system, intended to

BERCHTESGADEN

Near Berchtesgaden

To Vienna
To Vienna →
AUTOBAHN A-1

Freilassing
← To Munich
2 Kilometers
2 Miles
TRAIN STATION A-1
158
To Salzkammergut & Hallstatt
A-8
Salzburg ✈
N
HELLBRUNN CASTLE
AUSTRIA
A-10
SALZBURG SÜD EXIT
Bad Reichenhall
Untersberg
Bus #840 Between Salzburg & Berchtesgaden →
305
Hallein
21
GERMANY
Dürrnberg
SALT MINE
20
Unterau
Oberau
305
Bus #840/837 to Salt Mines
SALT MINES
Ober-salzberg
NAZI DOCUMENTATION CENTER
Berchtesgaden
Bus #838
Bus #841 →
Kehlstein
A-10
Königsee
Shuttle Bus #849 Only
HITLER'S EAGLE'S NEST
Watzmann
Königsee
To Villach (Austria), Italy & Slovenia ↓
St. Bartholomä

serve as a last resort for the regime as the Allies closed in. In the 1990s, a museum, the Obersalzberg Documentation Center, was built on top of one of the bunkers. The museum and bunker, plus the never-destroyed Eagle's Nest, are the two Nazi sites worth seeing near Berchtesgaden.

Obersalzberg Documentation Center and Bunker—To reach the most interesting part of this site, walk through the museum and down the stairs into the vast and complex bunker system. Construction began in 1943, after the Battle of Stalingrad ended the Nazi aura of invincibility. This is a professionally engineered underground town, which held meeting rooms, offices, archives for the government, and lavish living quarters for Hitler—all connected by four miles of tunnels cut through solid rock by slave labor. You can't visit all of it, and what you can see was stripped and looted bare after the war. But enough is left that you can wander among the concrete and marvel at megalomania gone mad.

The museum above, which has almost no actual artifacts, is designed primarily for German students and others who want to learn and understand their still-recent history. There's little English, but you can rent the €2 English audioguide.

Cost and Hours: €3 covers both museum and bunker; April-Oct daily 9:00-17:00; Nov-March Tue-Sun 10:00-15:00, closed Mon; last entry one hour before closing, allow 1.5 hours for visit, German tel. 08652/947-960, from Austria tel. 00-49-8652-947-960, www.obersalzberg.de.

Getting There: Reach the Documentation Center on bus #838 from Berchtesgaden's train station (Mon-Fri almost hourly, Sat-Sun 4/day, 12 minutes, 5-minute walk from Obersalzberg stop).

Eagle's Nest (Kehlsteinhaus)—Today, the chalet that Hitler ignored is basically a three-room, reasonably priced restaurant with a scenic terrace, 100 yards below the summit of a mountain. You could say it's like any alpine hiking hut, just more massively built. On a nice day, the views are magnificent. If it's fogged in (which it often is), most people won't find

it worth coming up here (except on David and Christine Harper's tours—described earlier—which can make the building come to life even without a view). Bring a jacket, and prepare for crowds in summer (less crowded if you go early or late in the day).

From the upper bus stop, a finely crafted tunnel (which will have you humming the *Get Smart* TV theme song) leads to the original polished brass elevator, which takes you the last 400 feet up to the Eagle's Nest. Wander into the fancy back dining room (the best-preserved from Hitler's time), where you can see the once-sleek marble fireplace chipped up by souvenir-seeking troops in 1945.

Cost and Hours: Free, generally open mid-May-late Oct, snowfall sometimes forces a later opening or earlier closing.

Getting There: The only way to reach the Eagle's Nest—even if you have your own car—is by specially equipped bus #849, which leaves from the Documentation Center and climbs steeply up the one-way, private road—Germany's highest (every 25 minutes, 15 minutes, €15.50 round-trip, *Tageskarte* day passes not valid, buy ticket from windows, last bus up 16:00, last bus down 16:50, free parking at Documentation Center).

▲Salt Mines

At the Berchtesgaden salt mines, you put on traditional miners' outfits, get on funny little trains, and zip deep into the mountain. For two hours (which includes time to get into and back out of your miner's gear), you'll cruise subterranean lakes; slide speedily down two long, slick, wooden banisters; and learn how they mined salt so long ago. Call for crowd-avoidance advice. When the weather gets bad, this place is mobbed. You can buy a ticket early and browse through the town until your appointed tour time. Tours are in German, while English-speakers get audioguides.

Cost and Hours: €15, daily May-Oct 9:00-17:00, Nov-April 11:30-15:00—these are last-entry times, German tel. 08652/600220, from Austria dial 00-49-8652-600220, www.salzzeitreise.de.

Getting There: The mines are a 20-minute walk or quick bus ride (#837 or #840) from the Berchtesgaden station; ask the driver to let you off at the Salzbergwerk stop. (Since buses coming from Salzburg pass here on the way into Berchtesgaden, you can also simply hop off at the mines before getting into town, instead of backtracking from the station.)

▲Königssee

Three miles south of Berchtesgaden, the idyllic Königssee stretches like a fjord through pristine mountain scenery to the dramatically situated Church of St. Bartholomä and beyond. To get to the lake from Berchtesgaden, hop on bus #841 (about hourly from train station to boat dock), or take the scenically woodsy, reasonably flat 1.25-hour walk (well-signed). Drivers pay €3 to park.

Most visitors simply glide scenically for 35 minutes on the silent, electronically propelled **boat** to the church, enjoy that peaceful setting, then glide back. Boats, going at a sedate Bavarian speed and filled with Germans chuckling at the captain's commentary, leave with demand—generally 2-4 per hour (€13 round-trip, German tel. 08652/96360, from Austria dial 00-49-8652-96360, www.seenschifffahrt.de). At a rock cliff midway through the journey, your captain stops, and the first mate pulls out a trumpet to demonstrate the fine echo.

The remote, red-onion-domed **Church of St. Bartholomä** (once home of a monastery, then a hunting lodge of the Bavarian royal family) is surrounded by a fine beer garden, rustic fishermen's pub, and inviting lakeside trails. The family next to St. Bartholomä's lives in the middle of this national park and has a license to fish—so very fresh trout is the lunchtime favorite.

PRACTICALITIES

This section covers just the basics on traveling in this region (for much more information, see *Rick Steves' Germany*). Unless otherwise noted, you can assume that the information about Germany in this section also applies to Austria (the city of Salzburg and the region of Tirol). You'll find free advice on specific topics at www.ricksteves.com/tips.

Money

Germany and Austria use the euro currency: 1 euro (€) = about $1.40. To convert prices in euros to dollars, add about 40 percent: €20 = about $28, €50 = about $70. (Check www.oanda.com for the latest exchange rates.)

The standard way for travelers to get euros is to withdraw money from a cash machine (called a *Geldautomat* in Germany, or *Bankomat* in Austria) using a debit or credit card, ideally with a Visa or MasterCard logo. Before departing, call your bank or credit-card company: Confirm that your card(s) will work overseas, find out the PIN code for your credit card, ask about international transaction fees, and alert them that you'll be making withdrawals in Europe.

To keep your valuables safe, wear a money belt. But if you do lose your credit or debit card, report the loss immediately to the respective global customer-assistance centers. Call these 24-hour US numbers collect: Visa (410/581-9994), MasterCard (636/722-7111), and American Express (623/492-8427).

Dealing with "Chip and PIN": Much of Northern Europe (including Germany and Austria) is adopting a "chip-and-PIN" system for credit cards. These "smartcards" come with an embedded microchip, and cardholders enter a PIN code instead of signing a receipt. If your US card is rejected at a store, a cashier will probably be able to process your card the old-fashioned way. A few merchants might insist on the PIN code—making it helpful for you to know the code for your credit card (ask your credit-card company). The easiest solution is to pay for your purchases with cash you've withdrawn from an ATM. Don't count on your US credit card being accepted at automated pay points, such as ticket machines at train and subway stations, parking garages, luggage lockers, and self-serve pumps at gas stations. But in many of these cases, a cash-only payment option is available.

Phoning

Smart travelers use the telephone to reserve or reconfirm rooms, reserve restaurants, get directions, research transportation connections, confirm tour times, phone home, and lots more.

To call Germany from the US or Canada: Dial 011-49 and then the area code (minus its initial zero) and local number. (The 011 is our international access code, and 49 is Germany's country code.)

To call Germany from a European country: Dial 00-49 followed by the area code (minus its initial zero) and local number. (The 00 is Europe's international access code.)

To call Austria: Follow the same directions above, but use Austria's country code: 43.

To call within Germany or Austria: If you're dialing within an area code, just dial the local number; but if you're calling outside your area code, you have to dial both the area code (which starts with a 0) and the local number.

To call from Germany or Austria to another country: Dial 00 followed by the country code (for example, 1 for the US or Canada), then the area code and number. If you're calling European countries whose phone numbers begin with 0, you'll usually have to omit that 0 when you dial.

Tips on Phoning: To make calls in Germany or Austria, you can buy two different types of phone cards—international or insertable—sold locally at newsstands. Cheap international phone cards, which work with a scratch-to-reveal PIN code, allow you to call home to the US for pennies a minute, and also work for domestic calls. While these work from any phone, they come with a big surcharge when used with pay phones (effectively negating the savings), and some hotels charge for calls to the "toll-free" access line—ask before you dial. Insertable phone cards, which must be inserted into public pay phones, are reasonable for calls within the country (and work for international calls as well, though not as cheaply as the international phone cards). Note that insertable phone cards—and most international phone cards—work only in the country where you buy them. Calling from your hotel-room phone is usually expensive, unless you use an international phone card. A mobile phone—whether an American one that works in Europe, or a European one you buy when you arrive—is handy, but can be pricey. For more on phoning, see www.ricksteves.com/phoning.

Making Hotel Reservations

To ensure the best value, I recommend reserving rooms in advance, particularly during peak season. Email the hotelier with the following key pieces of information: number and type of rooms; number of nights; date of arrival; date of departure; and any special requests. (For a sample form, see www.ricksteves.com/reservation.) Use the European style for writing dates: day/month/year. For example, for a two-night stay in July, you could request: "1 double room for 2 nights, arrive 16/07/12, depart 18/07/12." Hoteliers typically ask for your credit-card number as a deposit.

In these times of economic uncertainty, some hotels are willing to deal to attract guests—try emailing several to ask their best price. In general, hotel prices can soften if you do any of the following: offer to pay cash, stay at least three nights, or travel off-season. You can also try asking for a cheaper room (for example, with a bathroom down the hall) or offer to skip breakfast.

Eating

At mealtime, there are many options beyond restaurants. For hearty, stick-to-the-ribs meals—and plenty of beer—look for a beer hall *(Bräuhaus)* or beer garden *(Biergarten)*. *Gasthaus, Gasthof, Gaststätte,* and *Gaststube* all loosely describe an informal, inn-type eatery. A *Kneipe* is a bar, a *Weinstub* is a wine bar, and a *Keller* (or *Ratskeller*) is a cellar, usually serving traditional food. A *Schnell Imbiss* is a small fast-food take-away stand. Department store cafeterias are also common and handy.

The classic Germanic dish is sausage. The hundreds of varieties of W*urst* are usually served with mustard *(Senf)*, a roll *(Semmel)* or pretzel *(Breze)*, and sauerkraut. The various types of *Bratwurst* are grilled *(gebraten)*. To enjoy a *Weisswurst*—a boiled white Bavarian sausage made of veal—peel off the skin and eat it with sweet mustard. *Currywurst* comes with a delicious curry-infused ketchup. Particularly in Austria, the traditional favorite is Wiener schnitzel (breaded veal cutlet).

If you prefer smaller portions in this land of heavy cuisine, order from the *kleine Hunger* ("small hunger") section of the menu. Salads are big, leafy, and good; a *Salatteller* is a meal-sized salad. Europeans are passionate about choosing organic products—look for *Bio*.

Ethnic eateries—Turkish, Greek, Italian, and Asian—offer a

good value and a welcome break from Germanic fare. The Turkish *Döner Kebab* (sliced meat and vegetables served in pita bread) rivals *Wurst* as a fast-food staple.

This region has both great wine *(Wein)* and beer *(Bier)*. Order wine *süss* (sweet), *halb trocken* (medium), or *trocken* (dry). For beer, *dunkles* is dark, *helles* or *Lager* is light, *Flaschenbier* is bottled, and *vom Fass* is on tap. *Pils* is barley-based, and *Weizen, Hefeweizen,* or *Weissbier* is yeasty and wheat-based. When you order beer, ask for *eine Halbe* for a half-liter (though it's not always available) or *eine Mass* for a whole liter (about a quart).

Service: Good service is relaxed (slow to an American). When you want the bill, say, *"Rechnung* (REHKH-noong), *bitte."* To tip for good service, it's customary to round up around 5 to 10 percent. Rather than leave coins on the table, do as the locals do: When you pay, tell the waiter how much you want him to keep, including his tip. For example, for an €8.10 meal, give a €20 bill and say *"Neun Euro"*—"Nine euros"—to include a €0.90 tip and get €11 change.

Transportation

By Train: Europe's trains—speedy, comfortable, non-smoking, and fairly punctual—cover cities and small towns well. Faster trains (such as the high-speed ICE) are more expensive than slower "regional" trains. To see if a railpass could save you money—which is often the case in Germany and Austria—check www.ricksteves .com/rail. If buying tickets as you go, note that prices can fluctuate (you can save by buying tickets at least three days in advance). To research train schedules and fares, visit Germany's excellent all-Europe timetable: http://bahn.hafas.de/bin/query.exe/en.

By Car: It's cheaper to arrange most car rentals from the US. For tips on your insurance options, see www.ricksteves.com/cdw, and for route planning, consult www.viamichelin.com. Bring your driver's license. Germany's toll-free autobahn (freeway) system lets you zip around the country in a snap. While there's often no official speed limit, going above the posted recommended speed invalidates your insurance. Many German cities—including Munich—require drivers to buy a special sticker *(Umweltplakette)* to drive in the city center. These already come standard with most German rental cars; ask when you pick up your car. A car is a worthless headache in any big city—park it safely (get tips from your hotelier).

If you're driving in Austria, you're technically required to have an International Driving Permit, which is a translation of your driver's license (sold at your local AAA office for $15 plus the cost of two passport-type photos; see www.aaa.com). Note that to drive on Austria's freeways, you're required to buy a toll sticker *(Vignette,* €8/10 days, €22/2 months, sold at gas stations). Unlike Germany, Austria enforces a speed limit on its freeways.

Helpful Hints

Emergency Telephone Numbers: To summon the **police** or an **ambulance,** call 112. For passport problems, call the **US Embassy** in Germany (in Berlin: tel. 030/83050; consular services tel. 030/8305-1200—Mon–Fri 14:00–16:00 only, www.usembassy .de) or in Austria (in Vienna: tel. 01/31339; consular services tel. 01/313-397-535—Mon-Fri 8:00–11:30, www.usembassy.at). For information on what to do in case of theft or loss, see www.rick steves.com/help. For other concerns, get advice from your hotelier.

Time: Europe uses the 24-hour clock. It's the same through 12:00 noon, then keep going: 13:00, 14:00, and so on. Germany and Austria, like most of continental Europe, are six/nine hours ahead of the East/West Coasts of the US.

Holidays and Festivals: Europe celebrates many holidays, which can close sights and attract crowds (book hotel rooms ahead). For information on holidays and festivals, check the national websites: www.cometogermany.com and www.austria .info. For a simple list showing major—though not all—events, see www.ricksteves.com/festivals.

Numbers and Stumblers: What Americans call the second floor of a building is the first floor in Europe. Europeans write dates as day/month/year, so Christmas is 25/12/12. Commas are decimal points and vice versa—a dollar and a half is 1,50, and there are 5.280 feet in a mile. Europe uses the metric system: A kilogram is 2.2 pounds; a liter is about a quart; and a kilometer is six-tenths of a mile.

Resources from Rick Steves

This Snapshot guide is excerpted from the latest edition of *Rick Steves' Germany,* which is one of more than 30 titles in my series of guidebooks on European travel. I also produce a public television series, *Rick Steves' Europe,* and a public radio show, *Travel with Rick Steves.* My website, www.ricksteves.com, offers free travel information, a Graffiti Wall for travelers' comments, guidebook updates, my travel blog, an online travel store, and information on European railpasses and our tours of Europe. If you're bringing a mobile device on your trip, you can download free information from Rick Steves Audio Europe, featuring podcasts of my radio shows, free audio tours of major sights in Europe, and travel interviews about Germany and Austria (via www.ricksteves.com/ audioeurope, iTunes, or the Rick Steves Audio Europe free smartphone app).

Additional Resources

Tourist Information: www.cometogermany.com and www .austria.info

Passports and Red Tape: www.travel.state.gov
Packing List: www.ricksteves.com/packlist
Travel Insurance: www.ricksteves.com/insurance
Cheap Flights: www.skyscanner.net
Airplane Carry-on Restrictions: www.tsa.gov/travelers
Updates for This Book: www.ricksteves.com/update

How Was Your Trip?

If you'd like to share your tips, concerns, and discoveries after using this book, please fill out the survey at www.ricksteves.com/feedback. Thanks in advance—it helps a lot.

German Survival Phrases

When using the phonetics, pronounce ī as the long I sound in "light."

Good day.	Guten Tag.	goo-tehn tahg
Do you speak English?	Sprechen Sie Englisch?	shprehkh-ehn zee ehng-lish
Yes. / No.	Ja. / Nein.	yah / nīn
I (don't) understand.	Ich verstehe (nicht).	ikh fehr-shtay-heh (nikht)
Please.	Bitte.	bit-teh
Thank you.	Danke.	dahng-keh
I'm sorry.	Es tut mir leid.	ehs toot meer līt
Excuse me.	Entschuldigung.	ehnt-shool-dig-oong
(No) problem.	(Kein) Problem.	(kīn) proh-blaym
(Very) good.	(Sehr) gut.	(zehr) goot
Goodbye.	Auf Wiedersehen.	owf vee-der-zayn
one / two	eins / zwei	īns / tsvī
three / four	drei / vier	drī / feer
five / six	fünf / sechs	fewnf / zehkhs
seven / eight	sieben / acht	zee-behn / ahkht
nine / ten	neun / zehn	noyn / tsayn
How much is it?	Wieviel kostet das?	vee-feel kohs-teht dahs
Write it?	Schreiben?	shrī-behn
Is it free?	Ist es umsonst?	ist ehs oom-zohnst
Included?	Inklusive?	in-kloo-zee-veh
Where can I buy / find...?	Wo kann ich kaufen / finden...?	voh kahn ikh kow-fehn / fin-dehn
I'd like / We'd like...	Ich hätte gern / Wir hätten gern...	ikh heh-teh gehrn / veer heh-tehn gehrn
...a room.	...ein Zimmer.	īn tsim-mer
...a ticket to ___.	...eine Fahrkarte nach ___.	ī-neh far-kar-teh nahkh
Is it possible?	Ist es möglich?	ist ehs mur-glikh
Where is...?	Wo ist...?	voh ist
...the train station	...der Bahnhof	dehr bahn-hohf
...the bus station	...der Busbahnhof	dehr boos-bahn-hohf
...tourist information	...das Touristen- informationsbüro	dahs too-ris-tehn- in-for-maht-see-ohns-bew-roh
...toilet	...die Toilette	dee toh-leh-teh
men	Herren	hehr-rehn
women	Damen	dah-mehn
left / right	links / rechts	links / rehkhts
straight	geradeaus	geh-rah-deh-ows
When is this open / closed?	Um wieviel Uhr ist hier geöffnet / geschlossen?	oom vee-feel oor ist heer geh-urf-neht / geh-shloh-sehn
At what time?	Um wieviel Uhr?	oom vee-feel oor
Just a moment.	Moment.	moh-mehnt
now / soon / later	jetzt / bald / später	yehtst / bahld / shpay-ter
today / tomorrow	heute / morgen	hoy-teh / mor-gehn

In the Restaurant

English	German	Pronunciation
I'd like / We'd like...	Ich hätte gern / Wir hätten gern...	ikh **heh**-teh gehrn / veer **heh**-tehn gehrn
...a reservation for...	...eine Reservierung für...	ī-neh reh-zer-**feer**-oong fewr
...a table for one / two.	...einen Tisch für ein / zwei.	ī-nehn tish fewr īn / tsvī
Non-smoking.	Nichtraucher.	**nikht**-rowkh-er
Is this seat free?	Ist hier frei?	ist heer frī
Menu (in English), please.	Speisekarte (auf Englisch), bitte.	**shpī**-zeh-kar-teh (owf **ehng**-lish) **bit**-teh
service (not) included	Trinkgeld (nicht) inklusive	**trink**-gehlt (nikht) in-kloo-**zee**-veh
cover charge	Eintritt	**īn**-trit
to go	zum Mitnehmen	tsoom **mit**-nay-mehn
with / without	mit / ohne	mit / **oh**-neh
and / or	und / oder	oont / **oh**-der
menu (of the day)	(Tages-) Karte	(**tah**-gehs-) **kar**-teh
set meal for tourists	Touristenmenü	too-**ris**-tehn-meh-**new**
specialty of the house	Spezialität des Hauses	shpayt-see-ah-lee-**tayt** dehs **how**-zehs
appetizers	Vorspeise	**for**-shpī-zeh
bread	Brot	broht
cheese	Käse	**kay**-zeh
sandwich	Sandwich	**zahnd**-vich
soup	Suppe	**zup**-peh
salad	Salat	zah-**laht**
meat	Fleisch	flīsh
poultry	Geflügel	geh-**flew**-gehl
fish	Fisch	fish
seafood	Meeresfrüchte	meh-rehs-**frewkh**-teh
fruit	Obst	ohpst
vegetables	Gemüse	geh-**mew**-zeh
dessert	Nachspeise	**nahkh**-shpī-zeh
mineral water	Mineralwasser	min-eh-**rahl**-vah-ser
tap water	Leitungswasser	**lī**-toongs-vah-ser
milk	Milch	milkh
(orange) juice	(Orangen-) Saft	(oh-**rahn**-zhehn-) zahft
coffee	Kaffee	kah-**fay**
tea	Tee	tay
wine	Wein	vīn
red / white	rot / weiß	roht / vīs
glass / bottle	Glas / Flasche	glahs / **flah**-sheh
beer	Bier	beer
Cheers!	Prost!	prohst
More. / Another.	Mehr. / Noch ein.	mehr / nohkh īn
The same.	Das gleiche.	dahs **glīkh**-eh
Bill, please.	Rechnung, bitte.	**rehkh**-noong **bit**-teh
tip	Trinkgeld	**trink**-gehlt
Delicious!	Lecker!	**lehk**-er

For more user-friendly German phrases, check out *Rick Steves' German Phrase Book and Dictionary* or *Rick Steves' French, Italian & German Phrase Book.*

INDEX

Audio Europe

Rick's free app and podcasts

The FREE **Rick Steves Audio Europe**™ app for iPhone, iPad and iPod Touch gives you 29 self-guided audio tours of Europe's top museums, sights and historic walks—plus more than 200 tracks filled with cultural insights and sightseeing tips from Rick's radio interviews—all organized into geographic-specific playlists.

Let **Rick Steves Audio Europe**™ amplify your guidebook.

With Rick whispering in your ear, Europe gets even better.

Thanks Facebook fans for submitting photos while on location! From top: John Kuijper in Florence, Brenda Mamer with her mother in Rome, Angel Capobianco in London, and Alyssa Passey with her friend in Paris.

Find out more at ricksteves.com

Start your trip at

Free information and great gear to

▶ Plan Your Trip

Browse thousands of articles and a wealth of money-saving tips for planning your dream trip. You'll find up-to-date information on Europe's best destinations, packing smart, getting around, finding rooms, staying healthy, avoiding scams and more.

▶ Eurail Passes

Find out, step-by-step, if a railpass makes sense for your trip—and how to avoid buying more than you need. Get free shipping on online orders

▶ Graffiti Wall & Travelers Helpline

Learn, ask, share—our online community of savvy travelers is a great resource for first-time travelers to Europe, as well as seasoned pros.

Rick Steves' Europe Through the Back Door, Inc.

ricksteves.com

turn your travel dreams into affordable reality

▶ Free Audio Tours & Travel Newsletter

Get your nose out of this guide book and focus on what you'll be seeing with Rick's free audio tours of the greatest sights in Paris, London, Rome, Florence, Venice, and Athens.

Subscribe to our free Travel News e-newsletter, and get monthly articles from Rick on what's happening in Europe.

▶ Great Gear from Rick's Travel Store

Pack light and right—on a budget—with Rick's custom-designed carry-on bags, roll-aboards, day packs, travel accessories, guidebooks, journals, maps and DVDs of his TV shows.

130 Fourth Avenue North, PO Box 2009 • Edmonds, WA 98020 USA
Phone: (425) 771-8303 • Fax: (425) 771-0833 • www.ricksteves.com

NOW AVAILABLE:
eBOOKS, APPS & BLU-RAY

eBOOKS

Most guides are available as eBooks from Amazon, Barnes & Noble, Borders, Apple, and Sony. Free apps for eBook reading are available in the Apple App Store and Android Market, and eBook readers such as Kindle, Nook, and Kobo all have free apps that work on smartphones.

RICK STEVES' EUROPE DVDs

10 New Shows 2011–2012
Austria & the Alps
Eastern Europe
England & Wales
European Christmas
European Travel Skills & Specials
France
Germany, BeNeLux & More
Greece & Turkey
Iran
Ireland & Scotland
Italy's Cities
Italy's Countryside
Scandinavia
Spain
Travel Extras

BLU-RAY

Celtic Charms
Eastern Europe Favorites
European Christmas
Italy Through the Back Door
Mediterranean Mosaic
Surprising Cities of Europe

PHRASE BOOKS & DICTIONARIES

French
French, Italian & German
German
Italian
Portuguese
Spanish

JOURNALS

Rick Steves' Pocket Travel Journal
Rick Steves' Travel Journal

APPS

Select Rick Steves guides are available as apps in the Apple App Store.

PLANNING MAPS

Britain, Ireland & London
Europe
France & Paris
Germany, Austria & Switzerland
Ireland
Italy
Spain & Portugal

Avalon Travel
a member of the Perseus Books Group
1700 Fourth Street
Berkeley, CA 94710

Printed in Canada by Friesens.
Second printing May 2012.

ISBN 978-1-59880-689-2

For the latest on Rick's lectures, guidebooks, tours, public radio show, and public television
series, contact Europe Through the Back Door, Box 2009, Edmonds, WA 98020, tel.
425/771-8303, fax 425/771-0833, www.ricksteves.com, rick@ricksteves.com.

Europe Through the Back Door Reviewing Editors: Cameron Hewitt, Jennifer Madison
    Davis, Cathy Lu
ETBD Editors: Cathy McDonald, Gretchen Strauch, Suzanne Kotz, Tom Griffin,
    Samantha Oberholzer
ETBD Managing Editor: Risa Laib
Research Assistance: Cameron Hewitt, Ian Watson, Marijan Krišković, Rick Garman
Avalon Travel Senior Editor and Series Manager: Madhu Prasher
Avalon Travel Project Editor: Kelly Lydick
Copy Editor: Judith Brown
Proofreader: Lisa Noël Chrisman
Indexer: Stephen Callahan
Production and Typesetting: McGuire Barber Design
Cover Design: Kimberly Glyder Design
Graphic Content Director: Laura VanDeventer
Maps and Graphics: David C. Hoerlein, Lauren Mills, Laura VanDeventer, Twozdai
    Hulse, Kat Bennett, Mike Morgenfeld, Brice Ticen
Front Cover Photo: Steeples of the Munich Frauenkirche, Munich, Bavaria, Germany ©
    Konrad Wothe/Getty Images
Title Page Photo: view over Munich © koi88/www.123rf.com
Additional Photography: Rick Steves, David C. Hoerlein, Cameron Hewitt, Ian Watson,
    Dominic Bonuccelli, Gretchen Strauch, Karoline Vass, Robyn Cronin, Lee Evans

ABOUT THE AUTHOR

RICK STEVES

Since 1973, Rick Steves has spent 100 days every year exploring Europe. Rick produces a public television series (*Rick Steves' Europe*), a public radio show (*Travel with Rick Steves*), and an app and podcast (*Rick Steves Audio Europe*); writes a bestselling series of guidebooks and a nationally syndicated newspaper column; organizes guided tours that take over ten thousand travelers to Europe annually; and offers an information-packed website (www.ricksteves.com). With the help of his hardworking staff of 80 at Europe Through the Back Door—in Edmonds, Washington, just north of Seattle—Rick's mission is to make European travel fun, affordable, and culturally enlightening for Americans.